A Politics of
Virtue

A Politics of
Virtue

Hinduism, Sexuality,
and Countercolonial
Discourse in Fiji

John D. Kelly

The University of Chicago Press

Chicago and London

John D. Kelly is assistant professor of anthropology at Princeton University.

The University of Chicago Press, Chicago 60637
The University of Chicago Press, Ltd., London
© 1991 by The University of Chicago
All rights reserved. Published 1991
Printed in the United States of America

00 99 98 97 96 95 94 93 92 91   5 4 3 2 1

Library of Congress Cataloging-in-Publication Data

Kelly, John Dunham, 1958–
    A politics of virtue : Hinduism, sexuality, and countercolonial
discourse in Fiji / John D. Kelly.
        p.   cm.
    Includes bibliographical references and index.
    ISBN 0-226-43030-8. — ISBN 0-226-43031-6 (pbk.)
    1. East Indians—Fiji—History. 2. Fiji—Politics and government.
3. Fiji—Social life and customs. I. Title.
DU600.K38   1991
996.11'00491411—dc20   91-17326
                                                                                        CIP

Men make their own history, but they do not make it just as they please.

Karl Marx

We are troubled by a trouble which we know not yet how to name.

Rabindranath Tagore

Contents

Preface

This study is part of a larger whole, a part that developed momentum in its own direction. In 1984 and 1985 I pursued ethnographic and historical research on *bhakti* devotionalism and capitalism in the colonial past and postcolonial present of the Fiji Indians. In the archives and in discussions of history with Fiji Indians, I became intrigued by the spectacular events that took place between 1929 and 1932 in this overseas Indian community. In those years, in the midst of imperial political crisis and international economic depression, in a colonial environment hostile to Indian political efforts, Fiji Indian public discourse moved from anticolonial politics to a series of religious debates about the sexuality of gods and the propriety of different forms of marriage. At first glance the connection of the latter topics to their social and political context is hardly clear, but as we shall see, it was very real. In my research these debates and their principal protagonists and tragic heroes, the Arya Samaj, began to compete for the foreground with the central themes of my other study. It became clear that they needed a text of their own.

Inside larger questions about capitalism and colonial history, then, this is an inquiry into a history of dialogue in a colonial political field. With luck I will also be publishing soon a larger historical and ethnographic study that will examine grammars as well as discourses, of capitalism and *bhakti* devotionalism, in the lives of Fiji Indians. In contrast, this inquiry into a politics of virtue concerns colonial authority and the discourse of the colonized, the modalities of explicit resistance in Fiji's backwater version of British imperial order. It is about why Hinduism and its sexual morality became vital political topics, about the shapes countercolonial speech could and did take as Fiji Indians remade themselves in a colonial terrain.

To some scholars "colonial dialogue" would be an oxymoron, and surely I am using "dialogue" in its broadest sense. I take the term to describe not only the explicit exchanges between colonizer and colonized, but also the more frequent occasions wherein Fiji's colonial Europeans and Fiji Indians spoke about each other, but not to each other, and then spoke about what each was saying about the other, but still, not to each other. This is a very colonial form of dialogue, if we call it "dialogue" at all. I do see it as a form of dialogue, and I want to investigate how the contending voices are influenced by what they seek to reject, to respond to, and to preempt. This study is a history of dialogue especially in the sense that it examines a specific kind of historical dialectic, not a dialectic between analytical levels (such as an "infrastructure" and a "superstructure") but between real and changing sets of people, who engage, provoke, and change each other. The history I see is dialogical, despite differences in language and a "colour bar" separating the colonizers and the colonized, and despite the dominant position of the colonizers.

Why is this study about "a politics of virtue"? It is not a new attempt at a philosophy of "virtue" (cf. MacIntyre 1984). It is closer to what anthropologists call "structure and history." It is a study of discourse, a cultural history of contested uses of related ideas. Even as such, concern about a politics of virtue might seem misplaced in what is thought a modern world, a world in which politics is based on rights, interests, power, and empirically testable realities of material and human nature. It might still seem misplaced if we declare the world "postmodern" and identify the discourses of political economy, rights, interests, and material and human nature as no more than the "modern" discourse of power. From either point of view "virtue" conjures a double image of Platonic narcissism in politics and Victorian prudery in sexuality. The commitments of Fiji Indians and Fiji Europeans to forms of virtue sound like the centerpieces of prerealist idealism whose last historical appearances must be in immature bourgeois classes. In short, a politics of virtue would seem ineluctably "premodern"; concern about it could only be inquiry into forms of power long gone and not destined to return.

What I offer instead is not an argument that virtue belongs farther along a time line, but a query as to whether that time line itself interferes in analysis. The concept of postmodernism inescapably implies a modernization theory of history. In the face of the realities of colonial history, the naïvete in modernization claims is pathetic. Can we be "non-modern," "amodern," even "antimodern," rather than "postmodern"? I agree with those who argue that "modernity" was and is a discourse of power and not a natural reality, a discourse especially powerful in the form of political economy. If this is so, we validate its ontology if we arrange all human history, not only in a typology of relations to modernity, but in a system arranged in its favorite form, a linear evolutionary progression. I am trying to avoid an evolutionary model of history. I hope not to be read as saying that political discourse on virtue is a stage of colonial history, of westernization, or worst of all of modernization. If "virtue" conjures inescapably the double connotation of the Victorian form of body obsession and Platonic version of self-analysis and social engineering, this is precisely because colonial European, and especially British, culture combined these concerns under the general heading of "morality." The question of virtue entered colonial political dialogues when these particular colonizers raised it in their own interests. Organizing categories such as "virtue" and "modernity" are surely part of the content of history, a history, our history, not something intrinsic or inevitable in history's general form.

The impact on the colonized of the colonizers' discourse on virtue, and the ways the colonized dealt with virtue, are matters tied to the particular history of this earlier European discourse of power. Ideas of progress in virtue and "civilization" organized colonial relations, including colonial relations of production, before the discourse on political economy was realized, written, and accepted by a new nineteenth-century bourgeoisie in Europe. Insofar as European colonial practice was, in fact, reorganized along the lines of the discourse on political economy, we could inquire about how the colonized responded to this superseding version of the "modern" discourse of power; this is part of my larger study. One reason for this independent study of "a politics of virtue" is that new forms of a politics of "virtue" could arise wherever virtue (or, to strike closer to home, "values") is made a vehicle of power. Or this text might be read from another perspective, taking the focus on virtue as incidental to a study of colonial authority and the discourse of the colonized. From this point of view the important matter is not the virtue but the politics. In any case, this study is an attempt to reconsider the politics of colonial dialogue on a premise that colonial societies are not a superseded historical stage, but a type of social formation that is likely to recur, in new elaborations, many times more in history as it really will be.

This study is organized as follows. Chapter 1 lays out some of the paradoxes of the years 1929 to 1932 in Fiji, problems for investigation in what I will call, paraphrasing Foucault, the conditions of political possibility in a colonial social field. The principal issue is simple: the forms of political discourse that are possible for the colonized when their resources are fragmentary, complex, and incoherent and a colonial political authority seeks to deny them any political space. Chapters 2, 3, and 4 discuss Fiji, empire, and the Fiji Indians before 1929. Chapter 2 examines the dialogues on sexuality—between India and Fiji but principally within India—that played a central role in the end of the indentured labor system in 1919. Chapter 3 discusses the genres of dialogue and arrangement of legal and social relations between colonial Europeans and the Indians who were "free" of indenture, and chapter 4 discusses the further history of these relations and the Indian withdrawal from colonial Fijian society from the end of indenture up to the period of focus. Then chapter 5 introduces the Arya Samaj, a Hindu reform society whose project and fate are basic to the events we consider.

Chapters 6 and 7 begin the discussion of events in 1929–1932 proper, considering the reactions of Fiji European politicians and colonial authorities as they realized that the Fiji Indians, and especially the Arya Samaj leaders, were seeking to become political. Chapter 8 describes the shift of Indian public discourse from anticolonial politics to "sectarian" religion and questions of sexual morality and explains what happened to the Arya Samaj project. Chapter 9 gets to the point: why it happened.

An idiosyncrasy of this text is its frequent resort to paragraph-length, and sometimes longer, quotations of discourse. I realize that others would choose to rewrite the discourse they analyze for their own and readers' convenience. My sense is that much is gained by examining originals closer to their whole state. First, we get more access to the meaning of what is said, which resides grammatically in whole sentences, utterances, and dialogues and is always attenuated when a fragment is extracted. Second, we get a richer sense of some of the background as well as foreground circumstances of dialogue, in both the miscellany that find their way through and, more important, the matters of form, style, and genre that the larger units of discourse reveal. We can track changing Fiji European and Fiji Indian eloquence through the very languages and speech genres used. To this end, idiosyncrasies of spelling and diction have been retained in all quoted material. Working from and focusing on formal, written rhetoric of course limits our access to other verbal genres; we will pay close attention to accounts of important oral moments in dialogue, but (with the aid of interview material on events of fifty years past) we work from the written archive.

The source for the majority of the discourse quoted here is the Fiji National Archives, and within it the minute papers of the Colonial Secretary's Office. These files collected as exhibits the materials sent to or gathered by government for action, the letters and memos sent out by officials, and, of great interest to us, the numbered sequences of notes written by officials for other officials, about the exhibits and what to do about them. In these minute papers we can observe fragments of internal official dialogue and, in the relation of the notes to the exhibits and in the contexts of both, fragments of the dialogues between colonizers and colonized. We will also consider Fiji Indian discourse in genres apart from modes of address to the government, principally local newspapers and books published in India. The languages used for Indian discourse will be observed, but all quotations will be translated into English. Sometimes the Fiji government was interested enough to have something translated; we will examine their translations to see the way they received the Indian discourse at issue.

In this study I will be discussing the "Europeans" and "Indians" of Fiji, two different "races." None of these terms should be taken as natural. For good reasons many Fiji scholars and politicians want to substitute *Indo-Fijian* for *Fiji Indian,* to stress the connection to Fiji. Fiji's "Europeans" came mainly from Australia. And "race" theories in social and political discourse, then and now, are fraudulent biologically no matter how powerful ideologically. I talk about the "Indians," the "Europeans," and "race" not because these are natural realities but because people in colonial Fiji talked about them and used these terms to discuss themselves and others.

People familiar with Fiji have no doubt noticed that I have so far discussed Indians and Europeans but not "Fijians," a term restricted in local usage to the descendants of the indigenous Fijians. The British Empire remade Fiji into a place where Fiji Indians outnumbered indigenous Fijians; in my larger study I discuss the changing relations among the Fiji Indians, the "European" colonials, and the indigenous Fijians. However, indigenous Fijians have very little to do with the dialogues discussed in this study and consequently will come up only on occasion.

Further, the voices of women will be heard only rarely in this study, because they rarely entered the public dialogues examined here. This absence is itself significant to our story, as are the limits and pressures imposed on Fiji Indian women by both Europeans and other Indians. However, the private forms through which Fiji Indian women understood and dealt with their situation are not addressed here. We know from Kanwal (1980) that they did express themselves about past, present, and future in working songs; study akin to that of Abu-Lughod (1986) might be able to open further this side of Fiji's discursive history. However, as Naidu (1980: 38) makes clear, research by young men into the lives of older Fiji Indian women reaches significant limits quickly. I made no attempt to capture the hidden speech history of *girmitiya* women or to speculate about their influence on the public discourse we examine. For this history of public dialogues, we can only note how small a role these women, their virtue residing in their dependence on men, were expected and allowed to play while Indian and European men refashioned their own moral character in arguments about women's virtue.

Finally, I would like to note that this is not a story of victory for the colonized in resistance to colonial hegemony. Nor is it the whole history of colonial authority in Fiji and of Fiji Indian resistance to it. On both these counts, my larger study will be more satisfactory in its depiction of how Fiji Indians developed and used their own form of capitalism to evade colonial domination. In this account (and also in that one) the heroes are flawed and their successes mixed with failures. Both stories have elements of tragedy—the larger more terrible, with the coups of 1987. But this is the one I will tell as a tragedy, precisely in order to examine as protagonists the Arya Samajis.

Acknowledgments

This book is one product of a broader research project, and I do not seek to single out, from among the people who helped me with my research, only those who made particular contributions to this basically historical study. I thank the Fiji government for granting me permission to do this research, the Fiji National Archives (Setariki Tuinaceva, archivist) for access to relevant materials, and the Fiji Museum for scholarly collegiality.

I owe a debt of gratitude to many Fiji Indians, not only those listed here. For everything I warmly thank Shiu and Kamla Lal, Mrs. Phulbasi Singh, Anish and Neelam, Bijan and Uttra Singh, Prabhu, Anshu, and Shael. I also thank many religious organizations and devotional groups—including the Arya Samajs in Samabula and Lami, the Ramayan mandalis at Narere seven miles and Narere eight miles, the Sai Baba centers in Suva, the temple groups at Korociriciri, at Nasinu six miles, in Vatuwaqa and in Suva on Howell Road, and the Ramayan mandalis in Samabula and in Coboni—and the many businessmen I interviewed in their homes and work places. In each group many members were most helpful to me, but I should mention individuals for their gifts of time on my behalf and their efforts to help me understand: Shiu Sharan Sardar, Ambika Prasad Maharaj, Ganesh Prasad, Sukh Lal, Hari Charan, "Moce" Prasad, Bas Deo, Shiu Karan, C. M. Pala, B. B. Desai, Dhirabhai, Raojibhai Patel, Damodaran Nair, Tribuan Datt Sharma, Dr. Virendra Singh, Ram Mohan, Mahend Pratap, and Mahendra Rasiklal.

ACKNOWLEDGMENTS

For their knowledge of the Arya Samaj and insights into its history in Fiji, I thank Surendra Prasad, Narend Gaji, and B. N. Bhim; for the same concerning the Sanatan Dharm and its history in Fiji, I thank Devakar Prasad. For help and advice of many kinds, their encyclopedic knowledge of the history of Fiji scholarship, and most important, their knowledge of Fiji's colonial history and insights into colonial culture, I thank Margaret Patel of the Fiji National Archives and Fergus Clunie, then director of the Fiji Museum.

I thank the following people for their hospitality during my studies in Fiji: Ivan and Ateca Williams, Aseri and Nani Waqa, Epeli and Mere Nauwa, Jone Tuiwai, and the people of Drauniivi village.

Debts are also owed to teachers and colleagues here in the United States: Bernard Cohn, Marshall Sahlins, Ronald Inden, Ralph Nicholas, Donald Brenneis, McKim Marriott, Terence Turner, Stanley Tambiah, Edwin Gerow, Robert Foster, Nicholas Thomas, Vishvajit Pandya, William Sax, John Llewellyn, Diane Mines, Lee Weissman, Patsy Spyer, Rafael Sanchez, all my current colleagues, and especially Martha Kaplan.

Public Debates and Political Crisis, 1929–1932: The Strange Place of Discourse on Sexuality in Fiji Indian History

Between 1930 and 1932 public debates between religious societies dominated Fiji Indian public discourse and amazed and appalled colonial observers. In a time of political, economic, and social crisis in Fiji and in India, the Fiji Indians focused their energy and attention on "religious" disputation about sexual immorality. Why?

The Fiji Indians

The Fiji Islands became a British colony in 1874 when a group of indigenous "chiefs" assembled by the British for the purpose signed a Deed of Cession. Five years later the first Indian indentured laborers arrived in the coolie ships from South Asia, the labor for the sugar plantations and other enterprises that would make the new colony pay without exploiting its indigenous population. By the end of indenture in 1919, over sixty thousand Indians came to Fiji as indentured laborers; they called themselves *girmitiyas* (from the English word *agreement,* a reference to the labor contract). The British called them "coolies." The plan had been, in the words of an early governor, for the Indians to be "a working population and nothing more" (Scarr 1980: 88), but the Indians made their own plans. By the 1970s, not only was Fiji independent of colonial government, but the vast majority of European settlers had emigrated, seeing no future for themselves in the islands, leaving behind a Fiji with an Indian majority population and an economy based on Indian management as well as labor.

As indentured laborers these Indians came from North and South India. The first three-quarters were recruited in North India, mainly from what is now Uttar Pradesh, and departed for Fiji from a Calcutta depot, and the last quarter was recruited in South India and departed from a depot in Madras. The indentured laborers were 85 percent Hindu and 15 percent Muslim; in the 1976 census the Fiji Indian population of 295,000, 50 percent of Fiji's total population, was 80 percent Hindu, 15 percent Muslim, and 4 percent Christian. While continuing to be "Hindu" and "Muslim" (with changing forms and practices), Fiji's Indians lost caste every early in their Fiji history, in the radical pollution of indenture, and developed an egalitarian ethos.

The vast majority of social and historical studies of Fiji have concerned themselves with indigenous Fijians, but important research concerning the Fiji Indians has been conducted by Gillion, Lal, Mishra, Subramani, Kanwal, Nandan, Naidu, Mamak, Ali, Moynagh, anthropologists Mayer, Jayawardena, Brenneis, Brown, and others. Important historical research on overseas Indians including Fiji Indians has been done by Tinker. This study is not intended to replace any others, but rather to carry inquiry further into its particular point of focus, the politics of virtue among Fiji Indians from 1929 to 1932.

The Debates in Context

Consider the situation of the Fiji Indians in public politics when the debates on religion, sex, and virtue began. The first election of Indians to Fiji's Legislative Council in 1929 was accompanied by political turmoil and anti-Indian public rhetoric. The Indians had been promised electoral representation as early as 1920 in a concession to the government of India. The Fiji colonial government, in an ignorant misreckoning, had hoped that such concessions would lead to the resumption of "assisted" immigration of Indian labor to Fiji, but they did not. Even without the new labor, the Fiji government was forced by the Colonial Office in London to make good on its promise, which it did in the 1929 elections. The Indians were allowed three seats on the council. However, the Indians elected took those seats only briefly. For three days they read a long list of queries detailing Indian grievances on a wide range of topics, from the need for cooperative credit associations and reform of land-leasing systems to the unfairness of having Christian but not Hindu and Muslim public holidays. Then on 5 November 1929, Vishnu Deo, the leader of the Indian representatives, moved that the council recognize that political rights and status granted to Indians on separate racial[1] lines were not acceptable, and that Indians should be granted voting privileges on a common roll with other British subjects resident in Fiji. Only the Indian representatives voted to support the motion. When it was defeated, as all had known it would be, the Indians left the council and resigned their seats.

Behind the boycott stood a Fiji Indian National Congress. Before the walkout in late 1929 this congress ran successful Round Table meetings in which "all sections" of Fiji Indian society met and the boycott strategy was determined; after the walkout a congress meeting in Suva supported the boycott by acclamation. S. B. Patel, a lawyer sent by Gandhi to Fiji and an organizer of this congress, wrote to a London-based colleague:

We have decided upon the lines of future work. We have a National Congress of Fiji. The unity and solidarity among the Indian settlers here today are as they never were before. All sections stand united in one demand for the common franchise. We are all coming closer together day by day. We intend organising provincial and district congresses in all important quarters, and passing resolutions demanding the common franchise, in every Congress committee. We intend to take up the work of educating the masses for political consciousness. (quoted in Gillion 1977: 135)

By 1932 the Fiji Indian National Congress was moribund, never to reappear as a serious force. No Indians served on the Legislative Council until new elections late in 1932, elections for which Vishnu Deo was ineligible as a candidate because he had been convicted earlier that year of a felony, publication of obscene materials. The candidate put up in his place, and elected as his proxy, soon ignored his instructions and became a tool of the government instead. The inability of Vishnu Deo to stand for this election was effectively the end of the boycott and of the politics of open resistance to the colonial form of public order by an organized whole Indian political community.

Consider now some larger networks of dialogue, the topography of a larger colonial universe of discourse. As Joan Vincent notes in her "Prolegomena to the Study of the Colonial State" (1988: 151, 144), colonial officials "were expected to view politics as an aberration." In Fiji as in the African case she discusses, "administration and politics were viewed as worlds apart." In colonial Fiji, as in most polities, there was a space of power neither public nor private; in colonial Fiji it was particularly large. Debates on legislation concerning Fiji Indian "custom" and social organization were occasionally public, available in the published

1. Please recall the comments in the preface about the language of "race."

accounts of Legislative Council meetings. But laws and administrative policies were really shaped in the dialogues between colonial officials, dialogues kept oral or written in "minute papers" inaccessible to indigenous Fijians, Fiji Indians, and unofficial Europeans outside the halls of official practice. Official Fiji stood above the "public" sphere of marketplaces, streets, shops, and newspapers and by its own lights had ultimate authority over the order of both the public world and the private individuals in it. But official Fiji was not itself the apex of official hierarchy. In fact, Fiji was an imperial backwater. In the 1920s the integrity of official Fiji's authority was often breached by directives from London enforcing the advice of colonial India. India wanted more; it wanted an Indian Agent reporting directly to the government of India to control Fiji Indian affairs. In the late 1920s an arrangement among London, India, and Fiji compromised the integrity of official Fiji a bit more. J. R. Pearson, a civil service officer, was transferred from India to become Fiji's first "Secretary for Indian Affairs."

Especially from 1929 to 1932, Pearson waged a series of campaigns within official dialogue, most of which he lost, to find ways to give Indian "custom," "personal law," and "traditional" forms of authority official standing in Fiji. In marriage law, in court procedures, in rural government, and in educational policy Pearson sought closer articulation of Indian culture and Indian authorities with official power in the colony. His goal was to reward "moderation" and punish "extremism," to direct Indian development. But he was caught in a cross fire. He received no support from the Indian leadership, especially from the leaders like S. B. Patel and Vishnu Deo whom he and the rest of official Fiji regarded as "extremist." At the same time he alienated the official Fiji establishment, which feared Indian culture and politics in general. In 1932 his appointment was not renewed, and Fiji convinced London that it no longer needed the help of India to make policy for its Indians. Examining what separated Pearson from the rest of official Fiji on the one side, and the Indian leaders on the other, will help us measure the strange social and epistemological distances in this colonial universe of discourse; it will begin to suggest the gulfs countercolonial discourse had to bridge. Vishnu Deo and other Indians did not only discuss Hinduism, sexuality, and the exigencies of virtue with each other. They also lobbied Pearson and others of official Fiji, with varied results, over marriage law, child marriage, and custody disputes.

Questions of sexuality and virtue also arose in Indian efforts to develop their own public political space. The story of Vishnu Deo's fall is also the story of the failure of an effort to reform Fiji Hinduism, the story of the Arya Samaj and its fate in Fiji. In 1926 Fiji leaders of the Arya Samaj, a Hindu reform society, helped found and came to dominate a Fiji Hindu Maha Sabha, a national association that in its correspondence with government claimed to represent all of Fiji's Hindus. But controversy rose from 1930 to 1932. When *pandit* missionaries of the Sanatan Dharm, "the eternal religion," arrived in Fiji from India in late 1930, bitter public debates followed between them and the Samaj leaders, especially Vishnu Deo. The prospects for Fiji Indian political unity were destroyed by these debates, debates that were mainly about sexual morality: widow remarriage, child marriage, and the sexual conduct of prophets and gods. The reformist Arya Samaj was in favor of widow remarriage, against child marriage, and scornful of almost the entire corpus of Hindu myths, epics, and scriptures. Its project was religious but also social and political, building schools and involving its members in the developing nationalist movements in India. The Samaj was convinced of the need for a strong, "modern," and organized Hindu community. The Sanatan Dharm leaders advocated quite a different religious and social agenda: respect for a wide range of religious writings (especially the Tulsi Das Ramayan), support for child marriage, criticism of widow remarriage. The Sanatan Dharm had great appeal, especially among those knowledgeable about the myths, epics, and other religious texts the Arya Samaj sought to abandon.

The issue, how to build a politically, socially, and religiously strong community, became a debate about morality. While electoral politics was stalemated in boycott and a depression was reshaping world economics, the Fiji Arya Samaj found its position increasingly compromised and its reform agenda thwarted. In 1931 it launched an aggressive attack on the social and sexual morality recommended by the Sanatan Dharm. The Arya Samaj strategy was to reveal the immorality of the Sanatan Dharm by reading and ridiculing passages from texts accepted by the latter as sacred. As Vishnu Deo later put it, their argument was that "the Purans in parts accuse our ancestors, deities, seers and sages with gross indecencies and impure practices of most filthy and unnatural description and yet they are read to young and old alike."[2] The most famous debates, later infamous from the obscenity prosecution, occurred in 1931 between an increasingly belligerent Vishnu Deo and various representatives of the Sanatan Dharm. In January 1932 Vishnu Deo raised the stakes further, publishing what was nominally an account of the major 1931 debate and the victory of the Arya Samaj, an account that grew in size as more and better material was gathered for inclusion.

2. This quotation is from a confidential letter written by Vishnu Deo to the Governor in 1932 in a failed effort to obtain a pardon and, thereby, eligibility for the Legislative Council.

Official Fiji acted quickly, banning the book and destroying most of the copies. Vishnu Deo and another Arya Samaj leader, Babu Ram Singh, were brought to trial for selling an obscene publication. At their trial they changed their pleas from not guilty to guilty, and their attorney argued that (in the paraphrase of the *Fiji Times,* 9 March 1932) "this prosecution constitutes a singular and signal vindication of the principles for which the accused are contending. In effect, the publication is an attack on these offending passages and intended as a condemnation of them." However, the judge condemned their action. While leveling only a token fine, he criticized both men and the tenor of the Indian public debates more generally, calling for tolerance in the Indian community on the model of that between sects in the Christian community. In particular, he argued, the accused must realize that "no community will permit an outrageous and obscene attack upon the religious beliefs of any section thereof." By the middle of 1932 the Arya Samaj had moved from its presumed leadership of Fiji's Hindus to status as a sect, warned to leave the other Hindus alone. And Vishnu Deo was locked out of electoral politics for years.

The "religious" disputes of the Indian community destroyed the order apparently achieved in 1929. Debate and schism were not only between the Arya Samaj and the Sanatan Dharm: in these years Fiji's Muslims grew more orthodox and separatist through the leadership of their own missionaries, and Fiji's South Indians began to organize themselves into their own separate "Sangam" societies as well. But the clash of the Arya Samaj and the Sanatan Dharm was the most consequential. Official observers and their spies were disgusted by the level of issue and rhetoric in the key debates, finding the arguments about propriety in marriage and the sexuality of gods comic when they were not distasteful. Pearson wrote in his 1931 *Report on Indian Affairs* that the debate had "degenerated into an unseemly wrangle." But neither he nor others had a persuasive answer to our primary problem: why the public energy of this embattled overseas Indian community moved from countercolonial organizing to infighting over sexual morality. The matter is not explained, either, by existing histories. The leading historian of the Fiji Indians, K. L. Gillion (1977: 113), finds that

it was unfortunate that the Indian community could not stand together, that it was not better led, and that it had so much bad advice from narrow-minded though admittedly well-meaning people. Sectarian conflict weakened the Indians' claim to respect, enabled wedges to be driven between them by self-interested parties, and threw up the wrong type of leaders, who used sectional conflict to promote their own interests.

Without Gillion's ground-breaking research on Fiji's colonial history, this study and many others would not be possible. However, "unfortunate" though the events may have been, we will not follow Gillion in simply regretting them. Neither will we see in them anything natural or inevitable, nor follow Ali (1980: 113) in seeing them as "an exercise in status-seeking by aspiring new leaders desiring recognition." The question is rather, why was "the Indians' claim to respect" such an issue? Why, and in what sense, was status such a problem?

Our inquiry will take us back first to the arrival of the Indians in Fiji, into the "coolie lines" of the sugar plantations. The indenture system that brought the Indians to Fiji was, as Tinker has termed it, a "new system of slavery," the system that followed slavery as the mode of organizing plantation production in the British Empire. As we shall see, the sexual virtue of Indian women was very much an issue there, both in life as lived in Fiji and in the discourse about indentured labor that eventually led to its abolition in 1919. But before turning to these matters, a few more comments might help orient readers interested mainly in general questions about virtue and sexuality, discourse and colonial relations.

Virtue and Sexuality

What is "virtue"? Let us reconsider the double meaning in Western notions of virtue, the relations struck within the word between specifically sexual questions on the one hand, and the arguments about the more general sentiments that make the beast into a citizen on the other. This conjuncture is no accident: notice its presence, also, within the category "morality." A connection between the specifically sexual and the more general themes in these words is not hard to find. The interesting problem is rather that there are so many and different connecting logics, from varieties of Christian concerns about flesh, law, duty, and grace, to Freudian certainties that sexuality is the arena in which the beast is transformed into the citizen.

What then should we do with the category "virtue"? We will be entering some non-Freudian worlds of discourse on "virtue," "sexuality," and "human nature." The Indians, for their part, did not use categories quite like these—we will consider some of their categories at the end of this section. But it is not only the Indians, but also the colonial British, who have a view of human nature, virtue, "character," and "civilization" quite distant from Freud's synthesis. One way to use the category "virtue," then, would be the way Ruth Benedict uses categories such as "debt," "love," "sincerity," and "self-discipline" when studying Japan:

we could juxtapose different versions of "virtue" to enable comparison of different world views.[3] The cost of this approach is the "surgical operation" (Benedict 1946: 233) one conducts on one's own original understandings and commitments, high-risk surgery with outcome unforseen. Its promise is the greater wisdom of the comparative perspective. Another approach to "virtue" is that of moral philosopher Alasdair MacIntyre (1984: 2), who finds the "language of morality" in a "state of grave disorder" and tries to put it right. MacIntyre commits himself to the vision of a "classical tradition of the virtues," (p. 243) whose best features he can recover for us. The greater wisdom, here, is not breadth of historical and cultural understanding but precisely the recovery of philosophical gems such as the Aristotelian telos and "the threefold structure of untutored human-nature-as-it-happens-to-be, human-nature-as-it-could-be-if-it-realized-its-telos and the precepts of rational ethics as the means for the transition from one to the other" (p. 53). The cost is the need, in the recovery process, to prepare the jewels for their new settings. In MacIntyre's solution the human telos itself is set within a relativizing terrain, a human "virtue" defined as any acquired ability to achieve a good, such goods defined as "internal to practices" that vary culturally and historically (p. 191).

MacIntyre's effort to reconstruct "virtue" is bereft of discussion of the concept's sexual side, a startling indicator of the abstract nature of his search. Not only for this reason, I will begin by way of Benedict's method. I agree with MacIntyre that discourse on virtue has been fragmented historically, but the vision he stresses as Aristotelian I would locate as an early modern and even colonially inflected European reading of Greek, Roman, and Christian discourse. The emphasis in this version of "virtue" is on what people can become if they follow specially enlightened rules and rulers.[4] And rather than recovering the wisdom here for our context, I will examine its use in its own context, especially the colonial world. We turn then briefly to some of the major articulations of "vir-

3. See Benedict 1946: 100–101, 120, 215–18, 233. Benedict starts with received, dictionary-style equivalents and then deconstructs the equivalence in order to bring differences between whole patterns into focus. She clearly frames such discussions: "*Makoto* does not mean what sincerity does in English usage. It means both far less and far more. . . . Once one has accepted the fact that 'sincerity' does not have the American meaning it is a most useful word to note in all Japanese texts" (pp. 215–18). Once underway, she bends, breaks, and reconnects her key words to reveal the contours of the different pattern: "Love, kindness, generosity, which we value just in proportion as they are given without strings attached, necessarily must have their strings attached in Japan. And every such act makes one a debtor" (p. 113).

4. For some general issues in the history of reading and imagining the "classics," see Bernal 1987.

tue" in early modern Europe, to expand our sense of what was possible, and what was made real, in use of the category. Let us start with a notable colonial, Benjamin Franklin, to whom the virtues were a divinely fashioned prospect to pursue, as real and invariant as the vices that had to be suppressed to attain them.

Franklin's major text on virtue, a part of his autobiography (1791), was what would now be called "therapeutic" in intention, less concerned to establish facts about virtue than to determine how the virtues might be cultivated in practice. Citing Socrates and Pythagoras, quoting Cicero and multiple biblical passages, convinced that God "governs the world by His providence . . . [and] that God will certainly reward virtue and punish vice, either here or in the hereafter," (1962 [1791]: 92) Franklin sought to find the way "to live without committing any fault at any time" and determined that the problem was that "contrary habits must be broken" (p. 82). He therefore prescribed a practical regimen of adherence to a sequence of thirteen virtues: Temperance, Silence, Order, Resolution, Frugality, Industry, Sincerity, Justice, Moderation, Cleanliness, Tranquility, Chastity, and Humility. Practical mastery of each was to lead to practical mastery of the next. Prudent restraint of sexual practice "for health or offspring, never to dulness, weakness, or the injury of your own or another's peace or reputation" (p. 83), comes, as chastity, next to last in the hierarchy. What is particularly interesting about this late placement of chastity is that Franklin is certainly concerned to rein in the passions. Temperance (in food and drink) comes first "as it tends to procure that coolness and clearness of head, which is so necessary, where constant vigilance was to be kept up, and a guard maintained against the unremitting attraction of ancient habits, and the force of perpetual temptations" (p. 83). The Christian language of temptations of the flesh, encompassed later into libidinal sexuality, is regarded by Franklin as the organizing principle of a much wider field of vices, from pleasures, appetites, inclinations, and passions, bodily and mental, to avarice, ambition, and pride. The problem was a general struggle against "natural inclination," a need to subdue "natural passions" through disciplined practice (p. 90). Franklin portrayed his practical pursuit of his loosely structured telos, struggling against his nature as it was, as the basis for his success: "Tho' I never arrived at the perfection I had been so ambitious of obtaining, but fell far short of it, yet I was, by the endeavor, a better and happier man than I otherwise should have been if I had not attempted it" (p. 88). The classic bourgeois imperatives of frugality and industry, the commitments whose moral formulation so interested Max Weber, were to Franklin matters of (male) human telos rather than human nature; pursuit of them was not, as it was for Adam Smith, a natural expression of self-interest but a choice to seek that telos. Franklin constructed a book of tables in which he kept a daily record of his adherence to the virtues, and he prefixed to the books a prayer for daily use: "O powerful Goodness! bountiful Father! merciful Guide! Increase in me that wisdom which discovers my truest interest. Strengthen my resolutions to perform what that wisdom dictates" (p. 85). The good did not simply follow natural interests but were blessed with special wisdom about "truest interest."

To Franklin virtue was more important than the rest of philosophical wisdom and religious practice. He rejected existing organized religion because its advice was not practical enough. As in the natural philosophy of the day, so in relation to virtue God had less and less of a role to play in the world. It was not even necessary that divinity be ascribed to the precepts that shaped the virtues of sound human character, once a theory of the evolution of civilization made "civilization" in no way transcendent to natural history. After Hobbes, Locke, Rousseau, and Hume propounded their various accounts of God, man, and the states of nature and civilization, Adam Smith in *The Theory Of Moral Sentiments* (1759) refused to accept an irreducible telos, or any story of a single moment transforming rude savagery into civilized society. Smith generated the virtues within an ongoing natural history composed of natural social relations between men, their reason, and their faculty of "sympathy" for each other. For Smith, as for Franklin, sex and reproduction was just another matter to be contested between passions and reason; virtuous people reproduced according to the usefulness of children. But to Smith the virtues were still real, still the basis of character and fate, and the civilized were privileged, mentally and materially, because they developed them.[5] We can trace discourse on virtue and history from here into the dramatic reversals of much of Smith's position in Thomas Malthus's essay on population (1798). Malthus made sexual

---

5. Some who want Smith to be the founder of political economy also wish his moral philosophy could be summed up as "rational choice." But Smith attributes success to virtue, not reason. He could not accept the blurring of the difference between virtues and vices in Mandeville's *Fable of the Bees,* which argued that private vices were public benefits, even though Mandeville may have provoked Smith's own inquiry into what apart from benevolence guided people to prosperity. Despite his thinly veiled respect for Mandeville's argument, Smith sides with the philosophers who "suppose that there is a real and essential distinction between vice and virtue" and condemns the view of Mandeville, "which seems to take away altogether the distinction between vice and virtue, and of which tendency is, upon that account, wholly pernicious" (1976 [1759]: 485, 487). See also Smith's letter to the *Edinburgh Review* in 1755, which champions Rousseau against Mandeville on the principle that "pity," "natural to man, is capable of producing all those virtues, whose reality Dr. Mandeville denies" (1967 [1755]: 24).

questions more central to matters of virtue, not only because population increase had such dire consequences, but also because population conditioned the development of virtues and vices; he made reason a provocation of a divinely designed environment rather than a divinely inspired instinct; he was extraordinarily ambivalent about the position of sexual passions among the virtues and vices, pressured by the reception of the first version of the essay to make restraint of sexual practice a "moral restraint" rather than itself a "vice," as he had first depicted it.

If we follow Malthus in the direction his own work took, he leads us into the emergence of properly political-economic discourse, which, as Tribe (1978) persuasively argues, appears in the early nineteenth century. In nineteenth-century readings of Smith and in writings by Malthus and others, money value replaced moral virtue as the efficacious substance behind social evolution, quantities replaced qualities, and most importantly, a naturally "economic man" replaced a "civilized" one as the practitioner of rational ethics. Malthus held the first professorship anywhere in political economy, from which chair his writings grew more concerned with profits, rents, production, and value, less with God, reason, sexuality, and virtue. And no doubt the political-economic theory of this later Malthus helped reorganize certain aspects of colonial life. The professorship was at Haileybury, the East India Company's college. But before there was this college, or its chair in the new form of knowledge, there were colonial companies, plantations, and colonized peoples, a colonial world made by men, such as Franklin, who considered themselves "civilized" not "economic." And the promoters and defenders of "civilization" were far from finished in the early nineteenth century.[6]

Powerful new discourses do not immediately annihilate old ones—no news here—and I suggest that the colonies of the European empires were in the nineteenth and early twentieth centuries the context of a new and doomed efflorescence of European discourse about virtue, race, and civilization, even while that discourse was in a process of radical reconsideration in Europe as the alternative ontology of "political-economy" advanced. As political economy was propounded, the earlier image of human nature was increasingly challenged, concretely by such political economists as James Mill. In James Mill's view, as in his "Essay on Government" (1978 [1820]), "men" were by their nature maximizers of their own pleasure and minimizers of their own pain, and government a necessary evil that should be designed to minimize the power it granted

---

6. In a sense, the defenders of civilization are still a force in the 1990s, though it has become a specifically "Western civilization" that they seek to promote and defend.

to individuals who would inevitably, by their *nature,* impose their own interests on others. There was no special role in Mill's version for a human telos or "truest interests," or for men of greater virtue than others. In reply to such challenges, a new defense of civilization and its significance was propounded by such imperialists as Thomas Macaulay. Macaulay criticized Mill's assertions about "inseparable" parts of human nature and insisted on the importance of changes effected by civilization: "Civilized men, pursuing their own happiness in a social state, are not Yahoos fighting for carrion" (1978 [1829]: 117). Macaulay's vision was of a cultured superiority for a class that had achieved civilization and of a history that depended on their maintenance, propagation, and defense of it.

Macaulay's view was the license of empire. Its version of human nature is Aristotelian, centered on the prospect of improvement, and Macaulay's concern for human development is as practical as is Franklin's. But it is differently oriented: not simply to self-improvement and guidance for other individuals, but to extension and defense of the superior attainments of his group. Before and after Macaulay's day, Christian writers propounded even broader charters that included divinely inspired achievements and agenda as well as progress that was humanly made. But all that was necessary to define the colonial vision of virtue and civilization was the image of a cultural gap between rulers and ruled, a gap in social achievement, social-evolutionary time. This view of the gap between rulers and ruled as a gap in evolutionary time is of great importance in colonial discourse and, as we shall see, outweighed the political-economic image of natural marketplace behavior in the British colonial imagination. In India policy, much more than in British politics, James Mill concurred with Thomas Macaulay; both, of course, spent years of their working lives in service of India. Mill, the dominant European historian of India for the nineteenth century, explained India not as a different or degenerate form of civilization but as an immature one, retarded by a Malthusian effect, with a population history less conducive to advance (see, e.g., Hutchins 1967: 11).

More than half a century later, in the works of Conrad, we receive another powerful statement of the imperial view of human nature: hearts of darkness in uncultured people (perhaps made worse by eons of tropical climate) and a horrifying but exhilarating form of power there, to be repressed by the comforting order and power of civilization as expressed in the etiquette of the parlors of Europe. In contrast the political-economic version of history decenters civilization and ascribes capitalist order to rational choices springing spontaneously from human nature. To a V. S. Naipaul India is an "area of darkness" not because a dark human nature is unfettered there but because India's system of culture, its civilization (now conceived as a traditional closed-mindedness) is smothering individual freedom. Throughout the colonial era, in the West itself these two discourses clashed in myriad matters both practical and theoretical. After World War II, as a guiding principle of decolonization, the political-economic view of human nature and culture firmly replaced the colonial one, bringing us to the image of first, second, and third worlds, which (as Pletsch [1981] demonstrates) ascribes the problem of the third world to bad cultures while presuming a political-economic human nature.

What of sexuality in these discourses? Let us begin with Freud and sexuality in political-economic discourse. Freud's unconscious id could be depicted as the heart of darkness controlled by a civilizing consciousness. But more often Freud's own depiction of libido, sexual hunger, was of a psychic currency, and his image of human nature is thereby political-economic. In Freud's corpus one finds a developed model of psychic economy with currency, production, exchanges, and investments. The reality principle and the founding of society and civilization were both usually explained as products of cost-benefit reckonings. To be sure, Freud was no ordinary political economist. He saw interest in money and wealth as a transformation of other psychic currency and interests and viewed political economy itself as properly a branch of applied psychology.[7] Nevertheless his discourse was founded on a conception of an individual who calculates his or her way through various relationships, evaluating them all according to personal needs and preferences. His major innovations, the discovery of an unconscious and of a libido within it, actually serve to ground in a general human nature and its normal development a series of attitudes, self-conceptions, and social techniques that Marx had tried to prove profoundly social and historical. In this way Freud is a back door from Marx back to Adam Smith, or as Voloshinov argued (1987: 10–15), a servant of a bourgeois urge to deny the historical nature of the bourgeois self and to naturalize it. But more is provided by Freud's transformation and reaffir-

---

7. Freud wrote in the New Introductory Lectures, "even under the domination of those [economic] conditions men can only bring their original instinctual impulses into play. . . . If anyone were in a position to show in detail the way in which these different factors—the general inherited human disposition, its racial variations and its cultural transformations—inhibit and promote one another under the conditions of social rank, profession and earning capacity—if anyone were able to do this, he would have supplemented Marxism so that it was made into a genuine social science. For sociology, too, dealing as it does with the behaviour of people in society, cannot be anything but applied psychology. Strictly speaking there are only two sciences: psychology, pure and applied, and natural science" (1965 [1933]: 178–79).

mation of the Christian certainty that sexual passions lie at the center of human nature.

As Foucault argues, well before Freud sex was the "aspect of itself that troubled and preoccupied" the European bourgeoisie "more than any other." "It staked its life and death on sex by making it responsible for its future welfare; . . . it subordinated its soul to sex by conceiving of it as what constituted the soul's most secret and determinant part" (1980: 123–24). Sexual passions rose as the deepest truth and motive, as the organizing principle of the human "soul," precisely as God receded and was replaced by Nature.[8] Then it was Freud, not Malthus and Smith, who connected the passions and the interests most usefully. Freud depicted not passions simply given, or merely in conflict with rational long-run interests, but flexible, transferable passions capable of finding new objects, of underwriting any commitment, of saturating the world of things with meanings. In the world of political economy, the possibilities for sexuality as the answer to the mysteries of selfhood are easy to see. It supplies a nice starter-motor for a system that wants to take for granted the existence of individual tastes and preferences, wants, needs, and desires. In contemporary consumer culture, implicit and explicit sexual fulfillment has become a central quest, and advertisers strive to make their products into a sexual fulfillment. We are the children of Freudian economics. But our principal interest is in characters who had not been trained to respond to an implicit sexuality underlying other meanings.

The break in discourse that licensed and emerged with colonial social practice was the one that substituted a historically emergent "civilization" for a transcendent deity as guarantor of the telos of the virtues. Simply by knowing "civilization" a colonial European could rank people against its precepts, know the good, plan the future, and suppress the responses of the other with confidence in the logic and propriety of

8. When Freud's contemporary Durkheim argued that "man is double" and that our reasoning selves are irreducibly social, he defined ritual and religion as precisely those activities and conceptual frameworks that made and remade the consciousness in the person. He was then most perplexed by the observable historical decline in his "modern" world of what people unconcerned for his redefinitions, including himself, were calling "ritual" and "religion." Durkheim concluded that science, rising up as a "rival power," had changed the prospects for religion, submitting religion to its criticism and control; nevertheless religion was "destined to transform itself rather than to disappear" (Durkheim 1915: 478–79). While Durkheim's perplexity has spawned generations of student papers on whether science is the new religion, it is surely more reasonable to see as the new Durkheimian "religion" the discourse on sexuality, sex as the voice of Nature in our selves. In the "rituals" by which the European bougeoisie shaped the self-consciousness of themselves and their children, hygiene, health, fitness, and beauty became more basic to self than prayer and salvation; bathing and exercise, not communion, became what was obligatory (what the Hindu Mimamsaka ritualists would call *nitya*, necessary).

the actions. As many have pointed out, "character" was all-important in the colonial world, basic in European colonial self-image and, later, self-justification. Character could be imagined as God's will, history's vanguard, or white racial genius. But it was in any case "constructed out of a cultural consensus on Europeanness, rooted in a bearing and material standard of living to which all whites had to subscribe and from which Asians were barred" (Stoler 1989: 141).

In short, in expanding early modern Europe, before the reconstructions accomplished by political-economic discourse, virtues and vices were realities central to the explanation of character, the cultivation of virtues was central to the process of civilization, and the rise of civilization was the story of history. The pattern did not make sexuality into a matter of particular importance—at least, for men. Women were understood to be intrinsically different, both in their nature-as-it-was and as-they-could-be-if-they-realized-their-telos. As many have shown, their telos was different, usually associated with home rather than public action, faith rather than reason, body rather than spirit, children and dependency rather than adulthood and free agency. Unlike men they were identified as sexed and rarely considered apart from their sexual partners. Conrad's *Heart of Darkness* could tell the story of Kurtz with the most significant reference to his fiancée made while he is dying, "my Intended" along with "my station, my career, my ideas" in the list of things he gave up to pursue his fate in the darkness. His Intended, on the other hand, exists entirely through her relation to the dead Kurtz; "she had a mature capacity for fidelity, for belief, for suffering," remarkable for "the faith that was in her . . . that great and saving illusion that shone with an unearthly glow in the darkness, in the triumphant darkness from which I could not have defended her" (1963 [1899]: 76–77). "I could not perhaps understand," she says, but "I believed in him more than any one on earth" (p. 78). While hers is the only light that pierces Marlow's own darkness, he knows that its faith is in a lie. "He needed me! Me!" she says, and when Marlow lies that Kurtz's last word was her name he saves her faith. But of course Kurtz's last words were not her name, and he did not need her, whatever his path. It should not surprise us that, along these lines, sexual morality was a more important part of the virtue of women than it was of men, or that European women played a decidedly secondary role in the colonial project, often literally absent or even banned in the early stages.[9] The entry of European women into

9. In *Heart of Darkness* Marlow comments further, on the relation of women's telos and colonial adventure: "They—the women I mean—are out of it—should be out of it. We must help them stay in that beautiful world of their own, lest ours gets worse. . . . You should have heard the disinterred body of Mr. Kurtz saying 'My Intended.' You would have perceived directly then how completely she was out of it" (1963 [1899]: 49).

colonial societies, argues Stoler (1989: 147), was usually part of a planned domestication or stabilization of a colonial project already underway.

Ashis Nandy finds that an ideological promotion of specifically European masculine virility developed in European colonial society, seeing in the writings of Orwell, for example, "an unending search for masculinity and status before the colonized; the perception of the colonized as gullible children who must be impressed with conspicuous machismo" (Nandy 1983: 40). By 1924 British popular writer Philip Gibbs is moved to begin *The Romance of Empire* with this sentence: "The making of the British Empire has been a great adventure of which we may well be proud—an adventure in which the manhood of the race has proved its mettle, time and time again, through many centuries and in many lands; an adventure in which men have spilt their blood freely, with a genial courage, with a really rollicking spirit of gallantry, and with a fine carelessness of danger and death." Perhaps this self-consciously masculine telos of pride, bleeding, genial courage, and a really rollicking spirit of gallantry and carelessness—a telos for masculinity that is certainly not dead—is itself a product of colonial history. Or perhaps it is an undercurrent suppressed by the pieties of a Franklin or the earnestness of a Smith. In any case, the closer connection to body and sexuality of women's virtue than men's is not unique to early modern and colonial European discourses.[10]

Excellent studies of gender, race, and class now abound that seek to calibrate into one model of hegemony or domination the hierarchical relations of gender, class, and race in European history. For example, Gilman (1985) persuasively demonstrates interconnections in turn-of-the-century Viennese stereotypes about blackness, savagery, Jews, and promiscuity of primitives, low-class prostitutes, and women in general, concluding with a condemnation of the human tendency to stereotype. The force of such synthetic calibrations is to prove the profundity of gender domination, to dispel the illusions of all forms of paternalism, and to underline the protean possibilities of the rhetoric of European superiority. But do they clarify the historical particularity of assertions of European superiority? The European colonial discourse on virtue and civilization enabled, and still enables, its own form of domination on

10. For another example, Bauer (1985: 120) finds "local importance placed upon women's use of their bodies (or sexuality) and men's social graces in constructing moral behavior and concepts of self" in working-class urban Iran. Many other examples of the same or similar organization of identity, morality, and sexuality could no doubt be found. For interesting efforts to pursue the roots of British manliness, see Mangan and Walvin 1987, especially the contribution by MacKenzie on "the imperial pioneer and hunter."

lines of race, class, gender, and also on other lines of difference, notably culture, in each case first asserting the essential nature of a difference and then a moral ranking based on the difference. Current studies that measure all history on three connected dimensions of race, class, and gender domination can reveal and condemn dominators, but do they clarify the historical particularity of the larger strategy itself, the difference for example between the discourse on civilization, with its assertions of achieved superiority, and the discourse on political economy, with its assertions of universal sameness of agency? We can locate ideas of virtue and civilization, and their uses, in the dilemmas of people seeking not simply to understand colonial discourse but to respond to it, precisely what the Gandhians and other Indian nationalists had to do.

There is also a growing body of excellent scholarship concerned with gender and sexuality in particular colonial situations. Again concerned with the intersection of gender, race, and class, many of these studies question the proposition that white women incited or exacerbated the racism of colonial societies (see especially Stoler 1989). Fox-Genovese (1988) and Hansen (1989) examine relations between races within colonial households in the southern United States and in Zambia. On Fiji itself, Knapman (1986) chronicles the lives of "white women," 1835 to 1930, in order to prove that they were "ordinary": "By telling their story I hope to have restored in some measure the integrity of white women who crossed the seas, loved and endured living with their husbands, bore and wept for their babies, worked, relaxed, laughed, suffered and died—ordinary women" (p. 177). Knapman's archival work is thorough, and she details the suffering in the daily lives of these "pioneer" women, but her concern to vindicate them dominates her inquiry into their participation in the broader network of exploitation that supported their way of life. Jolly (1987) discusses Melanesian women in indentured labor in the Pacific, to keep their history from being forgotten, and shows that their labor emigration was controlled and limited by both Melanesian and colonial European men. On colonized women in India, Krishnamurty (1989) collects essays under the rubric of "economic and social history," and Sangari and Vaid (1989) collect essays that seek "to understand the historical processes which reconstitute patriarchy in colonial India" (p. 2), including several important studies of reform discourse. While Knapman's study of Fiji describes aspects of the history of gender and sexuality there, it is really the Sangari and Vaid collection that addresses questions most similar to those raised in this study: the dilemmas and resolutions, sources and consequences of colonial dialogue and the reform and anticolonial discourse of the colonized.

The key question for us is still, what is virtue? With the wisdom afforded by comparing different versions of it, we know that its form, content, and importance vary even within the history of European discourse. I will leave questions about the boundaries of these discourses on virtue open, and I will leave it to the examination of Fiji materials to decide which claims about character, virtue, and civilization were relevant there and how. The point in this section has been to examine presuppositions and open possibilities for a politics, to consider some of the fundamental questions about virtue on which challenge could be mounted and change attempted. How could the Fiji Indians live with the colonial realities of virtue and civilization? How could they live without them?

The tendency in historical studies of the Fiji Indians has been to portray questions of honor and virtue as concerns the Indians injected into colonial Fiji's political discourse. Gillion (1977: 130) sees in Fiji Indian politics a special emphasis on *izzat* ("honor" or "dignity"), product of the pollution of indenture and "a resentment of the inferior position assigned to Indians in the European dominated order." Ali (1980: 16, 37) begins the reification of *izzat*, writing of "*izzat* lost in the degradation of *girmit*," the free Indians having "their *izzat* compromised." Deryck Scarr (1984: 125, 146) completes the reification of *izzat* into an Indian cultural trait: "*Izzat* was at stake, the Indian sense of honour—lost, leaders felt, by three generations or more of Indian people being seen as a labour resource. . . . *Izzat*, the Indian sense of honour, was all." Scarr's rhetoric, especially, resonates with the colonial tendency to explain Indian motives according to racial traits. But the Indian political unity of 1929 did not follow from racial traits. Nor did Fiji Indian political problems. Although specificities of South Asian culture, discourse, and practice in Fiji will be irreducibly relevant to the dialogues we consider, we need not and will not attribute the fascination with questions of virtue, civilization, character, and female sexuality to peculiarities of Indian culture. An attentive reader may already have noted that this makes a deeper mystery of the Fiji Indian turn to questions about female sexuality and sexual morality, since we did not find them to be central themes of the animating European colonial discourses on virtue. This is, indeed, a mystery to be resolved.

We cannot move on without a final Benedict-style moment. Let us note a few significant differences in presupposition between South Asian and European universes of discourse on some specific questions of virtue, especially on the sexual side of the double connotation. When Gandhi called for sexual abstinence as a means of generating moral force in the quest for *swaraj* ("self-rule") and independence for India, his logic owed much to the South Asian discourses on *tapas,* or ascetically generated energy, as well as to the European sources of so much of his moral thinking. More consequential for our purposes, general conceptions of "chastity," especially women's chastity, differ between the two culture areas. As O'Flaherty stresses, a metaphor of flowing fluids underlies many South Asian analyses of human sexuality. If the ascetic is damming up this life-force, all binding of it is as dangerous as it is powerful; especially for women, "instead of boundaries, these rules [in the Dharmasastras] make channels to keep the fluids flowing," and a woman "increases her power, not by performing asceticism (for then she would be denied access to her supplementary source in the male), but by remaining 'chaste' in the socially sanctioned way: by letting milk flow. Thus she increases her power by letting her fluids flow freely" (O'Flaherty 1980: 60, 45). Marriage to a safe, perfectly balanced partner, generally a marriage within caste, is the precondition for this form of chastity. A woman's virtue (*satitva*) consists not in sexual abstinence or self-control but in proper attachment and subordination to her husband. Women are seen as vessels of power requiring control. Within marriage their power is creative; the woman takes semen from her husband, makes children by combining it with her own fluids, gives milk to children. Her sexuality then exists in balance with his. If these ideals sound similar, after all, to the "mature fidelity" of Kurtz's Intended, in some ways they are. However, in South Asia the powers and dangers of women not matched with men were and are used to justify child marriage, arranged marriage, and prohibitions on widow remarriage. They also provided the logic of the relatively rare practice made infamous by early European travelers to India, who never failed to claim they had seen it and to include a depiction in their travel narratives (Cohn 1989): *sati,* the self-immolation of a widow on her husband's funeral pyre.[11] *Sati* was the extreme statement of an ethos for women, *satitva,* virtue or chastity in devotion to husband. In *bhakti* devotional systems, the relation of wife and husband is even figured theologically: wife as devotee to her lord-husband. In Fiji, as we shall see, the *satitva* of "coolie" women became a major and mobilizing political issue. This was not only because the Indians thought it was important, but also because the British did not. And with such a discovery, we can begin to do more than, with Benedict's method, broaden our sense of the possible by comparing different conceptions of

---

11. Much more has been said about *sati* than can be addressed here. Important discussions include Nandy's (1980) discussion of the rise of *sati* in colonial Bengal and Lata Mani's (1989) discussion of images of tradition in the debates leading to the official abolition of *sati* in the early nineteenth century, another case in which the status of women is debated mainly by men.

virtue. We can also look further into the contours and consequences of dialogue between holders of such different conceptions, especially in a colonial situation.

Discourse and Colonial Authority

The European colonial project itself has been in the background so far, given in the circumstances of the discourse discussed here. To finish this introduction let us briefly bring it to center stage and discuss scholarly approaches to it. Colonial societies have come into new focus in anthropological, historical, and literary research. Anthropologists have come to regret previous neglect of the colonial terrain in their studies of "others"; historians and scholars of literature are beginning to realize that they may have underestimated the importance of colonial relations with others in the construction of the "modern" European self. Collectively, Europeans and others now debate what to do with the evolutionary and ethnocentric image of world history that we have inherited from the European intellectual tradition of the colonial era.[12]

Following Foucault, we can try to undercut the "transcendental" premises of our understanding of truth by "archeological" investigation of our discursive practices. In other words, we can give precedence to inquiry into the practice of knowing, over the search for new answers to old questions. In the terminology of Said (1985), this is to ask philological questions about our philosophical questions, to give philology privilege over philosophy. In the terminology of Durkheim, it is to take seriously the social nature of our collective representations. It is not clear that we can completely and consistently replace transcendental questions with archeological ones, philosophical questions with philological ones, ontological questions with questions about ontologies. But reconsidering the colonial era seems to be a philological project that may help us reopen and better formulate some very basic philosophical questions about history, politics, authority, and ourselves.

Many scholars of colonialism are now trying to stay within the discourse of "political economy." They write colonial history as an episode of capitalist history (Hobsbawn 1969), or they write colonial histories as functions of.the history of a capitalist world system (Wallerstein 1980), or they locate colonial history, and all history, in a political-economic terrain (Wolf 1982). Some of this work verges on a new func-

12. The most influential commentary on anthropological neglect of colonialism has been Asad 1973. Important contributions to the reconsideration of the relations between Europeans and "others" include Said 1978, Uberoi 1978, Ryan 1981, Nandy 1983, Todorov 1984, Bernal 1987, Brantlinger 1988, and Cohn 1988.

tionalism, some (especially Wallerstein; see Roseberry 1988: 167) is unambiguously a new functionalism, in which all events are explicable according to their contribution, not to social harmony, but to international capitalism. And even in the absence of new functionalisms, most of these studies depict European colonial projects as following the development of European industrial capitalism, especially for areas such as Africa where most of the colonization came so late.

However, the question of the relationship of European colonialism and European industry is reopened by other studies. Mintz (1985, reviving Williams 1944) shows that the industrial division of labor in Caribbean slave plantations preceded industry in Europe and was a condition of it. Scholars of South Asia, while finding what some would call "merchant capitalism" on both sides of the early colonial relations of Portuguese, British, and Indians in the sixteenth and seventeenth centuries, also find that most of the capital was Asian in origin (Pearson 1976; Chaudhuri 1985; Steensgaard 1985; Das Gupta and Pearson 1987; Bayly 1988). Long before Adam Smith and the first articulations of political-economic discourse, the British East India Company flourished, and its "factors" and "factories" in Asia became the envy of Europe for the profits they generated, not by production but by participating in trade of commodities produced in Asia. Whether in Asia or in the Americas looking for Asia, the Europeans of the European expansion were less agents of capitalism than pursuers of it, seeking access to the foreign opulence described by travelers such as Marco Polo. And like the Mongols, the Europeans' first method of extraction was plunder, especially in the more vulnerable new world.

If there are problems, then, with the image of capitalism moving from Europe to the world through colonial conquests, and the image of Europe as history's vanguard, there are also problems with the idea that capitalism determined the structure of colonial societies. As put succinctly by Frantz Fanon (1963: 40), race preceded class in the social organization of European colonies:

When you examine at close quarters the colonial context, it is evident that what parcels out the world is to begin with the fact of belonging to or not belonging to a given race, a given species. In the colonies the economic substructure is also a superstructure. The cause is the consequence; you are rich because you are white, you are white because you are rich. . . . Everything up to and including the very nature of precapitalist society, so well explained by Marx, must here be thought out again.

For all reasons, I find unpromising the current scholarly efforts to resolve colonial history into political-economic forms and the functioning of a "European world-system." Instead the problem as I see it is to understand specifically European colonial forms, functions, and discourses. Rather than seeing the European empires as the embodiment, determination, or function of a stage of the development of forces of world capitalism, we might see their version of capitalism as one appropriation and deployment of its mechanisms, intertwined with other relations, discourses, and projects. Many of the articulation questions this raises (in the Marxist sense of "articulation") I will leave for my larger study. Here, taking European and especially British imperial culture seriously in its own right, the questions are, how did the European colonials speak to "others," in what speech genres, with what in their discourses, how did "others" respond, and how did the empires manage to control their dialogues and other relations with "others"? For South Asia in particular, work has already begun on these matters (see, e.g., Ball-hatchet 1980; Cohn 1983; Oldenburg 1984; Inden 1990), and responses are still being fashioned in scholarship (such as Uberoi 1978; Nandy 1983) to the episteme of empire that was for generations in South Asia a problem both epistemological and practical, a problem addressed first by the social reformers Dayanand, Vivekananda, Tagore, Aurobindo, and especially Gandhi.

A method for study of European colonial discourse has been proposed within a more general scholarly project in the study of powers of discourse. A new synthesis is building around readings of Gramsci (e.g., Williams 1977; Said 1978; Comaroff 1985); it depicts the colonial situation as one type of hegemony, one example of the more general form of political order in which a hegemonic discourse establishes the authority of a ruling class, setting the terms of social relations from politics proper to etiquette to art and intellectual life. This model of the power of hegemonic discourse is ironically close to Whorf's cultural model of the power of grammar:

> We cut nature up, organize it into concepts, and ascribe significances as we do, largely because we are parties to an agreement to organize it this way—an agreement that holds throughout our speech community and is codified in the patterns of our language. The agreement is, of course, an implicit and unstated one, *but its terms are absolutely obligatory*; we cannot talk at all except by subscribing to the organization and classification of data which the agreement decrees. . . . No individual is free to describe nature with absolute impartiality but is constrained to certain modes of interpretation even while he thinks himself most free. (Emphasis in original; 1956: 213–14)

Whorf's image of the "agreement" sounds more like a social contract than a system of domination, but as such it is more like Rousseau's contract than Hobbes's, transforming the person and preceding social agency. And its terms are "absolutely obligatory" for anyone who wants to "talk." What is missing from Whorf's formulation is a theory of the politics of that desire, the specificities of the when, where, what about, and with whom of the talking. Whorf's interest in discourse ends with the grammar, without Bakhtin's (1986) recognition that there is no simple "flow of speech," that all discourse is generated in particular genres, contexts, and social relations. As Bakhtin shows, discourse is organized not only by grammar but also in dialogue.

But does the Gramscian approach enable us to distinguish the type of social influence Whorf is discussing, the epistemological and ontological grammars enabling agency and practice, and the more specific kinds of obligations and relations imposed in dialogue by a dominating discourse? Utterances in context make reference to particular things, located events, consequential actions, relevant relations. To deliver information they are dependent on grammatical forms that are obligatory, but the information they deliver is contestable. In short, I ask where hegemony resides: in control over obligatory grammatical forms for speech and action, or in control over what is contestable in dialogue? My own suspicion is that hegemony never really exists because no grammar can completely control the content of dialogue, and that authority resides in the manipulation of the boundary between the obligatory and the contestable, the boundary between grammar and content, not simply in incitement of discourse or suppression of it, but in attempts to direct it. Resistance is then a search for ways to contest or at least evade some of the things presented as obligatory while maintaining or even improving the things that truly enable effective speech and action.

The Foucault of *The Order of Things* is interested in how obligatory structures are necessary for and enabling of thought and, following his teacher Bachelard, in how resistance to them can dissolve one obligatory structure in favor of another. With Foucault, however, we lose Bachelard's optimism about progress inherent in such epistemological breaks. Foucault's reason still likes being in danger, but he is more aware of its Durkheimian social nature. Thus he writes (1973: xxii):

what I am attempting to bring to light is the epistemological field, the *episteme* in which knowledge . . . manifests a history which is not that of its growing perfection, but rather that of its conditions of possibility.

The later Foucault, as in *The History of Sexuality* (1:58–59), is less patient with questions about intellectual systems:

The "economy" of discourses—their intrinsic technology, the necessities of their operation, the tactics they employ, the effects of power which underlie them and which they transmit—this, and not a system of representations, is what determines the essential features of what they have to say.

If there is a difference between these two Foucaults, it is that the former was interested in conditions of possibility *for* discursive practices, the latter in the effects of the power *of* discursive practices. For our own inquiry, can we find another problem area in the space in between? Let us seek the conditions of political possibility *in* discursive practice. Perhaps we can know discursive practices not only by the effect of their power, but also by the entailments as one seeks an effect: how responses to external limits and pressures, and searches for something enabling, lead to effective, powerful discourse and also to unexpected epistemological and practical consequences. How does ongoing dialogue create new conditions of possibility and problem? Despite Foucault's interest in discursive *practices* and his resistance to structuralism, he still has the discourses like myths "thinking through the men," leaving little space for consideration of discursive choices *in* practice. Looking at speech genres and speech acts in and around social and political crises, especially, we can study historically individual and contextualized moments of discursive practice for their particular conditions of possibility and particular effects of power.

To go further with this, let us return to the question of colonial social fields. As many are aware (see, e.g., Fabian 1986: 5), colonial social fields are specially complex cases in the cultural constitution of agency and discourse, cases that frustrate attempts to bound neat "speech communities" or coherent cultures with members all sharing one Whorfian "agreement" about the world.[13] What is special about colonial social fields can be articulated very simply by working from an extended metaphor in *The Eighteenth Brumaire of Louis Bonaparte*. To explain how people make their own history, but not just as they please, Marx turns to a linguistic analogy:

A beginner who has learnt a new language always translates it back into his mother tongue, but he has assimilated the spirit of the new language and can freely express himself in it only when he finds his way in it without recalling the old and forgets his native tongue in the use of the new (1963 [1852]: 15–16).

This image of the revolutionary class finding the spirit of its new language and finally forgetting the ancestral tongue is underwritten by the

13. As this should make explicit, we have left aside the "Sapir-Whorf Hypothesis" reading of Whorf's intentions. Well beyond the question of whether language shapes culture or determines perception of the world is Whorf's real interest, which I share: in how people can come to find the grammars through which they understand themselves, society, and the world, and thereby find ways to change them.

evolutionary episteme, redolent with Marxist confidence in the vanguard. The same temporalization of relations organizes Gramscian discussions of superseded, hegemonic, and emergent classes. But in the colonial situation such an image of the relation of colonial and colonized culture, coming from the same European history, is itself the colonial premise. The beginner who learns the spirit of the new language and forgets his ancestral tongue is, more than anyone else, the hegemonized. But neither does his ancestral tongue, as it is, provide the way to contest colonial certainties. How, then, can the colonizer's authority be contested? By a search for the future, a return to the past, an insistence on the superiority of the colonized, a denial of difference? Fundamentally, the need is for a means to criticize.

I recall one of my teachers, Edwin Gerow, once saying something like this: that while the Indians were constantly accused by the British of being mystical, it was the British who mystified the Indians for centuries; that once the Indians figured the British out, it took very little time to get rid of them. Our story is of unsuccessful efforts, a fragment of this demystifying process. This of course puts it mythically, but then, so did Marx when he wrote of another episode of failure—1848 in Europe—that "the revolution made progress, forged ahead, not by its immediate tragicomic achievements, but . . . by the creation of an opponent in combat with whom, only, the party of overthrow ripened into a really revolutionary party" (1978 [1850]: 586). For me, the point here is not another (r)evolutionary ripening but the creation of the opponent, the transformation of the obligatory into the contestable. Of course, by a sort of social Heisenberg uncertainty principle, the colonial British changed as the Indians began to figure them out. The colonials became defenders, apologists, and advocates of things that used to reside not in self-consciousness but in presumption. Geertz (1968) claims that "modernity" transforms the piety of Muslims in Morocco and Indonesia from religiousness to religious-mindedness; in the same way the Indian discourses pushed the British from imperialism to imperial-mindedness, perhaps even from modernity to modern-mindedness. Resisting such change, the colonial Europeans in Fiji feared Indian culture and sought to deny Fiji Indians any forum for contestation; as a minor theme of our study we shall watch them reifying themselves in the process.

Indenture and the Discourse that
Ended It: Sexual Exploitation
and a Hindu Moral Rhetoric

Only five years after they determined that a Deed of Cession signed by
indigenous Fijian chiefs gave them sovereignty over Fiji, the British began what was to them an economic project, a plantation sugar
production project that would transform Fiji's future. The British decided on both moral and pragmatic grounds that they could not obtain the
labor necessary for a sound colonial economy from the indigenous Fijians, so in 1879 they began to import South Asians they called
"coolies." In the British view the Indian "coolies" were laborers who
agreed to an indentured labor contract, promising to work plantations
for five years in exchange for wages (paid by the task) and free passage to
Fiji. The "coolies" lived three to a room in rows of rooms called "lines"
or "coolie lines," and performed the tasks set by European overseers and,
under them, Indian work bosses called *sardars*. After five years the
"coolie" was "free" and, if he or she lived out five more years of indus-
trious residence in Fiji, entitled to a free passage back to India. Fiji's first
governor, Sir Arthur Gordon, intended that these Indians would become permanent residents in Fiji. Others locally were surprised when
the majority of Indians chose not to return to India and stayed permanently in Fiji.[1]

1. For more detailed studies of Fiji's indenture history see Gillion 1962, Lal 1983,
1985a, 1985b, Moynagh 1981, and Kelly n.d.b. For a history of Indian indenture in general see Tinker 1974. Breman 1989 is a detailed account of racism, labor relations,
violence, and repression of scandal in the treatment of Javanese and Chinese indentured
labor under Dutch control in Sumatra.

Fiji's plantations were sites of extraordinary violence: murders, assaults, and suicides, crimes of violence directed not against Europeans primarily but by "coolies" against other "coolies" or themselves. The contradictions generating this violence can be illuminated through a study of the discourses of the indenture system and their effects. For example, it is important that the system was economic, not in "fact" but in the European imagination of it. Once we understand this violence we can then understand the Gandhian counterdiscourse that revealed it and forced an understanding of it onto the colonial British in India, ending the indenture system.

Plantation Violence in Fiji

To describe plantation violence in colonial Fiji we have to operate between the plantations in the European imagination, following the lines of order of the European project, and the plantations as Indian immigrants received and responded to them. To resist colonial hegemony over our own inquiry, to reach matters not entailed within colonial formalities but hidden by them, we begin with Indian distance from the colonial descriptions of the plantations and plantation relations. This distance had three important entailments.

First, there was Indian ignorance of the legal mechanisms of colonial British society. Even politically sophisticated critics of indenture such as Sanadhya and Chaturvedi, authors of the most important text of the anti-indenture struggle, tell stories of fraud that concern not leases or contracts but "pieces of paper." For example, they tell the story of a "Biner sahab"[2] who had Fiji Indians sign "pieces of paper" while agreeing to lease pieces of bush land. Once the Indians had cleared the land and improved it for agriculture, "Biner sahab" threw them off it and took back possession. Was the "piece of paper" a legal lease Biner was ignoring? Was it itself a ruse, setting up the later expropriation? Sanadhya and Chaturvedi themselves do not know. This type of mystification, and a summary attitude that "pieces of paper" were simply European instruments of power, was a basic part of Fiji Indian life in the indenture period. The power of "pieces of paper" over Indians who could not read them was exploited by Fiji's Europeans in a variety of social and financial dealings. Not only were legal contracts enforced mainly according to European advantage, since Indians were not aware of their precise rights in dealing, but Europeans also wielded "pieces of

2. "Biner sahab" is possibly a descendant of the Binner of Levuka mentioned by Scarr (1980: 34–35).

paper" very freely to constitute illegal contracts, or to assert their existence. For example, barristers' offices, for a fee, drew up illegal divorce agreements for couples never legally married and ordered redistributions of property on the basis of them. In other cases "pieces of paper" were signed to seal illegal forms of contract, as when a "coolie" waived his right to sue an employer for return of personal property, or agreed to give up his marriage and his wife in exchange for the termination of his indenture.

Along with distance from colonial legal forms based on ignorance of them went Indian skepticism based on awareness of the leverage the colonial Europeans gained through their superior understanding and control of such documents. This skepticism extended to suspicion that the colonial Europeans intentionally used "pieces of paper" to debase and defraud Indians. Legal forms were then seen as themselves a sham and a cover for malevolent and exploitative intentions; the paradigm for this attitude was the indenture contract itself. Consider Sanadhya and Chaturvedi's scathing description of the indenture compact from their 1914 anti-indenture polemic, *My Twenty-one Years in the Fiji Islands*[3]:

> The recruiter explained things to the people there [at the depot]: "Look, brothers, the place where you will work you will never have to suffer any sorrows. There will never be any kind of problems there. You will eat a lot of bananas and a stomach-full of sugar cane, and play flutes in relaxation."
>
> After three days the recruiter began to prepare us all to be brought before the magistrate. Altogether there were 165 men and women. We were all closed into cars, and arrived at the courthouse in a half-hour. The recruiter had said to us before, that when the magistrate asked us any question we should say "yes." If we didn't do this then we would be charged and thrown in jail. Everyone was brought one by one before the magistrate. He asked each one, "Tell me. Have you agreed to go to Fiji?" The magistrate did not tell each person where Fiji was, what work they would have to do, or what punishment they would be given on not doing the work. The magistrate registered 165 people in some twenty minutes. From this the reader can estimate how the magistrate wanted to free himself from the work.

The conviction that the recruitment was a "dirty trick," a sham, that recruiters lied and deceived, seems to have been near to universal among the Fiji laborers. The laborers called "coolies" by the Europeans (until 1915, when the term was officially prohibited in a vain effort to deny its racist basis) named themselves after their labor contract, calling themselves *girmitiyas* (from the English word *agreement*, Hindi *girmit*). But

3. This and other quotations from *Fijidwip Men Mere Ikkis Varsh* (*My Twenty-one Years in the Fiji Islands*), are from the translation by Uttra Singh and myself, forthcoming from the Fiji Museum.

while the *girmit* was a constituting transaction, it was not a fair or clear one to those making it. In Fiji descriptions of the process became standardized, and the form of the story told by Sanadhya and Chaturvedi matches quite closely the narratives gathered later from surviving *girmitiyas* by Ali (1979), Naidu (1980), and Prasad (1974) and songs gathered by Kanwal (1980). The stories begin with the lies and tricks of sleazy recruiters (*arkatis*) and continue with the isolation and pollution of the new recruits, first in the depots and then on the ship in passage to Fiji. Food is mixed, black water is crossed, caste is ignored by the Europeans in command. Those refusing to eat are forced to eat off dirty plates. The new "coolies" realize, on the ship or even in the depot, that their lives have changed in fundamental ways, that they have lost caste and been lowered in personal substance. Once in Fiji, they are treated uniformly as people of the lowest rank, moved into the lines, and put to work.

The third entailment of the distance between Indian realities and the colonial imagination was European ignorance about the Indians. In the European imagination, the "coolies" were already low-class and low-caste at the time of their recruitment, a sort of street scum lucky to get the work. Even if the *girmitiyas* had all been low-caste, the imputation to them of low moral nature would have been an overdetermined stereotype of cultural "others," Hindu hierarchy in caste read through British ideas about race and class. But in fact they were from a broad cross-section of caste ranks. The British image of the "coolies" led them to project low caste origins onto them. As early as 1909, as we shall see, the Agent-General of Immigration sought to correct this impression in his testimony to the Education Commission. As late as 1983 Brij Lal made the same point a principal thesis of a new scholarly work. Yet even in the 1980s, in elite European and indigenous Fijian circles in Fiji the fiction of the Fiji Indians' low-caste and low-class background was taught as fact. The Europeans thought they were simply recruiting "coolies," Indians of a laboring race and class, to be laborers. But the Fiji Indians were aware that the "coolies" were being made.

Most of those recruited were already enmeshed in capitalist market relations, already offering their labor for sale, willing to travel for work and cash income. But they were also people with caste and home village standing, and according to many of their own accounts, they had hoped to use income to aid family or return home with wealth. These Indians, as Sanadhya and the other *girmitiya* sources articulate quite clearly, were totally and unexpectedly transformed by a transaction that took their labor power to be their total nature and made it into the first organizing principle of their social life.

When Indian critics of indenture emerged, they questioned the very premises that the system was based on contracts and concerned with labor, arguing instead that the system was based on deception and pollution and concerned with exploitation much more generally. The debates between critics and apologists for indenture then proceeded, as such basic political debates generally do, as a struggle more to define the questions than to provide the answers. Persisting in their own construction of their system as a labor system, legal and economic, the masters of empire commissioned official inquiries into the economics and penal ethics of the system. Major reforms were carried out. Concern about health and quality of life as construed economically led to lines made larger and more sanitary. Concern about abuse of workers led to better control over tasking and a lessening of the penal sanctions for work failures (Gillion 1962: 164–68). In many respects, in its late years the indentured labor system came to be monitored with excruciating exactitude, not only in Fiji but throughout the empire, as the volumes of official reports attest. In Fiji the Office of the Agent-General of Immigration reported each year, with impressive statistical elaboration, on the birth, death, and crime rates, on education, on return passages to India, on Indian savings, on health, and most exactly, on rates of "work, absence, and wages" on each individual estate. It was reported, for example, that in 1919 an average of 15.11 Indian men and 5.67 Indian women worked at Nasoli Estate in Colo East.[4] But this panopticon could only see what it understood to be there. On another crucial aspect of "coolie" life—crucial, in the long run, for the fate of the system—the Indians did all the reporting. This reporting was met by a vast embarrassed silence on the part of European officials of all rank, and when it finally caught social fire in India, it led to the abolition of the system as a whole. What the Indians made a center of discourse, and of dialogue in which the Fiji Europeans were puzzled, angry, and evasive, was sexual abuse of Indian women.

In Fiji, in the colonial imagination, the social and sexual life of the "coolie" was something that happened according to the desires and interests of the Indians within the coolie lines. The life of the "coolies"

4. These men worked 79.18 percent of the working days, missing 13.66 percent for "absence, court, gaol" and 7.16 percent for "sickness, bad weather, holiday, pass"; the women worked 76.97 percent of working days, missing 9.51 percent for "gaol," etc. and 13.52 percent for "sickness, bad weather, holiday, pregnancy, nursing, pass." Their average daily earnings were also listed, averaged both for total working days and days actually worked. The rates here quoted were roughly typical for the dozens of estates listed; the "gaol," etc. numbers and the percentage of days worked by the women are higher than the 1919 averages.

was their business, as long as it did not interfere with their work or cause other trouble. But trouble did come, in the form of the extraordinary rates of violent crimes: murder, wounding (with intent to cause grievous bodily harm), and suicide. Scholars who have sought to indict the indenture system for its economic exploitation highlight the proportion of these crimes that were directed against overseers and *sardars* or otherwise directly related to labor grievances (see, e.g., Naidu 1980). There were many such cases. However, an even higher, absolutely remarkable number of violent crimes were committed over what the colonial Europeans called "sexual jealousy." "Coolie" men killed and wounded "coolie" women, rival men, and sometimes themselves. To the Europeans the cause was partly contextual—the low proportion of "coolie" women—and otherwise was a matter of the racial character and temperament of Indians. To the Indian critics, the problems were directly related to European exploitation and revealed the real nature and problems of the system as a whole.

The Indian critics were right, as we shall now trace out. As basic to the operation of indenture in Fiji as the constructions of "coolie" labor identity, and more consequential for the eventual fate of labor importation, were the contradictions between the European imagination of "coolie" social and sexual life and its reality as lived by Indians, and the contradiction between European participation in an "Oriental" sexual world of their own imagination and their willful silence over, and official neglect of, the consequences of the very real abuses occasioned. Fiji's Europeans were, as their Indian critics argued, not only exploitative but, like Ravan in the Ramayan, themselves deluded about their own activity and its consequences. Precisely this delusion separates clearly the sexual contradictions of "coolie" social life from the legal and economic contradictions of indenture as a labor form, and it made the sexual contradictions the source of the greatest, unameliorated violence.

Let us consider first the European imagination of life in the coolie lines, especially in relation to the violence of "sexual jealousy," then the participation of Europeans in this world, and its consequences.

In 1914 Methodist missionary Cyril Bavin wrote a summary article about the Indians of Fiji for a volume on missions in the Pacific. He wrote,

> It is a matter of surprise and thankfulness that the life of the "lines" is not worse, considering the undue proportion of India's criminal classes who emigrate to Fiji. . . .
>
> It has been strongly argued by those who are averse to the indenture system, that the frequency and brutality of murders of women by their husbands or paramours are due to the numerical inequality of men and women brought out from

India. Only forty women accompany every 100 men, and the scarcity of women certainly is at root of a great deal of trouble and crime. It should be remembered, however, that the murder of an unfaithful wife is condoned by Indians. This national trait, coupled with the fact that the class of Indian women emigrating to Fiji is of low character, is responsible for the comparatively high rate of capital crime (Bavin 1914: 181–82).

Bavin's opinions were widely shared among colonial Europeans, key to the defense of the project as well as to its operation. Indian violence may have been contextually determined by the scarcity of women, but fundamentally it was produced by an Indian temperament that was excitable and condoning of sexual violence, and by the "low class" of Indians in Fiji.

Debate between apologists and European critics of indenture frequently focused on the morality of the system, but the focus was the ethics of indenture's virtual slavery, not sexual exploitation of Indians by Europeans. The apologists for indenture were sensitive to the charge that the Indians had been made "the helots of Empire."[5] They liked to emphasize the great benefits of indenture for this "low class" of Indians. Bavin (1914: 183) wrote:

Much has been said and written with regard to the merits and demerits of this indenture system. . . . No system of the kind can be perfect, especially where white races and black races, with their widely divergent ethical codes, come into close contact; but it is beyond dispute that the system does more good than harm to the class of Indians who have emigrated to Fiji. . . . As a result of his five years' training [the indenture contract period], the Indian invariably improves mentally, physically, and morally. He is trained usually by experts how best to apply his strength in carrying out modern methods of agriculture, to observe the laws of sanitation, to care for his children, and generally to become a useful member of society.

The divergence Bavin saw between black and white ethical codes did not relativize the ethical code of the whites, because Bavin, like many of the missionary writers especially, located the difference as a contrast between advance and degeneration in history. Colonial relations with the whites then "invariably" improved the black races. Twenty years before, another missionary writer, Henry Worrall, was not so sanguine. But like most European observers, he worried more about protection of the indigenous Fijians and their progress than about the Indians themselves:

In conclusion, we cannot too forcibly emphasize the vital fact that in evangelizing the Indian coolies we are protecting our Fijian Church of one hundred

5. This phrase was perhaps first brought into the debate by Henry S. L. Polak's 1909 pamphlet, *The Indians of South Africa: helots within the Empire, and how they are treated.*

and three thousand Methodists from one of the most serious perils by which it has ever been menaced.

The religious, social, and even physical life of the Fijian stand in jeopardy through being brought almost hourly into association with—what are to him— new vices and new diseases; but vices and diseases that through long centuries have become hereditary in the life and character of a race, . . . powerful for good or evil as intervening circumstances will decide.

Writing for a mission review,[6] Worrall portrayed the future "good or evil" of the Indians as a matter in the hands of the missionaries. In "character" the Indians were hereditarily degenerate, and in this were different from the innocent indigenes, "civilization's new-born babes," as Worrall described them in a later article (1912: 139). Whether or not it was inevitable, it was the moral duty of the Europeans to lead and guide the Indians out of degeneracy and the indigenous Fijians out of childhood, and this was the moral framework and justification for indenture and the rest of colonial relations.

Against this type of claim, the European critics of indenture built an impressive counterdiscourse. C. F. Andrews (1915: 8–9), the friend of Gandhi and Tagore who led the European critics of indenture, lectured to the Planters' Association of Fiji:

I tell you another thing. I went to the depot at Calcutta and saw Mr. Gibbs. I saw the actual material that was coming out to Fiji by the next ship that was going to sail. . . . I looked them carefully up and down, men, women, and children alike, and I can assure you, gentlemen, that the sight I saw in that depot of these coolies was very different from what I have seen in the lines in Fiji. A degradation has taken place; something has happened—a serious moral degradation. You may be able to make them more capable for work, and much more skilled and able to make their fortune in various ways; but there is one thing that is happening in the lines—they are morally depreciating.

The coolie lines are an apprenticeship of labour, I am quite ready to believe it. But I tell you, gentlemen, that I am absolutely certain from what I have seen about one thing. These coolie lines are an apprenticeship of vice.

Andrews and the other European writers critical of indenture sharply disagreed with the indenture apologists about the moral trajectory of the indentured Indians. They portrayed indenture itself as a degenerating force and blamed it for the moral condition of the "helots of Empire." But they accepted the claim that the "coolies" were degraded, and they agreed especially about what we might call the "harlots of Empire."

When describing Indian women, the apologists and the European

---

6. 1894 "Mission Work among the Indian Coolies in Fiji," *The Australasian Methodist Missionary Review,* 4 Jan. 1894.

critics of indenture shared many fragments of rhetoric. Both groups alluded to vice and testified to seeing it with their own eyes, but both found it inappropriate to fully describe the evil at hand. Both moved from summary judgment on the shameless immorality of the women to compassionate concern for the impact on Indian children. Thus while Bavin (1914: 193) assured his readers of "the dark and degraded minds of the Indian women of Fiji," Andrews also emphasized their indecency:

Vice has become so ingrained that they have not been able to recover their self-respect; this is what I have seen. . . . With the scarcity of women of marriageable age, bad effects must necessarily follow. This unnatural system cannot produce any other fruit—it simply cannot. You know the state of immorality in the coolie "lines." I have seen it with my own eyes. I have watched their faces, and have seen the children; I simply can't bear to think of children growing up in that atmosphere.

. . . The women of India are very chaste; but these women, well, you know how they are, and how can it be different, situated as they are, living the lives they do, brought up in this atmosphere of vice and degradation? (1915: 7–8).

When writing about Indian women, the critics disagreed with the apologists over questions of causality. But no more than the apologists did they hold other Europeans directly culpable for sexual exploitation. The point for the critics was simply that the degradation was not an inevitable part of Indian racial character; it was instead the impact of immediate environment and natural law, the lack of privacy of the lines and the disproportionate sex ratio.[7] Only one of the critics of indenture

7. To these factors, Andrews and some of the others added the loss of village and caste community, and its rigid moral controls, and the absence of any sort of accepted and enforced marriage law in its place. Andrews's most important text about indenture in Fiji is *Report on Indentured Labor in Fiji: An Independent Inquiry,* written in collaboration with W. W. Pearson. In that text Andrews and Pearson went so far as to suggest that some *sardars* (Indian work bosses) in some places "arranged, according to payment, the location of women with certain favored men" (1916: 17). When it came to European involvement, however, causality was reversed. Among the notes praising the willingness of the colonial government to aid in efforts "to remedy the moral evils which prevailed among the Indian population" was an assertion that overseers "clearly proved" to have "committed offenses" against women in the lines were always dismissed, and that this type of offense had "grown far less frequent." "We felt, however," Andrews and Pearson wrote, "that, with the state of morals among the Indian women which clearly existed (through no fault of their own, but because of the indenture system) it was altogether wrong to employ unmarried European overseers and unmarried Indian Sardars. The temptation of such a position was too great" (1916: 56). Thus the morality of the Indian women precedes any action by the overseers, though of course it is no fault of the women, either. It is possible that Andrews and Pearson believed what they wrote, also possible that they were being diplomatic. Whether ignorant or tactful, they participated in the European misrepresentation of the dynamics of the lines, despite their enormous effort to uncover and reveal the truth about them.

went farther than this and addressed the role of Europeans in the "degradation" of women. Praised for his courage by Indian writers, Methodist missionary J. W. Burton made many of the arguments later made by Garnham and Andrews, blaming the disproportion of the sexes and the absence of marriage law for the immorality of the women. He also shared some opinions with his apologist colleague Bavin, deriving the violence against women from a racial proclivity.[8] But despite finding that "morally, the Indian in Fiji is outside the decencies of description" (1912: 116), Burton did not avert his eyes from another aspect of the sexual relations in the lines:

Sometimes—much too frequently—it is the white man's relations with Indian women which are the cause of assault. Some Englishmen seem to imagine that because a woman is brown she has, therefore, no rights of person; and there is a certain class, happily growing less in Fiji, to whom no woman is sacred, and who profess incredulity if either a woman or her husband are above selling virtue. (1910: 290)

Burton provides the principal exception to the extraordinary silence of the colonial Europeans over the sexual relations between overseers and "coolie" women. More generally, the problems that the Europeans saw as "Indian morality" were indeed considered "outside the decencies of description." Apart from the pious and indignant accounts of the missionaries, "Indian morality" was not publicly discussed, and apart from Burton's declarations and Andrews's hints, European connection with it was not publicly recognized. The only documentary source rife with references to it are court records, more specifically the allegations of Indian witnesses and the confessions of Indian criminals.

My review of the court records for violent crimes, focusing arbitrarily on the years 1907 and 1912, found overseers implicated in one way or another in a large proportion of the violent assaults. In some cases the overseers were said to have refused to intervene in conflicts between men over women. In other cases they were asserted by defendants to have assigned rights to defendants' wives or women to *sardars* or other favored "coolies." Finally, in many cases the overseers were accused of appropriating women to themselves, or of attempted seductions or rapes. For two examples, let us consider Supreme Court cases 28 and 29 of 1912.

In case 28 a Taveuni plantation laborer confessed on arrest to having

---

8. "The shortage of women and the consequent immorality resulting therefrom, are a fruitful cause of quarreling. Nearly all the violent assaults and murders are attributable to these troubles. The Indian is a quick-tempered man, and when roused he becomes diabolical in his passion. He is also revengeful." (Burton 1910: 315–16)

killed his *sardar* and claimed to be part of a conspiracy to kill the European planter-overseer as well. Most of his alleged coconspirators appeared as prosecution witnesses against him and denied the conspiracy, but none contradicted his account of his motives. The *sardar* had at least twice tried to force the man's wife to have sex. In this case the planter testified. He did not mention, nor was he called to comment upon, allegations in Indian testimony that the woman involved had complained to him about harassment and that a delegation of five indentured men had come to see him about this and other transgressions against women by this *sardar*. Instead the planter noted the complaints of the *sardar* about the workers, particularly the accused:

One evening the Sardar told me that [the accused] had threatened him in the field with a knife. He said that this man had forbidden him to have anything to do with [the accused's wife]. He said that [the accused] declared he was married to her. [They] are not listed as married in the indenture papers.

Indeed, the couple were not noted as married on their indenture passes or in the General Register of Indian Immigrants. They had, however, registered for immigration at the same place the same day and had registry numbers, depot numbers, and ship numbers one digit apart. The planter did not offer an opinion as to whether the *sardar* did try to force the woman into sex, nor whether this was his tacit right if she was not married. He stated simply, "I have had no trouble before. I advised the sardar not to interfere with women." The accused was found guilty and put to death. At the time of the murder he and his wife had been in Fiji for three weeks. His wife was allowed to accompany him to his trial because she threatened to commit suicide if left behind. Two years later she married again. *Girmitiya* women had limited options.

In case 29 the dynamics were somewhat different. Here an indentured laborer in Rewa killed the woman, a woman he referred to as his "wife" despite acknowledging that she was formally married to a shipmate. She split her time between the two men and was having sex with the overseer as well. One morning she and the man on trial fought, she ruined his food, and he slapped her. She left to file charges against him with the overseer; he pursued her and killed her with his cane knife. When caught, he immediately confessed and led police and the planter (a different European than the overseer) to the body. His confession:

I want to make a statement. All of my money has been spent on account of my wife. I saw her on two nights at overseer's house—but when I complained to the overseer he called me a bugger and said that [the woman] wasn't my wife—she is not my wife she is the wife of [another man on the estate]. Overseer went with [the woman] to my room and took six pounds [money] away. I told the overseer yesterday that it was a bad thing he had done going with [the woman] and taking my money. I told him I was used to killing cattle and I might murder somebody. Overseer said that he would give me a note to the woman; that I wasn't to murder her then but on the sand bank on the other side of the river. [The woman] told me yesterday that overseer and [her registered husband] wanted to see me on No. 3 bridge. Sometimes [the woman] lived with me, sometimes with [her registered husband], and sometimes with the overseer.

Like much of Indian court testimony of this time, some of this is almost certainly false. In particular, the notion that the overseer instructed him to murder her is dubious, and other testimony disputed the notion that the overseer and the other man had asked him to meet them at a distant place. However, no one disputed the relationship between the overseer and the murder victim. The overseer was not called upon to testify, and the planter did not comment upon it. The accused "coolie" was convicted and put to death.

One does not find allegations of overseer and *sardar* involvement in the court records of every case of violence in the lines. Many, possibly the majority, seem to have been cases of conflicts among the laborers only. However, the rules for "assignment" of women, which clearly varied from plantation to plantation, were established by the attitudes of the overseers and the *sardars*. In the attitudes of the overseers specifically, the British construction of the native sexuality and moral character of the Indian women shaped the pattern of sexual abuse. This is borne out in a detailed account of one overseer's attitudes.

Walter Gill was an overseer in Fiji for fourteen years, and half a century later he published a memoir of his adventures there. Perhaps it was political activism that led him to write about Fiji, partly as an exposé of the evils of the capitalist system there. In any case, like the other European writers, Gill (1970: 65) is acutely aware of economic issues and questions of economic exploitation, but unself-conscious about racial and sexual ideology:

> If we, the overseers and sardars caught up in the rotten system of indenture servitude fathered by Big Business on that most fecund of whores, cheap Asiatic labour, had managed to survive in the tooth-and-claw jungle of the cane game, it was only by out-animalizing the horde of near-human apes in our charge. And I mean apes, because a percentage of men and women, regardless of what they were when they left India, had been changed by the terrors and conditions of the sea journey, and their years of servitude, into something like Simian humans.

Gill did not develop a single moral image of the Indians. He employed three different images, often in conjunction: Indians as sinister "Orientals" or "Asiatics," Indians as culturally primitive "natives," and, as here,

Indians as animals, subhumans. Finding Indian women highly erotic, he used all three images to explain why (1970: 33–40, 71–84). They were "feral," one at least "as joyously amoral as a doe rabbit." "If they moved on their bare brown feet with the grace of cats, it was because they all had the uninhibited instincts of animals." They were also "primitive." The rhetorical claim that public discourse was unable to capture Indian women's sexuality again appeared, but with a very different significance: "Who can paint a word-picture of a primitive telling a man with her eyes that she loves him?" And finally, the Indian women were exotic, from the seductive East: the woman he regularly called to his room was his "supple, supine Oriental thing of pleasure."

Gill claims not to have been promiscuous. As he describes it, he first pursued "his" Indian woman when he "caught her watching me, her eyes asking" provocative questions (1970: 79). He knew she lived with an Indian man in the lines, but he often made arrangements with her to stay the night with him instead. Once, he made the mistake of asking one of his *sardars* to fetch her and was horrified to find him dragging her down the road by her hair. Yet Gill truly believed that the woman was pleased with their relationship, that it fit naturally with her code of morality: "Hers was a wide-eyed acceptance of the reason for her being there. I needed her body, so she was content" (p. 80).

The way Gill tells it, the sensuality and manipulativeness of Indian women was the downfall of many overseers. It led the Europeans into injury or death in conflict with Indian men, or simply to a complete sapping of their dignity and vitality, until the Asian siren discarded the man she had used up and went on to someone else. He describes another Indian woman in detail (1970: 74–77) as a femme fatale with an innocent but predatory spirit:

It was not long before she selected her next man. I thought she selected her Europeans like a girl takes a chocolate from a box. First look over what it offers, then finger one daintily, before consuming it slowly, voluptuously, savouring it to the last morsel. Invariably she made the first approach, and she was never known to fail. . . . He asked me to help him get rid of her, but there was nothing I could do, and I said so. She was "free," and that's all there was to it. . . . What had begun as an isolated sexual experience rapidly became a habit. And as her ways of expressing her love diversified, he needed her, like a drug, more and more. . . .

Almost imperceptibly he became increasingly nervy, and instead of going out at night wanted to sit home talking. He worried me. Fiji was the last place for a man to let life get on top of him. . . .

In spite of what she was, she looked young, fragrant, vital. I remember thinking what little chance he had of resisting her with the silk sari framing her face, her breasts sheathed in that tiny jacket, leaving an area of smooth, warm, ivory woman between it and her waist. . . . With her was the music of bangles and anklets, and a clicking on the wooden floor of silver-ringed toes. One touch of gold was the tiny flower in the pierced lobe of her left nostril.

So if that was how I, who did not love her, saw her, what chance was there for the poor sex-saturated goop drinking her in from his chair across the room?

I was still being ignored. She stood looking down at him, and as I watched the expression in her eyes I wondered if she knew that she was killing him. Or was it that because her body was her loveliest possession, she wanted it to consume them both?

He broke the silence when he turned to me. "Stay put," he said, "I shan't be long." He was shaking when he got to his feet. She followed him from the room.

The company's matchboard walls were not built for privacy. I heard him cross the floor and throw himself on the bed. And then he said something so hideously revealing, I wished I had not heard it. "I'm too bloody tired, sweetheart. Help yourself."

We saved a nervous breakdown by shipping him home three weeks later.

To Gill, to the predatory overseers, sex with the Asian sirens was a dangerous but extraordinarily rewarding game of mutual consumption. The primitive, animal, Oriental sex was beyond the constraining bounds of the European civil society, a kind of gratification not only beyond its morality but outside its social forms. When Gill entered the world of Asian sexuality himself his major moral worry was not the moral code of the Indians, which was to him an amusing spectacle of little real consequence, but rather the prospect of gossip among the other Europeans, especially the "white women." In their first conversation, "his" Indian woman suggested that he should leave her alone. "I nearly agreed," he writes (1970: 79), "but then it seemed to me that if I did, I would be allowing the white women to make an unwarranted intrusion; interfering in a situation beyond their understanding."

Knowledge of overseer involvement with such putative sirens existed, in the form of gossip, in some social circles within the European colonial society of Fiji. In very specific contexts, this knowledge made official appearance. Police inspectors, for example, were quick to anticipate the existence of such troubles at the root of conflicts between overseers and coolies. When a laborer assaulted Gill and tried to kill him, Gill had difficulty convincing the investigating inspector that he was not having sex with the man's wife or daughter (Gill 1970: 43). Such knowledge, however, did not permeate the colonial social hierarchy. Burton's text excepted, it did not reappear publicly in any genre of discourse more formal or generalizing than gossip. Until the Indian protests, knowledge of it as a general phenomenon had not spread with credibility very far from the lines themselves. Consider for example a newspaper account of the murder cases discussed above, cases 28 and 29 of 1912. The account was first published in New Zealand from an interview with *Fiji Times* editor T. D. Taylor, and then reprinted in the *Fiji Times,* 5 October 1912:

> Both murders, committed before Mr. Taylor left the group, were terribly brutal. In the first an Indian employed at Suva was reprimanded by a superior for not having properly carried out his duties. Immediately after the rebuke had been administered, the Indian borrowed his overseer's sharpening stone, whetted his grass-cutting knife, and then cooly severed the overseer's head from his body, after which he carried on with his work. In the second case, an Indian boy was reported to his employer by an Indian girl for improper behavior. The boy retaliated by hacking the girl to pieces.

Much here is factually wrong: the first murder took place at Taveuni, not Suva; the murderer was not rebuked before the murder, and did not carry on with his work after it. The only correct details in this description were that the accused borrowed the whetstone first and that he severed the *sardar*'s head from his body. The second description was not inaccurate—it simply, like the first, omitted all the relevant details concerning the womens' relationships with the murderers, and the *sardar* and overseer. *Fiji Times* stories concerning violent crimes tended to omit reference to sexual involvement of *sardars* and overseers and often, as here, they omitted reference to social relationships entirely. The image portrayed was instead of a mysterious race of criminals to whom violence came naturally, for any slight, cool enough to return to work after a murder, or walk undisturbed to the gallows. The New Zealand account explained: "The fatalism of the Indian, and the belief in reincarnation, is considered by Mr. Taylor to be one reason why crimes of this description so frequently occur."

Images of Indian racial nature directed the colonial system of relations, but in different directions at different levels. To the overseers, these children of "that most fecund of whores," Asia, were a "horde" of animals to be feared and controlled, but also an erotic siren; to those more firmly ensconced within the confines of Fiji's nascent civil society, Indians were simply the necessary evil, a sinister presence to be watched, firmly controlled, and whenever possible, kept away. The overseers lived on the edge and knew what they faced: the call of the wild, the adventure of the East. Gill's memoir resonates with Conrad's mythos, from Gill's confidence in his ability to see "his" woman's thoughts (like Marlow's certainty that Kurtz's gaze was "piercing enough to penetrate all the hearts that beat in darkness" (1963 [1899]: 72), to his inability to capture what lay there in civilized words, to the danger he felt in its lure. If those on the edge—and nearer the bottom of European civil society— were constantly tempted, to the European elite the rough edges were to be smoothed, the worlds beyond civility distanced. As shown by Ball- hatchet (1980) and Stoler (1989), the sort of colonial world that included white women was incompatible with the one that allowed and acknowledged Asian mistresses. In Fiji at least, and quite possibly else- where, the incompatibility produced not respect but denial, a more covert exploitation and a further overdetermination in the projection of sexual motives onto the nonwhite women. The Indians and the lines were unfathomable, or at least indescribable. And yet the lines were a European invention.

Colonial Hegemony and Indian "Religion"

There were two sets of disabling contradictions in the indenture project in Fiji. One set, further explored next chapter, was legal and economic. The Indians were made free individual British subjects, precisely to facil- itate their conversion into "coolies." Being coolielike was thought to be their nature, but in order for this nature to be exploited, legal equality had first to be admitted. Outside of the lines, then, the colonial British could find no comfortable place for the Indians in their civil society. The second set was more pernicious and more consequential for the labor history itself, as we shall soon trace out. Europeans on the plantations not only exploited "coolie" labor, but also exploited the Indian women sexually, generating a world of extraordinary violence. Europeans at- tributed the violence to the same "coolie" nature of the Indians, and "coolie" morality was thought either beneath or beyond European reck- oning. But the acts of European overseers and European-controlled marriage laws were the major continuing causes of the disorganization and violence in "coolie" social life, acts and laws premised on the same illusions about Indian social nature. As a result, abuse and violence hem- orrhaged, beyond the comprehension but because of the actions of European authority.

What options did the Indians have, distanced from and exploited by the European authorities in Fiji? Bavin and the other Christian mission- aries offered a way to be saved, a salvation that would follow from admit- ting degradation and moral inferiority. But while indigenous Fijians became loyal Christian natives, the Indians resisted their assignment in the colonial moral universe. Told in implicit and explicit ways to perceive themselves and live as "coolie" labor units with a low racial nature, and as adherents of idolatrous heathenisms, they sought their own alternative terms of moral description and found them in their own "religions." The *girmitiyas* interviewed were quite explicit on the subject. As one put it (Ali 1979: 23):

Indenture was very harsh but nonetheless Hindus and Muslims retained their religion, without it they would not have survived or retained their identity. It was their religion which enabled both Hindus and Muslims to survive.

Another was even more succinct. He told Ali (1979: 35) that on his plantation there was no one to read the Koran or the Ramayan. Yet when discussing the Indians' survival of the abuses and oppressions, his opinion was firm: "It was our religion that saved us." To this day, while indigenous Fijians are self-consciously expressive about their "culture," its virtues and the need to respect and protect it, Fiji Indians are articulate about their "religion," its power and its importance to their lives.

The point here is not that the Fiji Indians used their religion to resist capitalism. Capitalism finds ways to coexist with multiple systems of belief and practice that Europeans type as "religion," and more than coexist. Simmel (1978: 360–61) suggests that powerful and extensive systems of monetary exchange provoke interest in transcendental unitary deities, deities whose absolute but intangible value anchor selves as "souls" against the monetary flows of tangible but wholly empty, relative value. Further, as the scholarly tradition following Weber (1958) emphasizes, religious orientations such as the "Protestant ethic" can be basic to the organization of capitalist projects. And in fact the Fiji Indians did not resist capitalism: this distinguishes our case quite sharply from, for example, the colonial experiences described by Taussig (1980) or Comaroff (1985). The Indians brought to Fiji by a particular capitalist project were already seeking to sell labor for wages, already integrating into a capitalist class structure. Certainly, the radical individuation of the recruitment process created an "individualism" in the Fiji Indian community far from Dumont's Homo Hierarchicus. But commoditized labor relations were already changing transaction-based identities in India itself. The point then is not that the *girmitiyas* resisted capitalism but that, while made "coolies" and "labour units," they did not become what their owners imagined them to be. They never accepted the status of a racially doomed proletariat. It was here precisely that "their religion saved them." Far from a working-class Methodism justifying labor-class status and relations (Thompson 1963), religion and especially *bhakti* became for the Fiji Indians a basis and tool for counterhegemonic discourse and action. The question then is, how? How did their religion become more than a solace, relativizing worldly realities by means of transcendental promises? How did it penetrate the forms of indenture realities and become capable of reorganizing them?

The *girmitiyas* were Muslim (15 percent) as well as "Hindu" but did not divide in religious practice as neatly as they did in immigration records.[9] Both Muslims and Hindus participated in the major ritual festivals held in the lines: Holi, the riotous Hindu ritual of reversals, and "the Tazia," the Shi'a Islamic Moharram reenactment of the martyrdom of Husain. Both also participated in Ram Lilas, dramatic reenactments of the Ramayan narrative, which in indenture days was told as a tale of Ram's exile, climaxing with the burning of a giant effigy of Ravan symbolizing destruction of the evil in the world. In these rituals the Indians found their social identity in relations to God outside of, and in tension with, the colonial racist and economic definitions of the "coolies." The reading and hearing of texts became a noncoercive basis for an open community; within that framework, the Ramcharitmanas of Tulsi Das rose in social prominence through salient readings of its teachings. In the example of Ram, this version of the Ramayan epic provided a paradigm for the struggle of the good in an evil world; in the example of his wife Sita, a model of devoted chastity under pressure; and in the example of their enemy Ravan, a model of the delusions of powerful evil. All the rituals of the indenture period provided a basis for self-respect in antagonism with colonial moral measures. The Tulsi Das text became more: it became a weapon against indenture itself.

This *bhakti* devotional text, while part of the religion of the *girmitiyas*, was not its only organizing form. It was left to the decades after indenture, and especially our years of 1929–1932, for the Fiji Indians to articulate and separate their "religions" and arrange the emblematic and empowering practices of each one. It was between 1930 and 1932 that a *bhakti* devotional Hinduism called "Sanatan Dharm," defined especially by this Tulsi Das text, established itself as the religion of the vast majority of Fiji Hindus, in part as a consequence of the debates we will examine.[10] The point here is not that the Fiji Indians of indenture days

9. *Hindu* is a term used by colonial outsiders to describe a wide field of South Asian religious discourses and ritual practices, a field without the focus of Islam or Christianity on the irreducible centrality of certain texts, rituals, historical figures, and premises about self, God, and history. To say that someone is Hindu is to specify very little about the person's religion. For more detailed discussions of the rituals discussed below, and their fates in Fiji, see Kelly 1988a, 1988b, n.d.b.

10. *Bhakti* devotionalism is one of many systems of discourse and practice internal to "Hinduism"; it could be opposed to systems, such as that of the Arya Samaj, based on *jnana* (knowledge) and systems based upon an ontology of fateful actions (*karman*). In

were all oriented by Tulsi Das's version of *bhakti* devotionalism, but that some Fiji Indians were able to use the Tulsi Das text to come to grips with, and attain a measure of mastery over, the circumstances into which the European indenture project plunged them: radical pollution and social isolation. Ram was an *avatar* (incarnation) of Vishnu, come to worldly existence to fight evil and restore good order. He allowed himself to lose his social status, to be banished; he endured hardships and fought the evil of his world. When portrayed as Ram and Sita, the *girmitiyas* could not be blamed for their polluted status. When portrayed as Ram's enemy Ravan, the British could be shown to be deluded and evil, whatever their social and spiritual achievements. Our interest, then, is to understand how this association of imagery empowered an effective countercolonial discourse and brought about the end of indenture.

Counterhegemonic Discourse and the End of Indenture

In 1948 a Fiji Indian named Gyani Das wrote a manifesto in Hindi calling for Fiji to be made a colony of a free India, condemning the British Empire. After describing other hardships faced by the Indians, from fraudulent recruiting to being out-casted on return to India, he wrote (to quote a translation-summary in English, the only version I have):

It is also heard that in the days of the Indenture, one woman was required to serve three men, but, in fact, this was not so. It may be that the British had this end in view when they sent Indian women out, but these women stuck to their principles and did not accept two or three husbands. Those women who were forced to submit to this practice saved their chastity by killing themselves. It was, of course, a different matter with prostitutes. Some prostitutes (for there are prostitutes in practically all countries) did get enlisted and came to Fiji and were given to debauchery, but because of their conduct it is wrong to say that all women who came from India during Indenture days were equally blameworthy. Indian men finding themselves unable to see their women prostituting with white planters and overseers, resorted to openly murdering them. The result was that these prostitutes became scared and corrected themselves. One hangs one's head in shame and shivers to write the stories of sexual indulgence and misbehaviour of the white planters and overseers in those days which are significant. It is difficult to understand how cruel, shameless and low those British planters

---

bhakti systems, such as that of the Fiji Sanatan Dharm, the relationship between God and devotee supersedes any other natural or moral law (*dharma*) and is a relation made not primarily by the knowledge (*jnana*) of the devotee but by the intensity and purity of the devotee's desire to find God. While many *bhakti* discourses portray the world and its relations as disintegrated when this longing becomes intense and divinity is realized, the Tulsi Das Ramayan emphasizes dutiful worldly practice as part of the search for divinity.

and overseers were who unashamedly committed such wicked deeds and revealed them afterwards. . . . When the pains of oppression caused by human demons could no longer be tolerated, they supplicated God for deliverance. Their cries penetrating all barriers reached their Motherland and made not only Indians but even a Britisher like Mr. C. F. Andrews, shudder. In face of a forceful agitation by Indians, iniquity had to give way and in 1917 the Indenture system came to an end.

This account captures the anti-indenture history from an Indian point of view, the vision of Gandhian nationalist discourse. It does this not 'even though' it employs a devotional metaphysic ("they supplicated God for deliverance, their cries penetrating all barriers"), but precisely because it is the story of a devotionally grounded struggle, not even though it exaggerates European immorality with images as crude as the overseers' of the Indians, but precisely because it does. The image of all the Europeans as "shameless and low," "human demons," was used to fix their place in the description of indenture as an epic of pollution and atrocity. The invocation of Ramayan imagery was explicit: "Those who passed through this ordeal and are still living tell us that the British people in their oppression of the Indians during the Indenture period surpassed even Ravan." Just as Ram came to earth to kill Ravan and save the devout, so too God would destroy the evil of the British: through the action of the devout.

Anti-indenture polemics written in the 1910s also related the Fiji narratives explicitly to Ramayan themes, notably the popular Totaram Sanadhya text, *My Twenty-one Years in the Fiji Islands,* which on page 1 "begins the tale of my own insignificant life, a sorrowful story of Ram." This 1914 Hindi text was written in fact by Benarsidas Chaturvedi, a schoolteacher, writer, and editor who had never been to Fiji, but it was for the most part the story of Totaram Sanadhya, a Brahman who spent twenty-one years in Fiji and then returned to tell Chaturvedi of conditions and events there. The text is uneven, shifting from first-person narrative to elaborate polemics and even to encyclopedia-style descriptions of such things as flora and fauna; Chaturvedi must have assembled it quickly from Sanadhya's descriptions and almanacs and gazettes. However, it is very consistent and powerful at the level of theme and argument. It depicts not only Sanadhya but all the overseas Indians as like Ram, banished from their homeland. In the manner of the text of Gyani Das, it depicts the British as evil oppressors of the devout and pure. Its most effective vehicles were stories, and perhaps the most influential of these was the story of the outrages (*atyachar*) against Kunti.

A missionary from the Arya Samaj named Manoharanand Saraswati arrived in Fiji in 1912. In 1913 he is said to have written a letter in Hindi

to *Bharat Mitra,* "Friend of India," a Hindi-language newspaper published in India. The letter, written as if the writer were the indentured
laborer Kunti herself, drew wide attention and was reprinted in other
forums. The following account of it was printed in the *Leader,* another
Indian newspaper, on 13 August 1913 and later sent to the Fiji government, attached to the Indian colonial government's official inquiry into
the matter.[11]

The writer is Kunti, daughter of Charan Chamar of Lakhuapokar P.O.
Belghat, district Gorakhpur. She left her home with her husband named Jal
and went to Gorakhpur where a coolie emigration agent induced them by
holding out tempting offers to have them registered for emigration to the Fiji
Islands and took them to Calcutta where he left them in the emigration depot.
They had to live there amidst great difficulties for some days after which they
were huddled together with other emigrants into a steamer bound for Fiji.
When the steamer reached a city named Suva in the island they were taken out
and were huddled like sheep into a boat and were taken to a depot named
Nuklab [*sic:* should be Nukulau]. Whence she and her husband were sent to a
firm named Wini Wakasi [actually a place, Wainibokasi] in district Rewa. She
worked there with her husband for four years and was able to maintain her
chastity although with great difficulty. Now the sirdar [*sardar*] and the overseer
were trying their utmost to violate her chastity. There is a great difficulty in
procuring evidence for all are afraid of the sirdar. When the sirdar and the overseer desire to violate the chastity of any woman they allot her to work in a
lonely place, where no evidence can be procured. A similar procedure is
adopted when they want to beat any coolie. Under such circumstances several
persons commit suicide by hanging or drowning themselves into a river. On
April 10, 1913, she was sent to work in an out-of-the-way field alone. The overseer and the sirdar then came there bent on violating her chastity. When the
sirdar attempted to get hold of her hand she ran away in utter despair and
plunged into the river, but was rescued by a boy in his boat and landed on the
other shore. When she referred the matter to the owner of the firm, he refused
to listen to her. Now both she and her husband were being treated with greater
harshness by the sirdar and the overseer and were alloted extremely hard tasks.
She and her husband were required to work separately at a distance of one mile
from each other. She says that she [one line of text unreadable] to maintain her
chastity.

The woman concludes the letter with a warning to such Indian women as may,
like her, be tempted to go to Fiji and with a stirring appeal to the leaders of this
country to try to put a stop to emigration to the Fiji Islands.

11. See, in the Fiji National Archives, Colonial Secretary's Office minute paper
8779/13. Hereafter, "CSO" will designate minute papers of the Colonial Secretary's Office held in the Fiji National Archives.

This letter, given the headline "The Cry of an Indian Woman from Fiji," was not the first call from Fiji for an abolition of the indenture system, or even the first account of sexual immorality in Fiji. But this story, in its reprintings and retellings, reached a wide audience in India, especially in the version of it told in *My Twenty-one Years in the Fiji Islands*.[12] The story of Kunti was told near the beginning of the text, the first of its accounts of outrages (*atyachar*) committed against Indian women in Fiji:

The arkatis [recruiters] fooled Kunti and her husband at Lakhuapur district, Gorakhpur, and sent them to Fiji. These people had to suffer great difficulties there. At that time Kunti was twenty years old. With great difficulty Kunti was able to protect her virtue for four years. Then a sardar and an overseer began a great effort to destroy her virtue. On 10 April 1912 [*sic*], at the banana plantation called Sabukere, the overseer gave Kunti the task of cutting grass, at a place apart from all the other men and women, where no witnesses could be found and no one could hear her crying. The sardar and the overseer went there to rape her. On the threat of the overseer, the sardar tried to grab Kunti's arm. Kunti freed her arm, ran and jumped into the nearby river. By god's will, the dinghy of a boy named Jaidev was nearby. Kunti was saved from drowning. Jaidev pulled her into his dinghy and took her across the river. When Kunti told the white plantation owner about this incident, he replied, "Go away. I don't want to hear about field things." Afterwards, Kunti did not go to work through the 13 April. On the 14 April she was given the task of weeding twenty chains of grass, and her husband was given a task one mile away. Also, Kunti's husband was beaten so much that the poor man was half dead. Kunti had someone write about the incident in a newspaper and it was published in *Bharat Mitra*. The government of India noticed this account, and an investigation of this incident was made in Fiji. An immigration officer arrived there and threatened Kunti. But Kunti said that what she had published in *Bharat Mitra* was completely right. No matter how much we here praise the courage and fortitude of Kunti, it is not enough. She jumped into the river and protected her virtue, and even when she was dependent on the immigration officer, she rebuked him.

Having listened to this story of Kunti, will not our brothers make an effort to stop this coolie-system?

From the circulation of this and similar stories, public outcry was raised in India over the sexual exploitation of Indian women in the colonies. With its simple Hindi narratives, the Sanadhya book in particular

12. Sanadhya, one of the early leaders of the Fiji Indians, had personal acquaintance with both Saraswati and Kunti. In fact, the Fiji government's investigation of the allegations by Kunti, conducted to satisfy an inquiry of the colonial government of India, alleged that Saraswati met Kunti and wrote his original letter in Totaram Sanadhya's house in Rewa. See CSO 8779/13.

was instrumental in bringing news and debate about indenture beyond the elite. "A deputation of prominent Indian women went to the Viceroy—an unprecedented event," writes Gillion (1962: 182). Protest was organized, mobilizing a wider public than any previous protest. The highest offices of the wartime British government, when deliberating the future of indentured labor, were informed of the depth of feeling of "the women of India." Protests of Indian women and Indian men were mobilized by leaders such as Motilal Nehru, H. S. L. Polak, C. F. Andrews, and notably, Gandhi's colleague Mrs. Sarojini Naidu. An Indian representative summarized the weight of telegrams sent to Lady Chelmsford, wife of the Viceroy: "There was an intensely strong feeling of concern . . . (which included) ladies who lived in purdah, but read the news" (quoted in Tinker 1974: 353). Largely from the pressure of this "Indian agitation"—the first successful "agitation" on a national scale of nascent Indian nationalism—the indenture system was not revived when shipping was again available after World War I, quite to the shock of colonial Fiji. By 1920 the last indenture contracts were commuted, and all overseas Indians were "free."

What gave the story of Kunti political power? Let us examine, in particular, the way Sanadhya and Chaturvedi tell it. Between their account and the first one there are major similarities, including the focus on the issue of chastity (*satitva*), the struggle, the flight into the river, the denial of justice or redress by European authorities, and the conclusion, a call for the end of the indenture system. Consider, then, the details added in the Sanadhya account.

In both versions Kunti's chastity and resistance to evil drive her to self-sacrifice; she plunges into the river. A classic devotional image is made literal. In Indian devotional literature, rivers are a paradigmatic metaphor for the tribulations of life, and God is sometimes figured as a boatman, who can be asked "to aid men to cross from existence or to cross the dangerous situations in existence" (Wadley 1975: 117). In Sanadhya's version, the devotional framing is made more explicit. Kunti plunges into the river; Sanadhya wrote: "By God's will, the dinghy of a boy named Jaidev was nearby." What has been glossed "by God's will" is in Hindi a standard form for describing coincidence, but on the other hand, Fiji Hindus at present often insist that coincidences are God's will. In any case, a devotional intention is also registered in the name of the boy. His name in the police records, Jagdeo, is itself a name of God, like many Hindu names. The name cited in *My Twenty-one Years* is even more apt: Jaidev, a compound of God, *dev*, and victory, *jai*, "victorious God," "God's victory." Kunti's purity and self-sacrifice are rewarded, she is saved.

The story goes on, and its terrain becomes political. Kunti is still opposed to European evildoers, now in the forms of government investigators demanding that she change her story and overseers punishing her and her husband. But now the audience itself must become the deus ex machina. She has sent her story to the Indian newspapers. She is controlled, abused, oppressed by the institutions of the labor system itself. "She jumped into the river and protected her virtue, and even when she was dependent on the immigration officer, she rebuked him. Having listened to this story of Kunti, will not our brothers make an effort to stop this coolie-system?" The audience must do God's work, work his will. The truth must be made clear, the good must force the truth upon the world, upon the British authorities in particular.

This devotional framing of political imperatives is what Gandhi came to publicize as *satyagraha,* activity organized by insistence on the truth. The pure suffering of the political agent forces the truth upon the oppressor, and the agent is rewarded by God with final victory. The evil foe is given every opportunity to purify his own ways, to realize the truth, before he is defeated by its power. The agitation against indenture brought the truth about exploitation of Indian women in the Fiji coolie lines to the attention of the Fiji authorities again and again. The Fiji government was forced into a dialogue about the sexuality of Indian women in Fiji and their treatment, a dialogue it despised but was unable to resist.

Following the publicity over Kunti's story in India, the Fiji government was presented with a series of official inquiries from the colonial government of India, concerning Kunti in particular and, as allegations mounted, other cases as well.[13] In response to the first inquiry, the Inspector of Immigrants conducted an investigation. He determined that Kunti was a troublemaker and a woman of low morals:

Mr. Cobcroft denies having ever attempted to molest Kunta [*sic*], but states that the woman has given him a great deal of trouble. . . .

9. It would appear that the trouble with Kunta arose shortly after the dismissal of a Sirdar named Sundar Singh. This man and Kunta were and are still on very friendly terms.

10. I was informed that Kunta had lived in Sundar Singh's house for nine (9) months, her husband Jal was in Gaol at the time, he had been convicted of larceny. During the nine months, so I was informed, Kunta did not sleep one night in the "lines." Kunta has at present leave on account of pregnancy, and I was told

13. These inquiries, and the reports of investigations they prompted, can be found in CSO 8779/1913, 3327/14, 6609/14, 10603/14, 3986/15, and 8865/15.

that most of her time was spent pottering about Sundar Singh's house and field, which are close to the Neuma "lines."

11. An indentured man named Rahman Khan, Reg. No. 38698, now acting as Sirdar, informed me that on one occasion when he visited Sundar Singh's house, for the purpose of obtaining orders for the next day's work, he found Kunta and Sundar Singh in bed together with the mosquito screen down. Kunta spoke to him and asked him what he wanted.

12. During the time Sundar Singh was on Neuma estate, it is stated that Kunta was allowed to do as she pleased, but always received full wages. . . .

15. The general impression on the estates, I think, is that improper relations existed between Sundar Singh and Kunta, and that on account of Sundar Singh being dismissed, and an Overseer and a different Sirdar appointed in his stead, Kunta has been dissatisfied and has made charges which appear to be false, against the Overseer and the Sirdar Ramharak. . . .

17. The only specific charge made by Kunta against the Overseer and the Sirdar Ramharak, is that on April 10, 1913, she was sent to work to an out of the way field alone, and that the Overseer and Sirdar Ramharak visited the field with the intention of committing a rape; I would like to point out that,

A. That the place where the woman was working was within a few yards of the public road leading from Nausori to Wainibokasi.

B. That the Overseer states that the Sirdar did not visit the field, but that he, the Overseer, did. The Overseer admits that he spoke rudely to the woman; he probably swore at her. He was angry because she had hardly completed any work and on account of the trouble she was causing.

C. The boy who is supposed to have rescued Kunta from drowning, states that the woman was standing with the water "Just over her feet." She asked to be put across the creek; Jugdeo took her across in his boat.

[points D & E: no Indian witnesses testify to confirm her version.]

The investigator found that Kunti was assigned separate work, that she was approached and at least treated "rudely" by an angry overseer, that she did flee and cross the river. But his reconstruction of context makes Kunti at fault for whatever actually befell her. Fiji's Colonial Secretary sent a copy of the Inspector's report to the Indian government, together with a commentary by the Agent-General of Immigration, who concluded:

7. I believe the whole statement to be a fabrication. It is absolutely untrue that female indentured immigrants are violated or receive hurts or cruel treatment at the hands of their Overseers, such as that ascribed. If such were the case it would be quite impossible to manage labourers on a plantation. It is only by fair and just treatment that labourers, at any rate in this Colony, can be worked.

The Indian colonial government was satisfied with this reply until further newspaper accounts were published in vernacular Indian newspapers. In these accounts an audience already told of the attempted rape was told of Kunti's new travails: "the Immigration Officer at Fiji" was pressuring her to change her story, accusing her of lies, and asking her to implicate others. Kunti was holding fast to the truth, and had even criticized the Immigration Officer to his face for his refusal to investigate previous complaints. To quote from a translated transcript sent to Fiji for explanation, the account in *Bharat Mitra* on 8 May 1914 concluded:

In this connection we cannot refrain from admiring the patience bravery and strength of mind shown by Kunti. In spite of her being of the cobbler caste, she has surpassed many well-to-do (high class) ladies by the courage shown by her in jumping into the stream to save her chastity. This will gain for her a place in the list of honorable and brave ladies. Our countrywomen should learn a lesson from the way in which she treated the Immigration Officer. Even on critical occasions one ought to stand by right (i.e. virtue?) [*sic*]. A time there was when our country had many ladies of Kunti type, but unfortunately that condition does not prevail now. . . . We beg to inform the British Government that it would be impossible to get on without putting an end to the indenture system. Kunti's case is but one of the few brought to light. God knows how badly indentured laborers are treated. . . . We hope she will get justice.

It was just as important to the critics to emphasize the quality of Kunti's character as it was for the Fiji government to deny it.

The Indian government was caught in the middle and did not like its position. "The Hon'ble Mr. R. E. Enthoven," Secretary to the Government of India, wrote to Fiji's Colonial Secretary on 10 June 1914:

2. As the matter has thus once more been brought to the notice of the Government of India, and as the circulation of such reports, if unrefuted, cannot fail to have the most mischievous effects, the Government of India are anxious to expose the falsity of the story before it attains a wider currency.

3. Before taking any steps to this end, however, the Government of India consider it expedient to strengthen their position by securing certain additional information, for which I am desired to invoke the courteous assistance of His Excellency the Governor.

The government of India wanted more and better evidence about Kunti's case. Enthoven requested that Saraswati be questioned "regarding the nature of the evidence offered by the woman when he wrote the first letter." He also asked for "any definite evidence of Kunti's relations with the dismissed Sirdar," evidence not "emanated from" another *sardar*, whose relations with Kunti and the dismissed *sardar* "might not have been altogether amicable."

The Fiji government was not happy with the requests. The first minute on the Indian government inquiry notes that "Saraswati is going to be troublesome person," and it took almost three months just to find him. However, like so many Indian witnesses when faced by European authority in Fiji's legal system, Saraswati denied any knowledge of the matter at issue, blaming all "mischievous reports" on others, in this case on Sanadhya, who had since left Fiji for India. Fiji government officials did not believe his denial but found it useful, leaving only the matter of evidence about Kunti's character to deal with. For this they ignored, or perhaps implicitly resisted, the Indian government's implied criticism of their investigating methods. They simply had the accused *sardar,* Ramharak, make a statutory declaration that "it was common knowledge in the Lines that Sundar Singh and Kunti had been living together that Sundar Singh kept Kunti." They sent copies of Saraswati's denials and Ramharak's declaration to India, making no mention of their doubts about the former, and baldly noting of the latter that "there is no reason to doubt the accuracy of the statements which it contains." The Fiji government sought simply to withstand the controversy and was not yet interested in any inquiry of its own into the standing or treatment of Indian women in the lines.

The Indian government accepted, for the moment, the Fiji government's explanations. The next inquiry from India to Fiji concerning sexual exploitation in the lines was in March 1915. It was not related to the Kunti story but sprang from a letter written by a "coolie" in Fiji to "The Governor General of India." A translation of the letter was enclosed:

> To
> The Governor General of India
> Calcutta
> May it please His Excellency,
> I most humbly beg to state that we have come to Fiji Islands to work and we do not get any money here. What we do get is not even enough for our food. There is one more thing I beg to add is that all the Europeans (male) in Fiji keep Indian women and the Coolie Agent and the Governor of Fiji takes no notice of our complaints but by force sends us to jail instead.
> The Government has brought us to the island of Fiji and the Europeans (male) here take Indian women by compulsion to their Bungalows and keep them there. May it please the Government to enquire into this matter otherwise this treatment given to us will be continued by threats in Fiji.
> (English words) he is Mr. James Harper Esq. Kept women. India. every day. Fiji dist: Taveuni Islands.

(Roman characters) Government do not now send
Indians from Calcutta as the Colony of Fiji is very bad. The
Sahibs here are no good. (English words) No good
Earopeans Fiji Dist: very bad. Every day keept to Indian
women. with sleep rooms. Fiji country no good. You give
the Fiji Governor reply. No good Mr. James harper kept
India women sleep rooms with:

(Sgd) Writer Jaisari Singh

The pathos within the structuring of this letter,[14] which was probably
dictated by an illiterate man in successive parts to others who could
write, suggests the inequity in the confrontation between the laborers
and the various agencies of economic and political power in Fiji. The Fiji
government replied to this inquiry that the letter writer had been convicted, three years before, for assaulting and severely injuring his wife.
He had never complained to the Immigration Department, they added,
about Mr. Harper and Indian women. Here they neglected the transcript of Jaisari Singh's trial, in which Singh testified in detail about
how another laborer, Harper's cook, paid Harper five pounds for
Singh's wife, how Singh was locked up for a night by Harper while the
woman moved in with the other man, how following this he assaulted
his wife, as he had vowed to do if she left him. The only person to cross-
examine the overseer about this aspect of the case during the trial (Supreme Court criminal case 7 of 1912) was Jaisari Singh himself; the
overseer denied that he was also cohabiting with Singh's wife.[15]

No reference to these matters was made in the official minutes plan-
ning Fiji's response to the inquiry. No serious investigation was contem-
plated. Instead, the contexts were again reversed. The conviction was
cited as evidence of Singh's unreliability; the Indian government was
supplied with the opinion of the Agent-General of Immigration, that
"the man Jaisari Singh is, I understand, a worthless character." The pattern of controversy developed: Fiji Indians appealed directly to the
Indian colonial government, and to Indian public opinion, about their
mistreatment in Fiji and the failure of the Fiji government to investigate

14. I have not seen the original, but only a transcript, in CSO 3986/15.

15. This case, like the two murder cases discussed above, was noted in the *Fiji Times*,
and again a reference there illuminates the themes of civil society understanding of the
lines. In 1912, following this case, a rape case emerged from Harper's plantation, and in
1913 no fewer than seven more of his laborers were up on various criminal charges, with
four more laborers waiting in the capital to be witnesses. Rather than expressing concern
about conditions on Harper's plantation, the newspaper commiserated with his economic
situation: "Mr. Harper will lose the services of no less than eleven units of labour for several weeks. He will be in a still worse position if the accused are convicted."

it. The colonial government of India, in the middle, grew increasingly dissatisfied as Fiji refused to take inquiry seriously.

In September and December 1915 came the final correspondence between India and Fiji directly concerned with the Kunti case. In August 1915 Kunti had returned to India and made a long and detailed complaint to R. M. Gibbes, the Government Emigration Agent at Calcutta, the document again enclosed in an inquiry to Fiji.[16] Kunti made a range of charges concerning work conditions, the way people of different castes and religions were forced to live, cook, and eat together, and other matters. The core of her complaint, however, was a reiteration of the attempt to rape her and the beatings and other punishments she and her husband received for publicizing her case, while government authorities failed to investigate properly. She ended with a scathing denunciation of the entire Fiji legal system:

> In the Fiji Courts the evidence of free men [free Indians] is of no use in such cases, while indentured labourers do not dare to give evidence against the superior staff or the Manager of an Estate. On one occasion my husband instituted a case but it was dismissed on the strength of the Manager's evidence who kissed the Bible and denied the charge. In short there is no redress. Neither the Manager nor the Coolie Agent nor the Courts care to hear or redress the labourers' grievances.

Gibbes himself wrote the letter to Fiji, referring also to the correspondence over Jaisari Singh's case. He wrote that Kunti was vigorously cross-examined on her various allegations; "I formed the opinion that there was probably a good deal of truth in them, in addition to much that was exaggerated." He added, in a warning again unheeded by the Fiji government,

> It seems evident that the anti-emigration party in India are engineering a campaign directed mainly against Fiji, and this new move of getting return "failures" from the Colony to make formal affidavits in regard to alleged ill-treatment there is one of which we shall probably hear more in the near future. In the meantime it is obviously desirable to verify the truth or otherwise of such statements with the least possible delay and I request that you will be so good as to favour me with a report on the enclosed affidavit after the necessary investigation.

Again the Fiji government made no proper investigation of the case. Instead it simply supplied Gibbes with copies of all former papers on the

16. This text is the only one in the dialogues we consider that is produced directly by one of the *girmitiya* women (though the original Saraswati letter may also have been dictated by Kunti). And this text is not only prefigured by the past dialogue about her conducted by men, but is itself appropriated into further dialogue about her conducted by men. See comments in preface about women's absence from these dialogues.

subject and with notes by the Agent-General of Immigration on Kunti's latest statement, here edited:

2. Caste distinctions are seldom observed in Fiji by the immigrants themselves. . . .

8. In regard to the assertion that immoral overtures are constantly made by Sardars and Overseers I have to state that the few authentic cases brought to the notice of this Department have been severely dealt with.

11. Kunta's statements regarding her ill-treatment at the hands of the Sardar and Overseers are mere fables. . . . Complaints made by indentured immigrants receive full and careful inquiry. It is significant that the complaints were made only after the dismissal of the Sardar (Sundar Singh) with whom she was living on intimate terms.

13. Kunta's statements regarding the procedure in the Courts of Justice in this Colony are unworthy of notice. The fullest investigation is made into all complaints of Indian immigrants.

In this strange conjuncture, the very production of this response to Gibbes's inquiry contradicted the claim made within it. They claimed to investigate fully but replied to a new inquiry with old papers and ungrounded generalizations. The essential fact from the "fullest investigation" into Kunti's complaint was the allegation that she lived "on intimate terms" with the former *sardar*. And in the case of caste, again, the cause of disorder was displaced from the managers of labor to the Indians themselves: the managers of labor did not force the Indians into polluting contexts and destroy caste statuses, nor did they sexually exploit the Indian women; instead, the Indian women themselves were immoral, the Indians themselves "seldom observed caste distinctions."

The Fiji government never understood the growing significance, as the Indian nationalist movement began, of Indian popular political opinion for the colonial government of India. In Fiji, press accounts of events in India through World War II presented Gandhi and the other leaders of Indian opinion as dishonest troublemakers whom the empire should keep in place. In its own responses to criticism the Fiji government branded its critics as troublemakers and their accounts as unreliable. Ironically one of its own reports, in 1918, raised the controversy that finally forced the Fiji government to launch a general investigation into the sexual lives of Indian women in the lines.

By 1918 the campaigns in India against indenture on moral grounds, especially indenture to Fiji, had already gathered enormous public momentum. The need for transport for the First World War had put a temporary end to the shipping of indentured labor to Fiji and other colonies, and C. F. Andrews was looking for evidence to convince the imperial authorities of the moral evil of indenture in Fiji and ensure that it would never be resumed. He found the following note in a Fiji government Health Department publication: "When each indentured Indian woman has to serve three indentured Indian men, as well as various outsiders, the results as regard syphilis and gonorrhoea cannot be in question." Andrews, an influential figure in India, showed this passage to the Viceroy in an interview. The Viceroy himself wrote to the Governor of Fiji:

> Dear Sir Bickham,
>
> The Reverend Mr. C. F. Andrews with whom you are probably acquainted came to see me recently on returning from a visit to Fiji and gave me an account of the conditions of indentured labour in Fiji which if true is deplorable.
>
> I invited him to submit a written statement containing his suggestions and I enclose the note which he has sent to me. I should be very much obliged if you would give your personal attention to the points he raises as the subject is one on which Indian opinion is greatly perturbed.
>
> The statement of facts published in Council Paper No. 54 to which Mr. Andrews draws specific attention seems to furnish a very sufficient justification for regarding the existing state of things as demanding prompt remedial measures.
>
> Sincerely Yours,
Chelmsford

The matter was given for investigation not to the Agent-General for Immigration, but to the Chief Medical Officer, a Dr. Lynch, whose subordinate Dr. Philip Harper had written the offending passage.[17] Lynch seems to have been infuriated by the matter, minuting:

It is not to be denied that among other evils in Fiji, there is much immorality, fostered no doubt by the existing condition of the disproportion of the sexes: but because of that, and because there is prostitution, it is foolishly inaccurate and purposely misleading to brand *all* the Indian women in the Colony in the way that this sentence implies. . . . Is it not known that there is at least as much immorality in India as there is any where else. Is Mr. Andrews equally insistent on reform in this and other directions in India as he is in this Colony? Here, it is admitted that there are abuses, which everyone concerned is doing his best to remedy—the remedies must take time, and owing to the war and the action of the Indian Government in closing emigration at once, the remedy must take more time. . . . The responsibility for prostitution here is due to the methods of

17. The inquiry and following investigation may be found in confidential Fiji CSO minute papers. In order to have access to these materials, I signed an undertaking required by the Fiji government not to reveal the particular sources.

recruiting, to the low percentage of women sent here, and in many instances to the class of women . . . The Indian Government has had full knowledge of all the evil methods of recruiting for many years past. It would seem therefore to be a little less than just that, now when a well organised agitation is afoot, the entire responsibility of any existing evils should be shouldered on to Fiji. That there are faults in the system of Indenture cannot be denied, and no attempt has been made to deny them, many attempts have been made to remedy them—that there are advantages in the system is also obvious. It is unfair to take all the faults and none of the advantages. The opponents to Immigration in Fiji lightly pass over any advantages and appear to think that everything is to be done for the Immigrant, in return for which the Immigrant is to do nothing, that they are to leave their lives of ignorance, dirt, poverty and insanitary conditions for a Colony where they are to receive every benefit and give nothing in return.

Thus investigation began with a tirade and with resort to the apologists' image of the Indians as more degraded before coming to Fiji than after. However, despite this more general contextualization, the alleged basic fact of Fiji Indian women's general immorality was also finally officially denied, now that the government was forced to investigate the matter.

Lynch claimed that he had meant, with Harper's permission, to delete the paragraph before publishing the report, because it was inaccurate. To begin to compile a proper rebuttal, he wrote to Harper. Unfortunately Harper, now working in New Zealand, stood by his version of the facts:

The idea may otherwise be expressed by saying that the average coolie woman is forced to allow sexual intercourse to the majority of the coolies in the coolie lines in which she lives as well as to various outsiders such as Europeans, free Indians, half-castes and, in many cases, Fijians. She is in fact demoralised.

The exceptions to this rule are the few women who are kept by Europeans, the women kept by such high-caste Indians as may find themselves living in a coolie lines in Fiji and a proportion of the women who come to Fiji with the men to whom they have been married in India according to Indian religious customs.

Marriage in Fiji, whether by the Government or even if accompanied by religious ceremonies, is looked upon by the coolie merely as a legal or social permit to keep a mistress. A woman under such circumstances may be hired out to a friend or even to a stranger. The woman finds such a union binding only as long as the man can keep her affection or supply her with luxuries and such unions are a source of frequent trouble and are the cause of most of the major crimes in Fiji. . . .

Nevertheless I do not presume to judge coolie women from the point of view of morality. Their views on such matters cannot be assessed by European standards, though their instinct of motherhood is obviously at least as unselfish and enduring as our own. The view point I wish to emphasize is the purely medical one.

Harper noted the fact that European men "keep" Indian coolies as mistresses, and he classed such Indian women as fortunate. His attitude compares closely with the views ascribed by J. W. Burton to "a certain class of overseer," the ones who professed surprise whenever they found that they could not buy the sexual services of any Indian women.

Faced with Harper's elaborate affirmation of his claims, the Governor ordered Lynch to survey other opinions. Eight district medical officers were surveyed, all with at least six years in their districts, many with more than a decade. These men were unanimous in refuting Harper's views, in such terms as the following:

After nearly 20 years in Fiji, 13 of which were spent in a district with considerably over 2000 Indentured Indians, and a very large non-indentured Indian population, and having kept careful venereal statistics for five of those years, I have no hesitation expressing my opinion that Dr. Harper's statement is most misleading.

A certain proportion, perhaps 20%, of the Indian women that arrive as immigrants in Fiji are "chinas" by which I mean, women who have been made outcasts from their villages in India, through some act of immorality, possibly they are girl widows not allowed to marry again in India, and having had their sexual passion aroused, will not submit to the life of slavery their husband's relatives wish to impose upon them; any how once they have "fallen" in India it is most unlikely that they will remain faithful in Fiji where, unlike India, the laws are enforced which will not permit individuals to punish the unchastity of their partners.

These "chinas" are, on arrival in Fiji, as every medical officer who has examined Indian Immigrants at the "Depot" knows, quite impossible to keep sexually moral, even there, where there is segregation of the sexes, and as soon as they get to a plantation, a proportion of them start very free living, certain of them do not, but settle down with one man, and perhaps a paying boarder, a bachelor whose food she cooks and with whom she probably cohabits. Beyond these two she is probably quite chaste. But the others of this class of women with perhaps a very few professional prostitutes from India are accountable for a great deal of the venereal disease, and general immorality of the Indians. The ordinary Indian woman arriving with her husband from India is probably quite as chaste as she is in India, and is kept so busy having infants, she has little time for unchastity, the same cannot be said of the man who not infrequently infects his wife. The custom of keeping a paying boarder is not by any means confined to Indentured Indians, and I remember one woman who only took a boarder, when her indenture expired and her husband was earning 5/- a day as a carpenter. So in my opinion the main factor in the spread of venereal disease is the presence of the incorrigible "china."

Attention was brought to distinctions within the lines: a vast majority of women were "chaste," some had a husband and a male "boarder" they cooked for and possibly also slept with, and only a few were promiscuous or professional prostitutes, part of a small class of aggressive, nonchaste women.

The picture Fiji drew to defend itself was quite different from the images of the missionary critics, in which chastity in the lines was impossible, Indian morality indescribable.[18] But Fiji's self-defense was too little, too late. Fiji was still unwilling to admit how many of its overseers shared the views of Harper, not the other officers, and how many of those participated in the world they imagined. In India, even the colonial government was fed up with the Fiji government's self-protective silences. Colonial Fiji's moral reputation had by 1918 been irrefutably challenged by the nationalist anti-indenture rhetoric. Not only was indenture finished, but Fiji lost all chance for further Indian laborers. In the 1920s India refused permission for labor emigration to Fiji even when Fiji, in a labor crunch, offered free transport for "free" labor immigration. Exposure of its sexual immorality had permanently undone the labor system supporting Fiji's colonial capitalism.

We deceive ourselves if we categorize the sexual relations and exploitation in indenture as part of a "superstructure" to a system that was primarily "economic" in a traditional sense. This is not only because these sexual dynamics followed in part from indenture's unique system for reproduction of labor (the indenture system, unlike even slave labor systems, reproduced its labor entirely from new recruiting and therefore had no economic interest in the sexual reproduction of its labor). It is also because the Europeans' racial and sexual imagination not only masked but also fostered the most destructive practice, not only hid but also generated the contradictions. Exposure of its sexual immorality was exposure of exploitation in indenture that was as real in its practice as its exploitation of the Indian labor. But we still might inquire further into how that exposure was accomplished: how the extent and nature of the sexual exploitation were discovered, how the silences and evasions surrounding it were penetrated, and how a public, a new national public in

18. For another example of such rhetoric, consider this passage from Florence Garnham (1918: 14–15), who was sent to Fiji by a consortium of women's groups in Australia and New Zealand. Her report, *The Social and Moral Condition of the Indians in Fiji*, states:

Life in the lines is unspeakably corrupt.

Indians speak of the lines at the mill-centres as "prostitution houses," and many men whose period of indenture had expired told me how glad they were to be away from the lines, and to settle in places where their wives were protected. It was quite impossible, they said, for a woman to preserve her chastity in the coolie lines.

. . . Sometimes I even found that husbands consented, for certain monetary considerations, to allow their wives to be shared by other men for a certain period. The degradation and unhappiness of such a life may be better imagined than described.

India, was made to understand the exploitation and led to protest it effectively.

Bhakti and the Power of Indian Nationalism

The dialogue on indenture was simple in outline. In the imperial British discourse, the British were the bearers of civilization and morality, the Indians, even the coolies, recipients. The Fiji Indians were freed from caste, in a healthier climate, making more money, "better off." Their status was defined legally, the quality of their lives was defined medically and economically. In the counterdiscourse, whether from Andrews or Kunti herself, the Indians were innocents and the Europeans mere exploiters and polluters, acting out of ignorance, moral laziness, or even actual malice.

However, there was also a difference within the counterdiscourse, between the Christian European writers (Burton, Andrews, and Garnham) and the Indian writers, in depiction of the condition and character of the "coolies" of the system. The Christian horror over the Asian squalor of the lines can be understood within the Orientalism of the European community as a whole, their conviction that the morality of the other was basically different, and lower. It can also be understood in relation to the more particular convictions of the Christian missionaries about heathen darkness in the souls of the Hindus, and about the intrinsically corrupting machinery of capitalism. The immorality of these laboring heathen Asians was hopelessly overdetermined; hope was restricted to the children.

For the Indian nationalist counterhegemonic discourse, the criticism of colonial authority and its forms was broader, in the end an attack on the morality of Western culture and empire as a whole. The innocents abused in indenture were also, like us all, devotees seeking God, trying to be good in a corrupted age the empire was making worse. The Indian writers depicted not fallen women unspeakably immoral, but chaste women, women struggling to devote themselves to lord and husband against all threats and pressures.

Indenture provided an excellent target for a *satyagraha* campaign, a campaign to find, beneath the surfaces of imperial discourse, immoral truths and grounds for rejection of imperial authority. For good reasons, the anti-indenture radicals chose the outrages against women as a focus and emphasized the "chastity" of the women oppressed. The economic issues of the indenture controversy were double-edged in a rapidly commoditizing home economy. Capitalist forms were not denied in whole by the Gandhian nationalists; workers needed work, and the government was expected to help arrange it. There was no prorape lobby, however. The issues were unambiguous and powerful as a metonym for the labor conditions faced by "coolies" in indenture. Further, insisting on the purity of such women as Kunti was of obvious rhetorical value. It made them a sympathetic focus for collective rescue efforts, made them worthy of the communally generated deus ex machina. It quite concretely brought to bear the devotional themes basic to Indian nationalist politics. Finally, the image of a Hindu woman defending her virtue served as a metaphor for the political action itself. Not only was she, like the colonized Indians, facing domination and concerned for her own welfare, but unlike the "coolie" more generally she was already engaged in struggle, already fighting back. The audience had to learn that like her they had no real choice. To be good they had to fight.

The stories about the exploitation of women provided advantages in imagery that help explain why the anti-indenture struggle was one of the easiest and most quickly successful of *satyagraha* politics. Not only did the stories shock British sensibilities, even those of the Viceroy, but the chastity imagery provided an excellent vehicle for teaching the necessity of political action. It brought a much wider group into antiraj activity, while offending no interest group. However, these advantages to this discursive vehicle probably explain its success better than its rise. We need not conclude that the exploitation of women was simply selected by the makers of countercolonial rhetoric for its shock value and other potential. Recalling the violence of the lines in Fiji, we might wonder whether the issue was thrust upon them because it was at the basis of the contradictions of indenture as practiced, a truth suitable for exposure in a *satyagraha* campaign. We come to a core issue: the power to articulate a truth.

We get a very clear picture of the gulf between the individual Indian "coolies" and the masters of the British Empire if we compare the letter of Jaisari Singh to the Governor General of India ("No good Mr. James harper kept India women sleep rooms with") to the letter from the Indian Viceroy to the Governor of Fiji ("The statement of facts published in Council Paper No. 54 . . . seems to furnish a very sufficient justification for regarding the existing state of things as demanding prompt remedial measures"). The authority of the Viceroy was reflected in his ability to reconstitute significances through manipulation of discursive forms. The facts as reported in a preexisting text, this Fiji council paper, became upon his pronouncement a "state of things" concerning Indian women in Fiji that required "prompt remedial measures." Before his pronouncement, the council paper had created no such emergency. Afterwards, the Fiji government could not change this reading of "the state of things" even when it denied the accuracy of the medical report, which was in fact inaccurate. In contrast, the specific allegations of the "coolie," even with the query from the Indian colonial government accompanying them, could not force a simple investigation. The "coolie" was a "worthless character" in the eyes of colonial authority in Fiji, powerlessness and exclusion reflected even in the pathos of his ungrammatical articulation.

It could be claimed that the real agency mediating between the powerless "coolies" and the colonial authorities was that of the European critics and reformers, notably Andrews, that Andrews had the power to articulate the issues in a way that could change colonial practice. Perhaps it did take a C. F. Andrews to frame the case about exploitation of Indian women in Fiji, and to marshal the evidence for it, in forms this Viceroy, in his time, could accept. However, the Viceroy's principal concern was not criticism of Fiji by Andrews, but the spectre, truly frightening to British colonial authority in India, of "Indian opinion . . . greatly perturbed." Essential to Andrews's own authority in the situation was his acceptance and esteem in the eyes of the nationalist Indians. Their emergence as a significant "party," in both their own and Gramsci's sense (1957: 146ff.), their ability to certify authority and mobilize public opinion, made their criticism of indenture effective. And the campaign against indenture itself helped constitute them as a party—not just an intellectual clique, but a political force representing a vast public. The story of the abolition of the indenture system is a significant part of the story of the rise of a counterhegemony to the British Raj in India, a nationalist movement that decades later accomplished its ambiguous triumph, driving British rulers, but not capitalism, out of India. The power of Indian nationalism was political, but also epistemological, not only the story of strikes and demonstrations, but also the story of how perceptions and articulations such as those of Jaisari Singh were generalized into an analysis of dynamics underlying the whole indenture system and even empire itself. The British saw no general phenomenon of sexual exploitation of Indian indentured women. How did the Gandhian nationalists find it and identify it?

First of all, the Indian critics were looking for ways to criticize imperial power effectively, ways to end its abuses. They were explicitly seeking political change; theirs was explicitly a counterdiscourse. They challenged interpretations and reversed symbols of the dominant political discourse, tried to capture the speech of colonial authority and turn it to countercolonial advantage. Thus their criticism of indenture was constituted with definite relations to the British discourse about indenture that it fought. It addressed arguments about health and welfare, ignorance and progress. Gandhi borrowed much of his theory of labor and critique of capitalism from Western anticapitalist discourses, from Ruskin, Tolstoy, and others, and his party was allied in the struggle against indenture with the continuing European anti-indenture critics. From such sources as Burton, they inherited the critique of the immorality of the lines that was grounded in Christian values and imagery and found the "coolies" to be degraded body and soul.

What Chaturvedi and the others then reconfigured was the terrain of the criticism. They left behind the Christian eschatology, obsession with body sinfulness, and convictions of heathen darkness, and they looked for Indian heroes in the stories they heard and read. Unlike the Christians, they were interested in leading readers to identify with indentured protagonists in accounts of struggle and hardship. Chaturvedi and the other Indian indenture critics found a story of people polluted, their most basic human relations ignorantly interfered with: even the devotion of wife for husband; even, as in the days of Ravan, the relations of devotee and God. The new discourse came together when framed within a *bhakti* ontology, as a story of people seeking proper relationships, pressured by misfortune and evil.[19] Anticipating the presence of ignorant, deluded agencies interfering in the lives of the devout, this version of the story had a place for villains and found them easily. It became possible to depict the British as both ignorant and malign, however remarkable and empowering their achievements, when colonial politics was reconsidered on a devotional field.

As Gandhi articulated it, the power of the Indian nationalist movement stemmed from its unique political action, *satyagraha,* insistence on the truth. Indeed, the Indian political movement revealed the presence of more at the base of colonial history, in colonial practice, than the British were willing or able to see. Confident in their searches, the Gandhian party exposed many exploitations in British colonial practice about which, for many reasons, British authority had been silent, evasive, and even on occasion truly ignorant. Gandhi argued that the practice of *satyagraha* did not have to be planned, that its "beauty" was that each issue "comes unsought" (1928: xiv), and in a sense this was true: the issue of the exploitation of "coolie" women was created not by the exigencies of nationalist rhetoric but by the contradictions within indenture as practiced, especially the anomalous blindness of the Europeans to their own acts of sexual exploitation.

19. Recall that *satitva,* the "virtue" or "chastity" of an Indian woman, is given a devotional significance in *bhakti* discourses: the proper wife's purity exists through her devotional attachment to her lord/husband. The issue returns, of course, in the dialogues of 1929–1932.

Is there a larger sense, then, to this power of *satyagraha* to challenge colonial authority and penetrate the forms of colonial discourse and practice? Many devotees of Gandhi or of revolutionary activity in general try to find an absolute spiritual, moral, or intellectual superiority to Gandhi's "nonviolent" *satyagraha* in particular, or a special power in revolutionary, "deconstructive" criticism in general. However, we must be wary. Gandhi's truths, and *satyagraha* as a new form of political practice, were themselves ideological, creations of a structured historical imagination enabled by cultural grammars. Gandhi lived in a fully figured and populated universe. He imagined his political career and the nationalist movement in a field he believed to be determined by a particular sort of divine will:

In a righteous struggle God Himself plans campaigns and conducts battles. A *dharma-yuddha* [righteous political campaign] can be waged only in the name of God, and it is only when the Satyagrahi feels quite helpless, is apparently on his last legs and finds utter darkness all around him, that God comes to the rescue. God helps when one feels oneself humbler than the very dust under one's feet. Only to the weak and helpless is divine succour vouchsafed. (1928: xiv)

Gandhi's politics were, in short, devotional. His penetrating criticism of the colonial world was made possible by his acceptance of a totalizing alternative, a universe based on *bhakti,* and his new deployment of *bhakti* grammar.

The power of Gandhian rhetoric to expose the truth about British colonial practice did not spring only from deconstruction of colonial discourse. To convince that the powerful British were evil required more than raising doubt that they were good; it required that the alternative be plausible. British colonial power presented itself as a historical inevitability and as proof of moral quality. The Gandhians made the inevitability into something contingent neither by calling for something new nor by calling for return to something past, but by reinscribing the realities and potentials of the world of the present. They found in a *bhakti* ontology the grounds to understand the practice of colonial power as effective but morally deluded. They made their countercolonial political party by defining a moral universe and history in which their suffering and heroism would make sense, and lead to something better.

As we have seen, Fiji Indians participated, in a small way, in the formulation of the mass nationalist party that was to redefine politics in India. By contribution and example, they helped develop the devotional imagery of Indian nationalist politics, including its use of the Ramayan as a vast political metaphor. The battles against indenture, and decades later against colonial power in general, were won in India through the power of a devotionally oriented nationalist movement; the values and successes of that movement were a public fascination in Fiji. However, our concerns remain in Fiji. In the Fiji of 1919 no battles had been won. The end of indenture in Fiji became a fact only through the command of higher colonial authority, not Fiji Indian authority. A devotional version of Indian nationalist politics would be attempted in Fiji too, but, as we shall see, in competition with other versions of an Indian nationalist project and in the face of sharp colonial antagonism to Indian nationalism in all its forms. In Fiji the indigenous Fijians were already favored sons of the land, and the Europeans knew they had an "Indian problem" before the Fiji Indians ever mounted a countercolonial rhetoric. In Fiji the outcomes would be different.

"The Indian Problem" Before the
End of Indenture

A term of indentured labor nominally began in a free-market transaction. Someone agreed to work for someone else for a specified term; in the case of Fiji, five years. Benefits of employment were also spelled out; for Fiji, wages of a shilling a day, and a promise of return passage to India. But beyond these appearances of marketplace form, this postslavery labor relation was a race-based commoditization of the whole agent rather than a market transaction between formally equal individuals. Once signed and delivered, for the five years of indenture the indentured laborers were subject to penal sanctions well beyond loss of benefits for failure to work. Throughout the term of indenture, they had little control over their person or their time. Like slaves, they had no incentive to work and like slaves were motivated by the threat and occasional reality of violence. Racial identity separated the managers of the system from its labor. The indentured laborers were Indian "coolies," the overseers, planters, government magistrates and inspectors, and others, all white "sahabs." Race defined place.

The indenture "contract" allowed the plantation system to continue in the Caribbean and elsewhere. The same lines that had once housed slaves were made homes to Indian "coolies," and much about plantation operation remained the same. The interesting thing about indenture in Fiji, most telling about race, class, and the limits of "political economy" within empire, was that in Fiji the coolie lines were built from scratch. More than fifty years after the abolition of slave trade, in a locale wherein slave plantations had never defined the genre, the "coolies" were still put in lines, denied control of their persons for the duration of their labor contracts, made servants to planter masters. The attempt of a new colonial government to make the colony pay for itself was framed within a system of well-established colonial agencies. However, this neat racial basis of the new colonial system had to resolve a major contradiction. After five years, the "coolies" became "free."

Fiji's first Governor, Sir Arthur Gordon, guided the introduction of Indian indentured labor in Fiji based upon his experience of the system as Governor in Mauritius and Trinidad, and he was sanguine about free Indians. He expected and even hoped that the Indians would stay and help populate the islands, a potential replacement if the indigenous Fijian "race" died away. Many of the other Europeans in Fiji had anticipated that the Indian "coolies" would return to India and were dismayed when the majority did not. Chiefs of the indigenous Fijians were concerned and protested the growing Indian population more than once. Not only the presence of the free Indians was a problem; there was also the matter of their social place. Here the political-economic, contract form of the indenture arrangement presented the particular problem. By its nature, it recognized the Indian as an economic, formally free and equal individual. The system was based upon a principle that the Indians too were citizens of empire. What, then, was to be their relation to colonial civil society?

Labor Commodities and Citizens of Empire: The First Version of "The Indian Problem"

Long before the end of indenture the Fiji Europeans were well aware of "the Indian problem"—an unchanging name for a changing cluster of problems perceived by Europeans in twentieth-century colonial Fiji. The first versions of the Indian problem concerned simply the undesirable consequences of the Indians' presence. Tellingly, the first regulations concerning "free" urban Indians were designed to control them and restrict their freedoms: a curfew, a prohibition on selling them alcohol, a restriction of municipal voting franchise to English-speaking and literate voters. These points are telling not because they reflect an interest in controlling the Indians, but because they point to a formal feature of the colonial legal situation. Apart from the restrictions imposed by such regulations free Indians could legally operate with a set of rights formally equal to those of the Europeans. This itself was the basis of the original Indian problem, an Eastern pollution of the young, and vulnerable, body politic of Fiji. Let us begin, then, with how this formal equality came to be.

Indigenous Fijians were never (and are still not) "free" in the formal sense that Indians were, even in the nineteenth century, once their indenture contracts ran out. Indigenous Fijians were always regarded as bound by what the British called the "customs" of their "communal" cultural systems—in practice, subordinate to their chiefs and their traditional kin groups (see, e.g., France 1969; Clammer 1973; but also Hocart 1970; Sahlins 1985). In colonial Fiji the indigenous Fijians became a polity within a polity. While the type and scope of the authority operating within the junior, indigenous polity was continually modified by the theories, advice, and interventions of various agencies of the superordinate colonial polity, the presence of the indigenous polity was a continuing and at times quite convenient principle for delimiting the rights and place of all the indigenous Fijians. This was of course simply "indirect rule" from the point of view of the settler, more interested in the land, profits, and his own colonial society than in "the natives." Our first problem is understanding why the Indians could not be socially bracketed by a form of indirect rule, and the consequences of this first form of the Indian problem.

The Fiji Indian indentured laborers were recruited in most cases as individuals. A small percentage of registrants were married couples, even families. But recruiting for Fiji was not generally done within villages or within recruiters' kin or caste networks. Instead, the recruiters (*arkatis*) directing recruits to the depots and thence to Fiji (or the Caribbean or elsewhere) generally worked in bazaar towns and pilgrimage centers, attracting individuals who were in transit, looking for work, or on pilgrimage (see Lal 1983). Thus the *girmitiyas* sent to Fiji were not organized by, or into, larger social aggregates in the process of recruiting. There was no theory of any sort of inherent, primordial, or legal social grouping of the Fiji Indian "coolies." They were conceived as having no leaders or social organization of their own. On arrival they were assigned in lots of any size as "labour units" to the planters and others contracting for that number. According to Sanadhya and Chaturvedi, overseers on the plantations actually went out of their way to deny Brahmans and other high-caste Indians forms of privilege or special standing. When an organized group of "Kabuli Pathans" arrived in Fiji in 1912, apparently promised work as a group, they were assigned together to a plantation. But when, in concert, they protested working conditions, they were met with violence, broken up as a group, and dispersed in reassignments (see Sanadhya 1914; Gillion 1962; Tinker 1974).

The Fiji Indians were taken to be individual and socially unattached in the modes of recruitment, in the legal terms of the contract, in the definition of "labour units," and in the arrangement of authority in the lines. Legally, Homo Hierarchicus died in the depots. While high-caste background was still invoked by many *girmitiyas* as a ground for social distinction, nothing existed to institute any caste rights, relations, privileges, or duties, and nothing akin to a "caste system" emerged.[1] Before the recruits left India, they appeared one by one before a magistrate who verified that they had contracted for indenture and understood its terms. We have discussed how these interviews were a symbol to *girmitiya* spokesmen of the emptiness of the colonial legal forms applied to them. Sanadhya and Chaturvedi wrote:

Recruiters fool them and take them to the magistrate. The magistrate asks, "Are you agreed to go to Fiji?" As soon as the word "yes" leaves the lips, the registry is done. What would be the registry? From saying only "yes," there was five years of black water!

However, as the focus of a particular construction of the Indians' social and political identity, this interview and the theory of contract it reified were far from inconsequential. They established the Fiji Indians, in the course of binding them temporarily to indenture, as British subjects otherwise adult, competent, and "free," capable of making contracts and enforcing them in British courts.

The Indian problem was the result of a contradiction in indenture. On the one hand, "coolie" identity began with the difference in conception between a "coolie" and a general "laborer," a proletarian in political-economic theory. As Breman (1990: 4) puts it, the colonial labor schemes "emanated from a state of mind that 'animalized' rather than 'commoditized' Africans and Asians." A "coolie" was a different type of human being than a "European." The "coolie" was suited to a particular type of labor and life by race: by physical, mental, and emotional characteristics, a "character" generally explained as the result of the action of the tropical environment over vast time. His or her identity and substance as an individual were not shaped by capitalist transactions—he or she did not relate to employers primarily as a seller of labor relating to a buyer of labor. Rather, the "coolie"'s suitability for tropical labor was determined by racial nature. In quite specific ways the inden-

---

1. Brahmans were the only group to consolidate a standing approximating that of a *jati* in India, with a degree of endogamy, a coherent social identity, and, as priests, unique functions in ritual exchanges accepted as vital. Even their precedence was limited, however, by doubts about the authenticity of any given person's claim to be a real or pure Brahman. The British discriminated against declared Brahmans in indenture recruiting, regarding them as lazy and troublesome, and many in Fiji who announced themselves to be Brahmans had declared a different caste in the official indenture papers.

ture contract, while a contract, was informed by these presuppositions. Wages were not mobilized as a work incentive—the wage rate was flat. Rather than a person working for wages, the "coolie" was considered a worker by nature, but a worker requiring discipline. While time wages were briefly experimented with before the tasking system was established, the rest of the plantation system of labor organization was never doubted. Labor discipline in this system was maintained by external constraints and enforcements, not education in proper attitude or incentives for internalization. The settlers and the CSR, the dominant refining company, were always against "coolie" education. But on the other hand, unlike slavery, indenture was based upon a contract. Even its discipline system depended upon giving the "coolie" standing in law as a competent adult: in marked contrast to slavery systems, the primary disciplinary locus of indenture in Fiji was the courtroom.[2]

These courts of law were a front line of the Indian problem, a place where official Fiji was continually called upon to resolve questions about the Fiji Indians' status. The courts decided, in one Fiji European's clarifying phrase, "justice as she was extended to the coolie." In the magistrate's courts hearing "coolie" discipline cases, the rules of evidence were extremely lax. Routinely assertions of overseers were sufficient evidence for conviction, while Indian allegations did not require investigation. Conviction rates in typical years were 90 percent and higher. Still, there were costs, as well as benefits, to the planters in the way justice "was extended to the coolie" there. On 15 October 1912 the *Fiji Times* editorialized against "coolies" receiving the death penalty for killing other "coolies" "solely on the ground of the insane wastefulness of it all." As in the case of Mr. Harper noted in chapter 2, planters lost money invested in laborers who went to jail or were hanged for violent crime. This aspect of what the *Fiji Times* called "the very incompletely defined diathesis called Justice" was unavoidable. But the Fiji Euro-

---

2. In one early year, 1886, a total of 8,853 charges of labor law violations were filed against a total indentured population of 5,237: the number of prosecutions was 169 percent of the number of laborers under indenture. Generally speaking, from 15 percent to 40 percent of the indentured laborers were convicted of at least one violation of labor laws each year: for absence from the plantations without permission, absence from work, refusal to work, failure to complete tasks (Tinker 1974: 194–95). Only in the last, reform-conscious years of the system did the rates drop appreciably, to under 10 percent. Until reforms of the system limited the powers of the magistrates, the penalties for "labour law violations," violations of the simple terms of the indenture contract, included both fines and extensions of the term of the contract. A "coolie" charged and convicted of failing to complete a task could be simultaneously paid nothing for what he did do, fined, and forced to accept an extension.

peans could and did manipulate other aspects of the rights of the Fiji Indians to appeal to European officials for justice.

In 1886 a pair of organized "coolie" labor actions brought quick reforms on the part of Fiji's new colonial government, on behalf of the employers. Gillion (1962: 83) describes the events. Following a strike by three hundred workers on a CSR estate, Walter S. Carew, then a stipendiary magistrate, jailed the "ringleaders" even though he found that the workers had been systematically overtasked. Two months later, 130 "coolies" from a Rewa Sugar Company plantation marched on Suva, carrying knives, axes, hoes, and sticks, protesting an increase in their daily task of more than 40 percent. The Inspector of Immigrants heard their grievances, and though Carew fined several of the protestors, he again found justice in their cause and ordered the original tasking standard reinstated. These two judgments led to planter complaints; then-Governor J. B. Thurston agreed that the Indian mobs presented "a positive threatened danger to the colony" and engineered the passage of new labor laws. It became illegal in Fiji for "coolies" to make complaints in groups of more than five, or to carry work implements when making complaints. At the same time, penalties were greatly increased for insufficient work. In this case and in others, the Agent-General of Immigration and the courts were the Indians' best protection and only recourse, however unreliable they were and however unsympathetic they were to Indian leaders. The only political role acceptable for the Indians was that of helpless individual, as Tinker (1974: 227) summarizes:

It was an absolute principle of the system that no Indian labourer should ever acquire a recognized position as a leader or even as a negotiator. Their only recognized role was that of petitioners: and humble petitioners too.

On the other hand, the officials of the European courts were not always comfortable when called upon to publicly and formally "extend justice" to Indian petitioners, or even Indian victims. For example, long prison sentences with hard labor were not uncommon for Indians, but it was news when, in September 1912, a white overseer received a prison sentence for his treatment of a "coolie." Under the headline "Overseer Sentenced," the *Fiji Times* of September 28 reported:

The Sub-Inspector of Police, who was prosecuting, at the conclusion of the evidence; said that though it was very painful to be obliged to do so, he was compelled to ask His Worship to inflict a severe sentence as the defendant had five previous convictions against him, and an example should be made in this case which would act as a deterrent to others.

His Worship found the defendant guilty and said that labour must be properly treated, and sentenced [the overseer] to 14 days hard labour without the option of a fine.

Much more commonly, evidence of overseer crimes against "coolie" (especially rape) led quietly to their transfer, in extreme cases to their transfer out of Fiji. John Wear Burton (1910: 290–94), a Methodist missionary and a leading European critic of indenture, defended the practice of informal punishment while decrying its necessity. Here I quote one of his case examples, then his explanation of the problem:

Din Muhammad was a man of good caste and education. He had a history in India, but it was more foolish than vicious. He was placed in charge of the women as sardar (head man) on a certain plantation under an European overseer. Din Muhammad was no saint; but he had spasms of ethics—and more than spasms of obstinacy. When his sahib made improper proposals to him regarding some of the better-looking women under his care, he became suddenly virtuous, and virtue mounted itself upon a mule-like intractability. He even preached a little on the subject, quoting from the Quran—of all books! The overseer was exasperated, and beat Din Muhammad so savagely that he had to be sent to the hospital. The coolie inspector heard of the case, and made some inquiries. The overseer sniffed trouble, and so laid a charge against the sardar of attacking him, paying four coolies two rupees each to swear that he himself struck only in self-defense. The four coolies told a consistent story—for two rupees is good money to pay in a country where a witness for any purpose can be obtained for a single rupee. Din Muhammad was sentenced to six months' imprisonment in the Suva jail. The coolie inspector, however, was not satisfied. He "Sherlock Holmesed" the case, and found out that Din Muhammad had been ill-used, and that he had really sought to protect the women under him. The facts were laid before the Governor: Din Muhammad was released; and the overseer had to leave the country.

[Again, in second example,] European prestige among these people suffered another loss.

It is really only by prestige that the people can be kept in check; and when that goes, there goes along with it all control. The Indian can scarcely be frightened. When his temper is fully roused, no power on earth can hold him back.

Thus even a critic of indenture hoped that its literal crimes, when officially discovered, would be dealt with as privately as possible—because European prestige was at stake, the real anchor of the colonial social formation. While the Indians were reduced politically to the standing of individual petitioners, there was embarrassment and resistance to allowing their protests to be formally and publicly heard in court.

In this light, let us consider one final case and the press reaction to it. By 1912 free Indians were living in and around Fiji's towns and cities in numbers that were already comparable to the urban European population; some were beginning to earn money at respectable levels and were even living among Europeans. In September 1912 a "Goanese" man appeared in Suva Police Court, suing a white police subinspector for assault (case 494; my account is compiled from court notes and press reports). This man from Goa, never a "coolie," claimed his true ancestry to be Portuguese but was thought by police and press to be an Indian. The night before the alleged assault a white neighbor had gone to the man's house, off Waimanu Road in Suva, to complain about the excessive noise of a party. A fight and some damage had resulted. The subinspector then came by to retrieve some of the white man's property (which the Goanese held to exchange for repairs to his own property) and to ask "why he was causing trouble," the subinspector testified. The Goanese claimed that the subinspector then said to him, "Take your pipe out when talking to a white man," and slapped the pipe out of his mouth, causing him to bleed. The subinspector claimed it was the Goanese who was abusive, blowing smoke in his face, and the court sided with the subinspector. The judge "considered the assault, such as it was, justified and was of the opinion that [the Goanese] was fortunate to escape being knocked down" (*Fiji Times,* 26 September 1912). The *Fiji Times* agreed, despite the fact that the same week it made several complaints of its own about police arrogance. In the same issue it editorialized:

There are *a certain number of people* in this town who seem to imagine that, under cover of *our all-protecting law,* they can by insolence and insults provoke *their superiors* to assault them, and then, by visiting a solicitor's office and issuing a summons, *further humiliate* them by bringing them before a magistrate who will fine them. His Worship's remark that the complainant was fortunate in not being knocked down should make it clear to *the gentry we have referred to* that even under the British flag, *where equal rights of citizenship are given to all,* there is a limit to the taunting behavior they can use to an officer of the crown, just as there is a still stricter limit with regard to the conduct of such an officer toward a civilian, and it is to be hoped that the lesson contained in the remarks made from the bench on Tuesday will be taken to heart *by those whom it concerns.* (emphasis added)

The newspaper took great pains not to argue based on race and to argue no explicit legal exclusion. But it also sought to make clear that it approved of a "lesson" to be learned from the case about a de facto limitation of rights to legal action. As for Burton, "prestige" was the crucial implicit issue. Equal rights were "given to" all, but a certain gentry was taking license from this magnanimous grant to seek to "humiliate" "their superiors"—the ones granting the rights. These rights as conceptualized were not universal "human rights," springing from a "human nature." They were instead imagined as the boons of a particular type of civilization, a benefit of social advancement. They were handed down by an authority that preceded their existence, an authority necessary for their existence. The authority was known metonymically; the "equal rights of citizenship" were given "under the British flag," given by "the crown." The agents of this high authority were "officers," who were, precisely as the guarantors of equality, superior. The senior officers, such as the magistrate, were described by forms of extreme deference, as here "His Worship."

In this decidedly non-political-economic imagination of social order, the elite, not the masses, made the social contract and named its terms, and rule descended and was justified by its prestige, not legitimated by its mass support. The issue in Fiji was, both literally and in rhetorical figure, how to "extend justice to the coolie." In the British colonial construction, even the most basic social values were supported in the first place not by an (imagined) human or other nature but by their purported authors, the authorities issuing and securing them. The values depended on the "civilization" to which they belonged, and more immediately on the high agencies delineating and defending the civil order. This construction of social order touches themes in legal discourse that run deep in the history of Europe as well as wide in the colonial discourses of Europe's empires. While it is often Germanic law that is singled out for top-down definitions of civil order and rights, Corrigan and Sayer (1985: 193–94) argue that the history of state formation in England itself has been a history of "revolutions from above." Terms such as *nation* and *society* applied first to the governing elite, who extended them to make a larger and larger ruling "class" in a series of compromises that always reconsolidated elite power. Voting rights became increasingly inclusive in successive expansions from the Magna Carta onward. Quite unlike the polities envisaged by political-economic theory, the British national polity was known and represented as descending both in history and in structure:

This set of cultural images provided the moral energy for English imperialism: the successive imposition of English civilization on the "dark corners" of England itself, Wales, Scotland, Ireland and eventually that British empire which covered a quarter of the globe. . . . It took a national culture of extraordinary self-confidence and moral rectitude to construe such imperialism as a "civilizing mission" (and in fact to rule with surprisingly little use of direct armed force, in comparative terms, from the "Mother Country"); *and* for long periods, with a fair degree of success, to bedazzle the domestically subordinated with the spectacle of empire.

The political manifestos of early political economy—the American Declaration of Independence, the French Declaration of the Rights of Man, James Mill's "Essay on Government"—concerned the natural rights of "man," political order as a construct of and for a citizenry, "legitimate" only to protect their interests, a construct in which it is not "the crown" but "man" (as seen from the vantage of "the market") that precedes all. Such manifests did not and do not form the foundation of the English state, even the English state of the nineteenth and twentieth centuries. Both Mill and Macaulay helped shape law and order for India. In Fiji, high Crown authorities deliberated whether and how to "extend" various rights and privileges of citizenship to the Fiji Indians and others. This process was not an aberration, an anomaly, but rather was the basic pattern of order of the British Empire and the British state—a British political grammar defining the "prestige" of those using it. The point, then, is the constraints upon the agents so empowered in the Fiji of indentured labor. The constant, through all the shifting situations, confrontations, and contradictions labeled "the Indian problem" in Fiji's colonial history, was the struggle of the Europeans to maintain their social height and contain Indians' social place in Fiji, against the implications of the Indians' formal and legal "equality" and "freedom."

In this light let us examine two areas of controversy concerning free Indians during indenture days: politics and education.

Politics and "Free" Indians in Indenture Fiji

The principal political issues labeled "the Indian problem" during the 1910s in Fiji related to political representation and voting. The problem was not the same as the one perceived two decades later, namely that Indian political rights were a threat to British authority, that Fiji was in danger of becoming an "Indian colony." The issue instead was that Indian voters polluted the franchise system, that Fiji's fledgling democratic systems needed protection from their meddling. In fact, in the decade of the 1900s, Indian voters in Suva's municipal elections had actually influenced the outcomes. Not only were white candidates affected by their votes, but a Chinese was elected to the Suva Council by "Asiatic" voters. The event was ridiculed as proof, not that Asians could come to dominate civic politics, but that Asian voters were capable of any level of nonsense.

Free Indians had the right to vote in municipal elections when they were ratepayers, paying city taxes on property they owned. Indians shared this municipal franchise long before they—or the local Europeans themselves—were granted (by their official superiors) a vote for

Legislative Council representatives. By 1903, however, Indian voting practices were already considered suspect. In that year, elective European representation to the Legislative Council was introduced, but the Governor of the time, writes Gillion (1962: 160) "said that he did not consider it necessary to provide for the representation of the Indians and Pacific Islanders because they had shown themselves open to corruption at the municipal elections, and because their interests were already safeguarded in the council by the Agent-General of Immigration." Then in 1912 the Indians lost their municipal franchise. Complex negotiations between the Fiji government and the Suva Municipal Council resulted in the council passing and forwarding to the Governor a provision for a new franchise requirement, a test in reading, writing, and speaking English. The test was originally to be applicable to "alien voters" only. But in the final version it was applicable generally in principle, to be applied in practice at the discretion of Suva's Mayor.

The rhetoric surrounding this revision of law matched that in the responses to the Goanese man's suit against the police. For example, Maynard Hedstrom, an influential merchant and city councillor, argued as follows in council for the measure:

> It is well known that in *our* midst we have a large number of ratepayers who cannot read or write their own language, and who have absolutely no knowledge of municipal affairs. The vote in the hands of people who have no idea what it is, and how they ought to use it, is a real danger to *the community*. If an education test were enforced . . . there would be an end to the "40 votes for 1 shilling each" business. (*Fiji Times,* 23 Nov. 1912; emphasis added)

The *Fiji Times* (7 Sept. 1912) itself carried even further the imagery of the Indians as alien and outside of the true civil society, when it defended the version of the law that applied the education test only to "alien voters":

> It is just as well that his motion was not amended to apply to whites. It is, as Cr. Johnson suggested, establishing a most dangerous precedent to put the illiterate black on the same level as the illiterate white, especially in the cases where the former's conception of the duties of citizenship is so very vague as is that of the great majority of local coloured voters. . . . It is anything but elevating that a white man of repute should, in a council election, have to stand or fall by the chance vote of electors who, at the bidding of any Babu, would vote "Brown sahib" or "Jones sahib," just as their memory served them. We congratulate Cr. Scott for having brought this important matter forward, and trust that his colleagues on the Legislative Council will sufficiently emphasize the matter as to impress the Colonial Office with the need for an alteration in the law. That this conviction will take a lot of pressing home we know, but the day has arrived

when the progress of this town demands that legislation shall not be in the interest of one class or race.

"Progress" was seen to "demand" the exclusion of the Indian voters, "alien" to the "conception of the duties of citizenship" basic to the new civil society. In a startling rhetorical twist, this exclusion was taken as a paradigm of legislation not in the interest of one race or class, presumably because it was intended to elevate what Hedstrom called "the community" as a whole. It was instead the obstructionists in the Colonial Office and elsewhere (notably the government of India), resisting such laws, who promoted class and racial interests.

This rhetorical snarl is notable not because it seems so transparent—for it is transparent to us, not to its audience—but because it demonstrates how the legal exclusions and restrictions of the Indians had to be, and were, couched as evenhanded promotions of the colony as a whole. Further, this very rhetorical requirement prevented the differentiation of the Indians as "alien voters," despite the efforts of the *Fiji Times* and others to avoid the "most dangerous precedent" of their inclusion. The Indians were subjects of the Crown (excepting the few from princely states in India) and were not, legally, aliens in Fiji. Thus the voting education test had to be universal de jure.

In fact, the Fiji colonial authorities had no qualms about representing the Indians officially and formally as equal citizens of their colony, even while they fought to restrict their political rights. Increasingly as the indenture system was criticized in the 1910s, they made special efforts to represent the free Indians as equal citizens of Fiji. In 1916, responding to pressure both from Fiji Indian petitions and from India, the Fiji government arranged for a special representative for the Fiji Indians on the Legislative Council—but one chosen by nomination, not election. In 1921, when negotiating for further labor immigration from India, they proposed to adopt the following ordinance:

An Ordinance to make clear the status of British
Indians resident within the Colony

WHEREAS it is deemed expedient to define the present and prospective status of British Indians in the Colony of Fiji BE IT ENACTED by the Governor with the advice and consent of the Legislative Council as follows;—

1. All British Indians resident in the Colony shall have equal rights and privileges with other subjects of His Majesty the King to hold lands practice professions follow any trade or calling in the Colony in common with all other British subjects resident in the Colony, subject nevertheless to the provisions of the Liquor Ordinance of 1911, and any and every amendment thereof.

2. The Municipal Institutions Ordinance 1909 and the amendments thereto and by-laws and regulations thereunder shall be deemed to apply to all subjects of His Majesty the King resident in any Municipality in the Colony without any distinction of race or origin and absolute equality of rights of all British subjects shall be maintained in any further amendments of the said Ordinance by-laws and regulations.

3. The Political rights of British Indians resident in the Colony reserved by the Letters Patent passed under the great seal of the United Kingdom constituting the Office of Governor and Commander-in-Chief of the Colony and providing for the Government thereof and the Instructions and Regulations thereunder shall be maintained.

4. Subject to the provisions of the Ordinance and to the said Letters Patent the position of British Indians resident in the Colony shall be equal to the position of other British subjects resident in the Colony.

This proposed ordinance, as the colonial government of India noticed, did not actually change the legal standing of the Indians in Fiji at all—they were still banned from purchasing alcohol under the Liquor Ordinance and excluded from municipal voting (under amendments to the Municipal Ordinance) and from Legislative Council elections (under the Letters Patent). Fiji's Attorney General assured the officers of the Colonial Sugar Refining Company "that the ordinance simply guaranteed existing rights, that Indians 'shall be equal' merely meant 'are equal,' and that there was nothing in the ordinance to place the Indians in the future on the same plane as the Europeans" (Gillion 1977: 70). Even so, it was never adopted, both because India was unimpressed, and because indigenous Fijian chiefs were alarmed.

The same year, 1921, the Attorney General was asked to prepare a memorandum on the status of Indians in response to a question in the Legislative Council by the one nominated Indian representative, and he found that within and despite the restrictive terms of particular laws, the Fiji Indians were equal, even without the ordinance (CSO 6707/21). After reviewing Indians' voting rights, land acquisition rights, trading rights, and "differentiation in any other direction" (the liquor law restrictions, the nonentitlement of nonwhites to juries, the need for nonwhites to get special permits for gun licenses, the nightly town curfew on nonwhites, etc.) the Attorney General concluded:

It will be seen that except in a few instances in nearly all of which the differentiation is for their protection and is shared by Fijians and other Pacific Islanders the Indians are on exactly the same footing as Europeans—in some respect, indeed, they are on better footing, e.g. the Indian Land Settlement Ordinance 1916 provides for the appointment of a Board to acquire land on which to settle Indians.

Even the fact that Indians could not buy land, but had to lease it on terms set by the government, became here not a restriction but a privilege. All such provisions were deemed for protection: the land reserves for protection of indigenous Fijians, the restrictions on alcohol for protection of indigenous Fijians and Indians from themselves, and so on. Indians and indigenous Fijians were not seen as unequal to Europeans by law—but rather, by nature.

Education and Citizenship

"The Indian problem" as originally conceived was a contradiction between the requirements of civilized law and the realities of Indians' nature. From the extraordinary violence of the coolie lines to the voting habits of the urban Indian ratepayers, Indian action was read not as a response to social and political contexts, but as the expression of a dark Indian mentality. Sanadhya and Chaturvedi complained bitterly, in *My Twenty-one Years in the Fiji Islands,* about the restriction of municipal franchise to those literate in English, which eliminated virtually all Indian voters. In Fiji, they pointed out (in 1914), there was little opportunity for an Indian to achieve the required literacy. "Will the Indians come out from the womb speaking English?" they asked. For the Europeans, the nature of Indians "from the womb" was precisely the issue, especially when education itself was debated.

Because the Indians were conceived as different by nature, the question of Indian education became a major focus of debate over whether and how the colonial authorities ought to "extend" justice, civilization, and citizenship to the Fiji Indians. One battleground for this debate was the testimony before the Education Commission of 1909. Education for Indian children was the matter of last rank in the original charge for the commission, which was primarily concerned with "the Education of Europeans and Natives in Fiji" (just as, in protocol, the Indian members of the Colonial Legislative Council always ranked lowest, beneath all indigenous Fijian nominees as well as European, regardless of seniority). Only the last two of the twenty-five questions prepared for committee and witness consideration concerned the education of Indians, while the first thirteen concerned European children, and the next ten, indigenous Fijian and other Islander children. However, in the eighteenth of its eighteen resolutions, this commission established the Fiji government's commitment in principle to Indian education, and its general form—a limited number of public schools and "grants-in-aid to private schools . . . provided these latter conform to regulations made by the Board of Education with the sanction of the Governor in Council." In a pattern that was maintained at least until the 1987 coups, the Fiji government posted teachers, provided grants-in-aid, and controlled curriculum for Indian schools once the Indian community organized and built schools for itself. In 1909 this was highly debatable policy.

The official questions concerning Indian education were vague, simply a call for suggestions on education of indentured and nonindentured children and a query whether Indians should be educated separately from other races. The answers, however, raised several specific controversies, concerning the advisability in principle of Indian education, concerning its content, especially its religious and moral content, and concerning control of the Indian schools. To begin with, in written submissions the Christian missionaries said that Indian education should continue to be entrusted to them.[3] Wrote Brother Claudius:

The Indian with a good moral education can be turned into a very serviceable citizen. I think nobody is more suitable for that work than the missionary.

Remark—The Indians with their 32,000 gods are divided into as many creeds, all averse to one another. Thence, strifes of every shape and form; add to that the blind state in which they live, &c. But, with all that, their belief in God, under one form or another, is in them, and pretty strongly too. Along with it, they reverence and respect the missionary. This being the case, if their children were brought up through religious influence and unity of belief, it would, I think, strike a severe blow at the source of their discord and subject of quarrels. Nobody, I think, could do any better work with them than the missionary.

. . . Indian lads can be turned into splendid teachers; through education they lose almost entirely their backward national spirit and replace it, willingly, by a good English spirit.

Richard Piper of the Methodist Mission was even more emphatic, stressing dangers as well as benefits as the Indians became more educated:

The present low moral condition of the Indian is used by some as an argument against their education. But from the standpoint of Britain's own history as a race rescued from barbarism . . . the obligation is increasingly clear to uplift these peoples intellectually and morally, and not leave them merely as human machines for the production of wealth. It will be generally admitted that the education of the Indian needs to proceed upon special lines. The ordinary secular education is not calculated to do much good but in many cases harm. Secular education does not make men better. But the primary object of educating Indians will be to make them better citizens and reduce their average of criminality which, at present, is alarmingly high. The danger is that of all education a purely

3. Before 1909 the few schools educating Indians were almost all run by Christian missions, Methodist and Catholic. Frustrated in their efforts to convert adults, the missions had made a major financial commitment to education, in the hope of gaining influence on the Indians before it was too late (see Burton 1910, Thornley, 1973).

secular one will place sharper and more formidable weapons in the hands of those whose moral and religious sanctions are lamentably weak, but whose predilections to theft, deceit, duplicity, conspiracy, rapine and murder are terribly real and strong. Education, I submit, must be decidedly moral and religious. Opinions may differ as to the advisability of christianizing the Indian, and it is hardly to be hoped even by the Christian missionary that the Government will become an active proselytiser. Nevertheless . . . until ethics is recrowned and reseated on an equality with religious beliefs and practices, all education will fail to obtain the desired result—a trustworthy Indian.

The issue raised by Piper was of concern to the commission and rose again in testimony, for example in this exchange between a commission member and a Catholic missionary:

In your opinion do you think that the mentalization of the Indian is always inclined to go ahead of his moralization?———I can hardly say. He is very sharp-witted.
Do you not think then that to educate him and leave him to his former associations is to make him a public danger?———I do not think so. The moral influence of his teacher would help him.

Others were less sanguine about the moral influence of teachers, and of education and even Christianity generally, on the "lower races." E. W. Fenner, a CSR official, approved only of a minimal education program for Indians, "the three R's—sufficient to keep from running wild." If indigenous Fijians were taught English, he thought, "we would require more police. . . . It would only tend to make them despise manual labour which, after all, must be the source of livelihood of most natives." With respect to the Indians, both English and Christianity were sources of trouble:

A coolie who speaks English and professes Christianity is generally worth watching. I am speaking from my own experience, and any one who has anything to do with coolies will tell you the same.

This skepticism, worry over the danger of educated Indians and indigenous Fijians, was less uniformly (though occasionally) anti-Christian than it was concerned to maintain the racial structure of Fiji, a concern presupposing that the racial structure of indenture days was natural and therefore the most harmonious and progressive order possible. W. A. Scott was concerned that indigenous Fijians, even with education, "continue to be 'Fijians,' and not 'neither one thing nor the other'—a class which many of them are drifting into at present." He thought that "speaking generally there is at present no scope in the Colony for highly-educated natives"; further:

I am not in sympathy with teaching Indians English. I consider the class of Indians in this Colony to be agriculturalists, and I think they should be confined as much as possible to that sphere of usefulness. If any of them desire an academic training there are liberal and ample means for their acquiring it in their own country.

The placement of the Indians in a subordinate racial "class" within the colony was coupled here with the idea that their real "country" and rights to education lay in India. But on the education question, as later with respect to directly political questions, the attempt to construct the Indians legally as "aliens" in Fiji was a failure, at least in colonial days.[4] However, the rest of Scott's position was well supported by others, including J. W. Burton, the missionary critic of indenture. Burton's submission to the committee endorsed limited education for Indians through mission schools but was mainly concerned with indigenous Fijian education. It elaborated on the racial theory underlying most of the submissions and testimony heard by the commission:

The Fijian of To-Day must be studied, and the system of education drawn up in sympathy with his special needs. What type of instruction will benefit him most? What class of facts is he most capable of assimilating and turning to good account in social efficiency? None would look upon the Fijian as an intellectual type. Charming and naive as he may be in his manners, he belongs to the category of the "lower races." This fact must be recognised, and education must approach him accordingly. The training which suits admirably a boy at Eton or one in our Australasian High Schools may not only be useless, but most probably vicious, in its effect upon a Fijian native. We have made a tragic mistake in India in raising up a few to inordinate heights of unsuitable education and thus divorcing them from usefulness to the commonwealth. A half-educated Indian

---

4. As late as 1921 the governor of Fiji resisted Colonial Office demand that Indians be granted elected representatives on Fiji's Legislative Council on the grounds that the Indians might yet abandon Fiji and return to India (CSO 718/21). But the Colonial Office was not impressed and insisted on political representation for Fiji Indians in Fiji. This argument, that the Fiji Indians are really and legally aliens in Fiji, has resurfaced in postcoup Fiji in the rhetoric and political program of Rabuka and the *Taukei* Movement. It is the principal vehicle for denying the implications of the original *girmit* contracts. Now it is the elite indigenous Fijians who must be impressed by legal and moral arguments, and thus far they seem unimpressed by the claim that a century of residence, political "freedom" and economic activity makes the Fiji Indians real citizens of Fiji. The colonial debate over what legal and social rights *girmit* entailed for the Indians has taken a new and ominous turn. A more exclusively racial definition of "nation" than ever before is now publicly discussed, and criticized mainly in hushed tones when no soldiers are around. In the new "republic," "nation" and "public" are being transformed in form and content simultaneously; the public space for an Indian position in national dialogue is disappearing at the same time that Indian alienness is proposed. For further discussion of these issues and accounts of the Fiji coups, see Kelly 1988c, Kaplan 1988, and Lal 1988.

babu, with his staccato English and metronomic syllables, is torture enough; but a Fijian babu—! May Heaven forfend!

. . . The brain-work of the community, for many years to come, will be undertaken by the European element in the country; but the native has land—land that he should be encouraged to use; he has labour stored away in his splendid physique—labour that he must call forth or die. . . . Education, etymologically, is a *drawing forth;* and we must draw forth that which is already in the native. Make as many rungs in the ladder of his progress as we will, but let us see that the first rung is near enough to the ground for him to commence the ascent.

Burton himself, like the witnesses before the committee taken as a whole, could not resolve an image of the nature and capacities of the indigenous Fijian "natives" and the Indians, swaying between concepts of universal human potential and images of racial limitations and characters, "lower races" with vices and a backward national spirit. It was clear to the Europeans that the Indians (and the indigenous Fijians) had unrealized potentials, some sort of telos, but not as clear how much progress was possible or desirable. Furthermore, the measure of desirability was not only each race's potential but also the implications for the other races of various sorts of attainment. While European advances were obviously good for everyone, serious questions had to be answered about the purpose of education provided to Indians and indigenous Fijians. There was not only the threat of mentalization outstripping moralization, but also the tragedy of the good agriculturalist or manual laborer made over into something betwixt and between, "divorcing them from usefulness to the commonwealth." Unlike later, more Social Darwinist, Fiji European visions, what Burton perceived was not a threat to the future of his "race" in the colony, but only a threat to the indigenous Fijians and the Indians themselves, and a prospect of public discourse polluted by half-educated *babus.* So what would the wise policy be?

Until a rude awakening in 1920 and 1921 (when the government turned its back on Fiji Indian strikers and even orchestrated violence against them) the vast majority of Fiji Indians had greater respect and affection for the high officials of the Crown than for any other part of the white society. Even such critics as Sanadhya and Chaturvedi hoped on many occasions that the good will and superior insights of high officialdom would intervene and suppress the evils of those operating the "coolie system" below them. Though such respect was dependent on a series of illusions, it also followed the inner lines of law and order in the British colonial social formation itself. What measures of privilege the "coolies" did receive were extended to them down from the top, from Royal Commissions, from Governors, from the Colonial Office, and through the interventions of the government of India. Crucially, their legal status as "free" individuals, with rights in courts of law as subjects of the Crown, were constructions of colonial India, the Colonial Office, and the laws establishing indentured labor itself, all beyond the control of the Europeans of Fiji. As many witnesses to the Education Commission noted, Fiji really had a duty to educate the Indians, who were, as Brother Claudius put it, "British subjects here just as well as in India."

Therefore, the commission decided to extend the benefits of education to the Indians. They rejected and criticized the opinions of those who would deny it to them. Among all the witnesses they heard, they quoted and endorsed the following advice from the official with the highest rank who wrote to them on the matter, the Agent-General of Immigration. There were, he said, very good reasons to educate the Indians:

I feel impelled to point out to the Commission, in conclusion, that in this Colony the checks and restraints of religion and custom, under which the population of India are largely governed, are much weakened or are entirely absent. Contrary perhaps to the opinion of persons not sufficiently informed in this respect, the class of Indian recruited for service in this Colony does not include a large proportion of the criminal class; but under conditions existing here, and no doubt also owing to the great preponderance of males introduced, there is an amount of serious crime committed by Indians, recorded yearly, which should give good cause for reflection. As three-fourths of the immigrants who arrive here do not return to India but make their permanent homes in Fiji, it is to be considered whether the younger people are to be assisted to receive such education as may fit them to become useful and law-abiding citizens—and my personal experience of the Indian is that he has the inclination to become so if properly guided—or whether through ignorance or discontent many of them are to become in the future a race of helots regarded with suspicion and a menace to the public order.

Indian criminality in Fiji was understood to be caused by the indenture context, but only insofar as that context "weakened the checks and restraints of religion and custom" and let the Indians' brutish nature express itself unimproved, to the peril of those more civilized. Thus perceiving a contradiction between Indians' racial nature and the imperatives of their own civil order—and neglecting the way in which their order was founded on their construction of the Indians' racial nature—the authorities of the Crown proposed and, over time, attempted to enact a solution. By education, they would impress a new social form onto the Indians' nature, "fit them to become" a type of citizen, the type both "law-abiding" and "useful."

No Fiji Indians were asked to discuss the future of Fiji Indian education in 1909. But Badri Maharaj, an early Arya Samaj leader, is said to have opened a school for Indian children at his own expense in 1898. In a sense, this was the beginning of the Samaj competition with the Christian mission schools in Fiji. The question for the Indians as for the Europeans was not only whether there would be schools, but what the curriculum would be. What indeed were they to teach their children to become? The education of the Fiji Indian educators depended upon the flow of texts and teachers from India to Fiji. Current Fiji Arya Samaj authorities name Behari Lal, a twenty-two-year-old Punjabi on his way to the Americas, as the first visitor to educate Samaj educators. Lal was not indentured, but he broke his journey in Fiji and found clerical work in Navua for the Vancouver Sugar Refining Company. On weekends, present-day Fiji Samajis describe, he came by punt to Suva and joined in social gatherings of a Fiji Indian leader, Babu Mangal Singh, in Samabula, outside of Suva, sometimes staying in a guest house, a *kuti*, Mangal Singh had built for religious visitors. Lal brought with him a book, an Urdu-script version of *Satyarth Prakash*, "The Light of the Truth," the major work of Swami Dayanand Saraswati, founder of the Arya Samaj in India. The text was discussed and a group was formed that found the light of its truth to fit their situation in Fiji. In 1904, the first Fiji Arya Samaj was founded by Behari Lal, Babu Mangal Singh, Gaji Pratap Singh, and others. In his hagiographic, Hindi-language *History of the Arya Samaj in Fiji* (1966: 15–19) later Arya Samaj missionary Shri Krishna Sharma describes the founding of the Fiji Arya Samaj as a dramatic moment, using imagery of light and darkness, seeds and growth. The majority of the Indians were illiterate, and "the imperial shadow of the darkness of ignorance" had fallen on them. In India,

publicity about Vedic religion was everywhere. As a result, the bonds of old conventions were breaking, and among the thoughtful, young and old, Arya sentiments were rising like the morning sun. Some of these people with modern Arya Samaji ideas then arrived in Fiji, pledges made, gripped in the chains of the coolie-system. Among their beloved possessions, a priceless book named *Satyarth Prakash* was with them in Fiji. . . . On December 25, 1904, in Samabula at Babu Mangal Singh's *kuti*, an Arya Samaj was established. From that day's planting, a small sapling has been made into a vast *kalpataru* [a tree that grants wishes], and into the cold shadow of the whole Pacific Ocean, happiness has carried itself.

Behari Lal left for the Americas shortly thereafter, but the Arya Samaj kept meeting. Education quickly became one of its principal interests, and in 1908, the year before the Education Commission's report, it bought its first piece of land, for a school.

The 1920s: Policy Debates
and Indian Withdrawal

When Fiji Indians were "free," where did they go and what did they do? They were still part of a colonial capitalist society; the 1922 census profiled their occupations. A reported 854 of them, about 3 percent of those with occupations other than "domestic duties," were employed in commerce, mainly as hawkers and traders, storekeepers and assistants. Indian rural shopkeepers had driven the European "country store-keepers" out of business by 1912 (Gillion 1962: 157), and by 1921 the competition of "Asian" merchant houses, Chinese as well as Indian, in the towns and cities caused European merchants to sell some items below cost (Knapman 1987: 87). Another 3,179 (11 percent) of the Indians were employed in "industry," mainly as labor; this category also included 88 goldsmiths, silversmiths, and jewelers, 79 tailors, 98 cabmen, stablemen, and carters, and 89 motorcar proprietors and drivers. However, in 1922 roughly 80 percent of the Fiji Indians reporting nondomestic occupations were working in agriculture, mainly as sugar cane–growers. Those who did not work for others leased land in units of eight to twelve acres from indigenous Fijians. They were effectively barred from buying their farmland by an official policy: before the Indians even arrived in Fiji, Fiji's colonial government had reserved 83 percent of Fiji's land, all the land not already sold to Europeans, for inalienable collective ownership by indigenous Fijian kin groups. The Fiji Indian farmers, when not working directly as laborers for the dominant (by 1926, the monopoly) sugar refiner in Fiji, the Colonial Sugar Refining Company, were most often selling their cane to the company at prices the company fixed. The "free" Indian sugar growers were locked in between their land leases and the company payments in 1922, and they still are today (though by 1976 the eighty percent in agriculture had dropped to 40 percent).

The free Indians developed their own network of credit and debt, their own commercial circuits of goods and services, and eventually their own productive enterprises, evading this structure of colonial economic domination. This withdrawal began in the 1900s, as Indian money stopped finding its way back to European banks and stores. Indian withdrawal from colonial society was also reflected in resistance to the Christian missions, in absurdly low marriage registration rates, and most dramatically in a pair of major strikes in 1920 and 1921, the latter closing the sugar mills for most of a milling season. We will examine this Indian withdrawal in its relation to a series of public and official discussions about Fiji Indians and policy on Fiji Indian questions, starting with the dramatic strikes. As we shall see, at the same time that the Fiji Indians withdrew socially, official Fiji remained comfortable talking about them rather than with them; it was not until 1929 that official Fiji came to regard its distance from the Indians as a serious problem.

Strikes and Political Leadership

As the Indians left the indenture lines they entered a political vacuum. There was literally no system devised for the local government of the free Indians. The pattern of settlement of the majority continuing to work in agriculture was determined by their leases, and therefore as time went on by the leasing schemes of the CSR Company and the government. Within settlement areas generally known by their indigenous Fijian names, the free Indians did organize free associations such as *mandalis* or religious "circles," groups that would meet to read religious texts, and even *panchayats*, councils of "big men" who would sit to resolve disputes. The question, however, was the legal standing of these organizations and other forms of order. In the 1910s and 1920s the government denied Indian organizations any official legitimacy but provided no alternative forms of its own. The government regarded the organization and control of the Indians as the business of the sugar companies, especially the dominant CSR, and expected the Indians to abide by what the Indians called *kampani ka raj*, government by the company. The company, in turn, was concerned mainly with keeping up its control over cane production, managed by European overseers working with Indian *sardars* leading the cane gangs of the various localities.

If official Fiji accepted no Fiji Indian forms of authority at local levels, neither did it accept any Indian leaders as legitimate representatives of colonywide Indian interests. When the sugar company and other Fiji employers resisted raising Fiji Indian wages despite a doubling of prices in postwar inflation, and the Indians struck, official Fiji responded by exiling the Indian leaders they blamed for the strikes, Manilal Maganlal Doctor in 1920 and the *sadhu* Bashishth Muni in 1921. This response was extreme, and to contextualize it, it may help to understand how official Fiji had dealt with Indian leadership and proposals about local Indian political institutions before the antagonisms of the major strikes.

When official Fiji was given no choice but to appoint an Indian to its Legislative Council, in 1917 it appointed a Fiji Indian Brahman and relatively rich planter in Ra Province named Badri Maharaj. He had been chosen in preference to the more popular candidate among Indians, the barrister Manilal Maganlal Doctor. Manilal had come to Fiji from Mauritius in 1912, after reading a published letter from Fiji Indians (including Totaram Sanadhya) to Gandhi, requesting a lawyer to help in Fiji. Unlike Manilal, Badri Maharaj was regarded by the government as "a man of character" (Gillion 1962: 161). In 1918, before the strikes and before the end of indenture, their "man of character" suggested to the government of Fiji a way to establish an administration over Fiji Indians. In a letter to the Agent-General of Immigration (CSO 4549/18), he outlined a scheme for establishing legal *panchayats:*

At the present time the Government are put to much trouble and expense in endeavouring to trace crimes which are, unfortunately, all too frequent among Indians; with the Panchayat in existence things would be simplified. The parties before proceeding to extreme measures would submit their case to the Panchayat and in all probability a settlement would be arranged.

In the event of a crime the perpetrator would be known and easily traced. Then in cases of immorality which have been, and still are, very prevalent with the lower caste Indian, these practices would be known to the Panchayat, and when proved, punished. Should the parties involved refuse to acknowledge the authority of the Panchayat then the parties could be brought before the Court to answer to a higher authority.

Another matter that would be dealt with by the Panchayat is the Mohomedan custom of sacrificing a cow. To a Hindu this is a gross affront and one that if not stopped is likely to cause a great deal of trouble. To a Hindu a cow is sacred and for a Mussulman to make a sacrifice of it is for him to deliberately go out of his way to make trouble. On the Panchayat would be both Hindu and Mohomedans and a satisfactory arrangement could be arrived at whereby no ones religious views need be outraged.

Finally in the case of Marriages the Panchayat would in all cases have cognizance, and, in the event of the parties being unsuitable, would step in and prevent the marriage taking place. As you are aware marriages amongst our people are arranged at a very early age, and sometimes the betrothal is only arranged in order to extort money or the equivalent from the man.

While the Government have no power to prevent these things the Panchayat could and would do much toward the abolition of these pernicious practises.

I would suggest a Panchayat, authorised by the Government should be established in each district vested with authority to deal with all questions relating to Indian customs and religion. In the event of my suggestion meeting with the approval of the Government, should they need assistance in choosing men to form the Panchayat I would be prepared to go to the various centres and personally choose suitable men. This matter is deserving of the gravest consideration at the present crisis. Preserve Indian Customs and there will be less difficulty in getting Indian labour. The Panchayat is recognised in India and its good work is known to all. Let its good work be extended to Fiji and there will be less dissatisfaction and greater unity than has ever been known before, amongst our people here.

The handpicked leader for the Fiji Indians was quite willing to lead and rule them. He proposed a scheme, couched in terms of preserving Indian custom, that would establish a network of official authority. The *panchayats* envisioned by Maharaj resemble neither the *panchayats* of village India nor the contingent, ephemeral *panchayats* known in Fiji Indian settlements, which made rulings but could rarely enforce them. Badri Maharaj's *panchayat* system, like British colonial government itself, was to be a top-down exercise of authority, empowered to solve crimes and mete out punishments to the limits allowed by higher authority. It would also regulate matters of Indian custom, distinguish between suitable and unsuitable marriages, and control the obnoxious behavior of certain "Mussulmen," matters beyond the regular scope of the authority of the colonial government.

The government took Maharaj's letter seriously (CSO 4549/18). The Agent-General of Immigration noted that *panchayats* of this sort would be a good thing, and literature on *panchayat* law was solicited from both India and other indentured-labor colonies. It was found, however, that no *panchayats* of similar sort existed in other indentured-labor colonies, and it was judged that even under the leadership of government's chosen man the enterprise would be too risky, that the time was not ripe. This reticence exemplifies the remarkable difference in attitude and procedure of the same government toward its two subject "races." In Fijian affairs, chiefly authority was quickly identified and readily enabled by administrative support and endorsement; customs were regulated and improved with regularity. The Fiji colonial government confidently established its own novel institutions in such matters as land tenure. But the Indians were different.

This difference stemmed mainly from the continuing identity of the Indians, in the colonial imagination, as laborers. As Badri Maharaj knew, official Fiji evaluated all Indian affairs in the late 1910s and early 1920s in relation to its attempts to arrange a new scheme of labor importation. When regarded as labor the Indians were not desired to have any form of organization at all. If indentured labor had been a variation on the social organization of slavery, the political attitude of the colony to its "free" Indians continued its attitude toward the Indians under indenture. This became quite clear during the 1920 and 1921 strikes.

The Fiji Indian strikes of 1920 and 1921 have been described in detail elsewhere (Gillion 1977; Ali 1980), and I will not provide an elaborate description. The 1920 strike of Indians in Suva and Rewa concerned wages and prices and a long roster of Fiji Indian political hopes; the Indians were suffering from postwar inflation and imagined that the end of indenture and the victories of nationalists in India would mean further favorable changes in their situation in Fiji. As in indenture days the Indians also thought that the high officials of the government and courts were their best hope for redress. They exempted the houses of the Governor, the Colonial Secretary, and the Chief Justice from the walkout of servants, and they petitioned for the recently appointed Governor, Cecil Rodwell, to come to Rewa to met with them and hear their concerns. Rodwell, whose previous colonial experience was in South Africa, chose instead to call out troops, including reinforcements from New Zealand and licensed indigenous Fijian deputies. As Gillion (1977: 30) describes, Rodwell cabled to London "that the Indian unrest was assuming the character of a racial outbreak rather than a strike, that bloodshed was inevitable, and that Indian agitators were trying to disaffect the Fijians." The next day his troops stopped a crowd of Indians trying to come to Suva "for food and to see those in custody" and fired shots into the resisting crowd, killing one and wounding several. The strike soon ended. As Ali (1980: 65) emphasizes, the 1920 strike was decisive in disillusioning the Fiji Indians about the attitudes of Fiji's colonial government, and when Manilal was deported in its aftermath, it left them without urban, legally trained leadership. Intense colonywide distrust of the government was manifested in 11,369 registrations for repatriation to India.

A few months later, another strike began, this one to be much longer. Its focus was the cane-growing western side of Viti Levu, where postwar inflation had made unlivable the stingy crop payments of an apprehensive postindenture sugar industry. This strike was led by a *sadhu,* a holy man, called Bashishth Muni. Bashishth Muni arrived in Fiji in 1920 and toured Viti Levu in 1920 and 1921, preaching. He described himself as an exponent of the "Sanatan Dharm," the true "eternal religion," and called for school-building and other efforts at communal uplift. He praised Gandhi and, like Gandhi, called upon his audiences to take solemn oaths of to assist in the planned social projects. He also focused on questions of wages and prices, in the context of "a rhetorical flourish, comparing his people to a people living in perpetual darkness with only a sporadic gleam of light." This quote, and much of the rest of what is known about his meetings, comes from a confidential report by Badri Maharaj, who had the *sadhu*'s visit to Ra province closely observed on behalf of the government. The *sadhu* was (and still is) widely popular in Fiji's west. Among his followers were not only laborers, Badri Maharaj reported, but "business men, planters and civil servants. Four persons in Penang [Maharaj's part of Ra] were enrolled but these are all renegades."

This indirect confrontation of Badri Maharaj and Bashishth Muni might be considered the beginning of the rivalry, in Fiji, of the Arya Samaj and a "Sanatan Dharm," two contesting efforts to organize Hinduism. Maharaj was, in his time, Fiji's leading Samaji. His political life did not set the pattern for later Samaj politics, which quickly grew more separate from and antagonistic to colonial authority. However, much of his social and reform agenda was the same, including most of the principles embodied in his *panchayat* proposal: antagonism toward Muslims and, as here, "renegades"; an interest in organizing the Indian community by discipline and firm leadership; marriage reform, especially raising of the marriage age; and interest in developing the political rights and structures of the Indian community. To this list could be added also a principle shared with the Sanatanis, including the *sadhu:* a commitment to advancing Indian education. The *sadhu,* in contrast, represented a more utopian and less organizationally oriented politics, a politics of commitment and will in which religious images described economic realities and communal issues were devotional—a Gandhian politics proper, begun in Fiji. However, in the strike of 1921 it sputtered, and the *sadhu,* like Manilal, was deported.

The 1921 strike shut down Fiji's sugar industry for most of a growing season. It went on long after the *sadhu* was deported. For the Indians the direct economic outcome of the strike was minimal: concessions on prices, rather than a raise of wages, by a CSR company never forced by the government into any particular action to meet the strikers' grievances. But Bashishth Muni articulated as a matter of morality the drift that had been a matter of fact in newly postindenture Fiji: communal withdrawal, insofar as it was possible, from the European colonial society. A deputation to Fiji from the colonial government of India in 1922 (quoted in Gillion 1977: 56) found that Bashishth Muni had taught Fiji

Indians that "it was an indignity for an Indian to work for a European," especially for less than equal wages, and had also promoted the identification of Gandhi with "Indian" identity. Indeed, they found that "wherever we have gone we have been welcomed with cries of 'Mahatma Gandhi ki jai,' [victory to Gandhi] a piquant experience for a deputation from the Government of India."

Led by Rodwell, the Fiji government despised such adulation for Gandhi. In India in December 1920, just two months before the beginning of the second Fiji strike, Gandhi had led the rewriting of the Indian National Congress Constitution to make it call explicitly for "the attainment of *swaraj* by the people of India" (Wolpert 1982: 303). *Swaraj* was "self-rule"; as expounded by the Gandhians *swaraj* was simultaneously about moral improvement and political emancipation, a call for self-control and for independence. The Fiji authorities wanted nothing like it to be discussed among their Indians, and they deported the emerging Indian leaders who did not declare loyalty and submit confidential intelligence reports. In the two strikes, the political orientations and strategies of the Indians had shifted radically, from naive hopes for government intervention to the search for an effective separate course. However, as an interesting set of exchanges demonstrates, the government's attitude remained consistent with the principle of indenture days, denial of legitimacy to all Indian political spokesmen. In his report to the Colonial Office on the 1920 strike (quoted in Gillion 1977: 27), Rodwell wrote:

The proposal that the Governor should make a journey of 14 miles, in order to parley in a clandestine fashion with strikers, was one which I need hardly say I should not have been prepared to entertain for a moment, and I regret that the leaders did not put forward their requests in writing and so afford me an opportunity of telling them what I thought of the suggestion.

In time, he got his chances for rebuke. On 15 February 1921 he sent a telegram to be read to strikers in Ba (in CSO 5718/21), which stated in part:

Governor fails to understand allusions at last Sunday's meeting to lack of sympathy of Fiji Government. During past year Government have (1) cancelled indentures [and so on through eight points]. Therefore those who charge the Government with lack of sympathy in their administration of Indian affairs are wilfully misrepresenting Government's attitude.

In the same telegram he noted his hope for an early resolution to the strike. He received a reply dated 13 March (in CSO 1656/21):

We the distressed Indian labourers, starting from Raki Raki to Sigatoka districts, heartily thank Your Excellency for the kind sympathy shown by you towards our Industrial Strike and the desire expressed of its early settlement.

This generous information of Your Excellency has given a great consolation to the distressed Indian Labourers for which we are grateful to Your Excellency.

The Governor had a letter sent in reply that flatly denied his sympathy:

His Excellency has at no time expressed sympathy towards the strike. On the contrary His Excellency has requested the strikers to resume work forthwith.

"His Excellency" would allow the Indians to describe him as neither sympathetic nor unsympathetic. Logically, his potion was consistent— he claimed sympathy for them, but not for their strike. But the purpose of his responses was not to clarify his attitudes or to open new dialogue with the Indians. He had sought, and taken, his chances to rebuke them.

More consequentially, in 1920 between the strikes, N. B. Mitter of Nadi wrote to the Colonial Secretary to announce the formation of a "Fiji Indian Labour Federation" and to ask for government recognition (CSO 7793/20). A draft letter was prepared instructing Mitter in the procedure for establishing a trade union, but Rodwell rejected it. He substituted a letter in which the first paragraph noted the previous correspondence and its topic, and the second allowed the association to correspond with the government, but only "so long as it is understood that such communications are only to be regarded as representing the views of those who are actually members of it and provided that a list of members is furnished." The third and final paragraph referred to the federation's stated opposition to further labor immigration from India (until conditions improved, the federation had noted) and argued, "You cannot reasonably expect the Government to view with favour an organization of whose declared objects one at least is diametrically opposed to the Government's policy." Rodwell explained his letter in a note: "I prefer my alternate draft. The second paragraph of my draft really means nothing at all and the third administers a little cold water for Mr. Mitter." As Gillion notes (1977: 51–53), Mitter's Labour Federation, rejected by CSR as well as government, was already moribund by the outset of the 1921 strike, and the "conciliatory, dignified, and moderate" Mitter lost all influence to the *sadhu*.

The Fiji government's policy effectively aided the "radicals" and separatists by snubbing the "moderates." The so-called moderates seeking liaison were hurt far more by government hostility than were the leaders who sought to lead the Indians away from colonial European society. However, neither complete Indian separation nor unremitting government hostility was possible. Fiji Indians were constrained by relations of capitalist production, and the colonial authorities in Fiji were themselves constrained by higher authorities. London, influenced by colonial India, was insistent in the late 1910s and early 1920s that the Fiji Indians be granted more political voice than they had. In the 1910s the Letters Patent of the colony had been rewritten to allow a nominated Fiji Indian representative to the Legislative Council, and Maharaj was appointed. However, in India and elsewhere this was not considered enough, and as Fiji lobbied for more immigrant labor further pressure was brought to bear on Fiji in return. Fiji was instructed by the Colonial Office to provide the Indians elected representation—two elected members on Fiji's Legislative Council—and in August 1920, between the two strikes, Rodwell appointed a commission to establish the means to effect this.

Reporting in April 1921 (CSO 718/21), the Indian Franchise Commission was a crystallization of the relations that distanced the Indian community from power in Fiji, but also put them out of reach of the authorities exercising the power. The commission was chaired by the Chief Justice of Fiji's Supreme Court and included other high-ranking elected and unelected Fiji government officials. It took testimony and received submissions from a wide range of official and unofficial witnesses. Unlike the 1909 Education Commission, which had put Indian matters last on its agenda, this commission was devoted to Indian questions, included Indians among its witnesses, and even had an Indian member. However, this was not because Fiji Indian viewpoints had been empowered in the interim, but only because their formal inclusion had become necessary to the public simulation of decision-making. The one Indian member, Badri Maharaj, was not influential. He was not even present at the most important deliberations.

The commission addressed two major issues primarily: first, how to divide Fiji into Indian voting districts, and second, whether the voting should be direct or indirect, or as the commission discussed it, whether or not it should involve *panchayats*. On the first issue, most witnesses and commission members agreed that Fiji could not be divided into two Indian voting districts. Wide support was offered for a threefold scheme, dividing Fiji into eastern Viti Levu, western Viti Levu, and the other islands. However, the commission did not and could not consider such an option. By the terms of its appointment it was bound to a two-representative scheme. The commission therefore suggested election of two representatives by a single, colonywide Indian voting roll.

The commission received an extraordinary range of advice on the second matter, a so-called *panchayat* indirect voting system versus an electoral roll, and in relation to the latter, the qualifications for voters. However, it had already made its basic decisions at a closed session in early January 1921. With Maharaj absent, and before gathering evidence, the commission decided against *panchayats* and for a direct election, with literacy (in Indian or English languages), property, and income qualifications to ensure that only a "better class of man" would be voting. The *panchayat* idea involved general meetings that would appoint a *panchayat* of electors to represent the meeting as a whole, who would then go on to the next stage of meeting to elect the Indian representatives. In its closed session the commission was concerned about such meetings. Two issues were closely associated: how to ensure that the meetings would come to definite agreements in their appointments; and more generally how to supervise the outcomes. One member argued that "the Immigration officer should preside at a meeting—call if a 'panchayat' if you like." Others pointed out that it would be easier to accede to the wishes of the Indians, which was to say, to the wishes of a particular group of them. As another member put it, "The better class of Indians looks down on the lower-class Indian just as much as we do, or more so." All would be better off if the better class were simply given a direct franchise. This was the scheme agreed upon, and though a considerable volume of evidence was yet to be gathered, the commission proceeded to debate the details of the franchise qualifications and settled most of the points. Europeans were not to be allowed to stand as candidates to represent the Indians, because only "a certain class" would attempt to do so and they were "undesirables." Stipulations would be made about both income and property to ensure that the voters were really part of the "better class of men."

In short, the commission settled in a single meeting (with Maharaj absent) all the principal matters not predetermined by the terms of their charge from the Governor. Then public notices were issued, inviting all interested to submit evidence or testimony, and many days of hearings were held. Finally the commission issued a report, recommending what it had already decided. The testimony of the Indians was largely irrelevant, and in substance much of it did not comprehend the issues debated by the committee. Consider for example an excerpt from the (clerk-translated) submission of Manoharanand Saraswati, the Arya Samaj missionary:

> The voters should not be lunatics, turbulents, cruels, self-opportunists, covetous, drunkards, stupids, shameless, &c. . . .
> The voters and the members should ordinarily know these: History, system of both Government and its subjects, logic, chemistry, science, arithmetic, astronomy, theology, philosophy, &c. . . .

If true decision is given on real rights, then it is the duty of reliable educated persons to consider without prejudice the following points so that no one can be debarred from rights bestowed by God. The voting right is a natural one to both man and woman, &c, &c.

In my opinion each and everyone should be allowed to vote whether male or female, literate or illiterate, rich or poor, Government servants or private employees, &c.

Saraswati and many of the other Indian witnesses argued on a prescriptive plane that was irrelevant to the commission as it proceeded, presenting suggestions that must have seemed self-contradictory and unworkable to the commission. A letter from two South Indians in Ba suggested, as voting qualifications, that a voter should "bear good character" and "be a man of wisdom." Other Indian witnesses addressed the commission in its own terms, but they were capable of doing so precisely because they were members of the "better class of Indians," notably the government clerks and translators, whom we will discuss in greater detail below. Many of their proposals were also found by the commission to be unreasonable, for example the complex scheme of clerk S. S. Chowla, in which Indian Christians were reserved one seat in five in every *panchayat,* along with one for Muslims and three for Hindus, and in which major shopkeepers, government clerks, and other Western-educated Indians gained special voting privileges on a par with members of *panchayats* representing the rural population generally.

The 1921 report of the Indian Franchise Commission did not become the basis of new legislation for many years. First, the government of India intervened, wanting the matter held until its 1922 deputation had visited Fiji and reported. Further, a major issue remained to be settled in the commonwealth as a whole, a question first debated in Kenya: whether Indians would become voters on a common roll with Europeans.[1] In August 1921 Secretary for the Colonies Winston Churchill declared at an Imperial Conference that "there should be no barriers of race, colour, or creed which should prevent any man of merit from reaching any station if he is fitted for it" and then wrote a confidential memo to the Governor of Kenya entitled "Equal Rights for Civilised Men." Only degree of civilization, and gender, were to provide grounds for discrimination. In practice, "civilization" was to be measured in language skills and class; Churchill directed Kenya to admit to a common electoral franchise with Europeans all Indian men with a "reasonable knowledge" of written and spoken English and capital of a thousand pounds or an

1. The details on imperial debates over common roll in Kenya are taken from Tinker 1976: 63–77, 93–115.

annual income of 150 pounds. Such franchise restrictions, later called "civilisation tests" and "an equal franchise of a civilisation or educational character, open to all races" by British proponents, were never accepted or enacted by Kenya. Kenya's white settlers threatened boycott of Indians and government, a tax strike, even expulsion of Indians from Nairobi. Fearing another African white settler breakaway from empire, London did not push. And as important for Fiji, officials in Kenya and London developed new arguments against common roll for Indians. In 1923 the British cabinet accepted the argument that imperial government was "a trust on behalf of the African population," that Indian common roll would threaten African interests, and that "the interests of the African natives must be paramount." Official India still argued for common roll in Kenya, Fiji, and elsewhere, but in 1925 the Colonial Office determined, for Fiji, that Indian common roll would conflict with the terms of Fiji's Deed of Cession, which had ceded rule only to the Crown (and somehow, to only one of the races governed by the Crown). In 1927 the Governor of Kenya turned the rhetoric of "civilisation tests" into a case for separate "communal" voting rolls, with proportions not demographic but based on each community's relative "character, its education, its enterprise, its civilisation, and the contribution it makes in all ways to the development of the country."[2]

Official India did not acquiesce to communal voting rolls for Fiji's Indians until late 1926, and this resulted in no form of Indian representation to the Legislative Council elected that year in Fiji. It was not until 1929 that elections for Indian representatives to Fiji's Legislative Council were held, direct elections in three voting districts for three representatives, with no *panchayats*. It was in 1929, after the bureaucracy of empire had already ruled against common roll and in favor of separate rolls for overseas Indians, that common roll was to become the principal issue of Fiji Indian politics.

Law and Marriage

Most of the laws about the Indians on the books in Fiji concerned their situation as laborers. Some laws became irrelevant when indenture was

---

2. By 1927, interestingly, the frustrated East African Indian National Congress "had virtually collapsed" (Tinker 1976: 94). Tinker quotes a Kenyan Indian journalist who wrote to C. F. Andrews in 1927, "All political activity has come to a standstill—the Congress office is locked up. The community is divided into mutually antagonistic groups and we are all indulging in the unprofitable pastime of mutual abuse and vilification." However, unlike the Fiji Indian National Congress, the Kenyan Congress recovered and was, on occasion, a political force in future years.

abolished, others when Indians found occupations outside of direct service to European masters. Fiji's laws concerning the Indians were rewritten piecemeal, according to circumstances. A decade after the end of indenture, laws were still on the books referring to the Indians collectively as "immigrants," even defining them as immigrants "for the purpose of being employed as labourer or servant." This led to legal snarls concerning the "Fiji-born" and to protests from Indian leaders finding such laws "humiliating to us as a race" (CSO 3339/27). More generally, as Indians went their own way the government of Fiji was confronted by situations for which it had, simply, no law at all. For example, the government sought to thwart Indian plans to commemorate the fiftieth anniversary of their arrival with a Gandhian *hartal* (day of prayer, strike) in 1929, only to realize that it had no laws concerning Indian festivals except the one governing the celebration of Holi and the Tazia on plantations. New, broader regulations were passed, and "moderate" Indian celebrations of the anniversary were sponsored and monitored carefully. The piecemeal approach caused its own problems for both official Fiji and Fiji Indians.

The simplest problem the government faced was keeping track of the Indians for such purposes as taxation. As the Indians moved off the plantations, it lost sight of many of them. And by the 1910s free Indian immigrants were arriving in Fiji, Gujarati traders and Punjabis seeking land for farming. But in the decade after indenture the favorite indices of Indian population continued to be the old indenture records, especially the individual indenture passes themselves and the registers recording plantation assignments, labor law convictions, extensions of indenture, and so forth. The direct tax levied against Indians in these circumstances was a hut tax, keyed to residences that could be surveyed and identified.[3] Still, the Ba annual reports suggest that organizing this tax and collecting from the proper individuals was a task largely beyond the capacity of his office. Another vehicle the government insisted upon was the maintenance of vital statistics. Here birth certificates, though they were not always issued, were less of a problem than death certification. In hopes of accuracy, colonial authorities required that constables see the dead bodies before funeral arrangements could be executed—but constables were not always available, especially in rural areas. The dead were sometimes buried before they were official, and in other cases saved for inspection. But reform, including Indian requests for cremation facilities, would take years.

3. From 1923 the hut tax was replaced by a residential tax of one pound per Indian male aged fifteen to sixty. Collection problems persisted. See Moynagh 1981: 112–13.

Among the gaps in legal form for the postindenture Indians, none was as important as the problem of registering Indian marriages. The original provisions for Indian marriage in Fiji law sought to avoid the issue of what the Attorney General once referred to as the "so-called marriages" of Indian custom. Through most of indenture, those not already married and registered as such when entering indenture could marry legally only by registering their marriage with the Inspector-General of Immigration. A census was taken in 1922 and found 12,497 of the 24,886 adult (over fifteen) male Indians reporting themselves to be married, and 10,600 of 12,326 Indian women (over fifteen) so reporting. However, nowhere near this number had registered their marriages legally, and despite legal reforms the registration numbers decreased as the Indians moved out of the lines and dispersed. The new laws intended to lead all Indian marriages to be registered had provided for a licensing of Indian *pandits* and *maulvis* to conduct and register marriages. However, from 1920 to 1925, only sixty-eight marriages were registered by licensed *pandits* and *maulvis* (CSO 2602/28). This legal reform and its problems explain much about the constraints on official Fiji and about its evolving methods for deciding Indian questions.

Fiji officials liked the simple, controlled marriage registration system of indenture days, and as we shall see they tried to return to a similar system even in 1930. However, in the late 1910s they were under moral fire and sought measures to appease Indian and Indian government opinion. Critics such as Sanadhya and Chaturvedi, and most importantly C. F. Andrews, made Fiji's marriage system a focus of attack. In their *Report on Indentured Labour in Fiji* (1916: 32–33), Andrews and Pearson wrote:

As if to make the evil more deep-seated, Government had done its best to banish Hindu and Muhammadan religious marriage altogether from the land. . . . The only valid marriage was said to be that drawn up in the office of the Immigration Department, and this was a mere matter of payment and registration. An Indian had merely to go to the Immigration office and register his name and that of his intended wife, and pay five shillings. Then if no objection was lodged, after three weeks he received a certificate from the office declaring that he had been married. There was no ceremony: no solemn declaration: no mutual promise in the presence of witnesses. . . .

The following story was told to us by a missionary, who knew the two brothers concerned, and tried to get their sentences commuted. Two brothers of a respectable Hindu family were guardians of their younger sister. They caused her to be married by Hindu religious rites to a husband whom they regarded as suitable. The Hindu ceremony was fully and duly performed. Then another man intervened and induced the sister to be married to him by means of a "marit" at the Immigration office. This "marit" was legal. The Hindu marriage was illegal. There was no redress. When the brothers knew that there was no other remedy, they went and killed their sister and gave themselves into custody. They declared at the trial that they had done it for the honour of their family and their religion. They had done it, they said, to preserve Dharma. They were condemned to be hanged.

This sort of criticism tied marriage law questions to general concerns about immorality and sexual abuse of Indian women in Fiji. In the face of such criticism and the official protest from India that followed, Fiji had to change its marriage law, and it had to get and take the advice of a suspicious Indian colonial government while doing so.

The colonial government of Fiji drafted an ordinance to license *pandits* and *maulvis* and require them to register the marriages they conducted. They sent it to the government of India for comment and approval in 1916. The reviews were largely negative, several of them written by "native" Indian legal experts within the colonial government of India (CSO 5552/16). Criticisms were raised against the attempt to continue to include all Indians under the term "immigrant" and against clauses concerning "ministers of religion" and religious "denominations," which were meant to apply only to Europeans and Christians, while "Hindus and Muhammadans, Quakers, Jews, and Fijians" were designated in separate parts of the law as simply having "marriage officers." More important, the law was criticized for forcing Indians to accept Christians forms and procedures for marriage. Wrote a Hindu representative to the Legislative Council of Madras, asked by a Secretary to the Government of Madras to provide the opinion of "the Hindu community": "The Bill virtually overrides the principle that a Hindu or a Muhammadan carries his personal law with him wherever he goes." Specifically objecting to provisions "essentially like the preliminaries to Christian marriages such as the publication of banns, consent to the parents and the like," the Hindu representative determined that "the provisions of the Bill . . . affect the religious usages of Hindus and Muhammadans and . . . impose a form of marriage to which they are not accustomed in the country of their domicile."

This criticism was founded on a flawed premise, that India was and should remain the "country of domicile" of the Fiji Indians. While this question was ambiguous as a legal and technical one, the reality of a permanent Fiji Indian community was presenting Fiji officials with legal problems they were only beginning to confront. The new marriage law was one of the first attempts to address that reality, to write law for Fiji Indians. The major problem for such legislation was here raised, perhaps for the first time: the question of the "personal law" of the Indians.

In his analysis of the Government of India's criticisms and redrafting of the law, Fiji's Attorney General made few changes. He defended the continuing use of the term *immigrant,* citing similar legislation in Trinidad and British Guiana, and arguing incongruously that "so long as a person is of Indian descent and professes the Mohammedan or Hindu religion, I see no reason why he should not be allowed to avail himself of such provision." On the larger question, whether to prohibit Islamic or Hindu marriages not following the procedures laid down in the bill, he concluded that since "Indian priests" could become marriage officers, "it seems only logical that persons seeking to evade the marriage law of the Colony should be punished, and a stop put to the ceremonies purporting to be marriage ceremonies which are now performed by Indians among themselves without interference" (CSO 5552/16).

Further correspondence over the bill passed back and forth between Fiji's Attorney General, the Government of India, and the Colonial Office, and it was not until 18 April 1918 that a marriage bill was ready for consideration by Fiji's Legislative Council. As the Attorney General explained to the council that day, Fiji was required by the Colonial Office on advice of the government of India to include provision prohibiting prosecution "of any person performing these irregular marriages between Indians. Personally I regret having to include any such words in the Bill. I had hoped that we were going to wipe out once and for all these irregular forms of marriage."[4] This requirement sparked a heated and complex debate. Slightly more than one year later, on 7 July 1919, the process was repeated. Fiji's Legislative Council had to consider, and accept, another amendment to the Marriage Ordinance of 1918, again at the wishes of the government of India and by instruction of the Secretary of State. Fiji's Attorney General noted that "this amending Bill is not entirely satisfactory to this Government," but that "it is desired, at the present time, to conciliate the Government of India as much as we can in the present state of labour." He then proposed to further amend the marriage law to include explicit recognition of "the personal law of the parties" involved. Again a heated and complex debate ensued, but the amendments were acceded to. In these debates, Fiji's official and elected European leaders revealed their conceptions of Fiji Indian "custom" and Fiji Indian problems, articulated the grounds for evaluating Indian policies, and, in sum, allowed reforms of law to push Fiji Indian marriage even farther from the legal domain of colonial Fiji than it had been in indenture days, because they refused to accept the alter-

4. All information and quotations concerning the Legislative Council Debates over the Marriage Ordinance of 1918 and its amendment are from *Fiji Legislative Debates,* 1918 and 1919, Fiji National Archives.

native: giving legal power to Fiji Indian authorities on "custom" and "personal law."

The concern of Fiji's colonial authorities about "irregular" marriage often fixed on polygamy and incestuous marriage. But the label "irregular marriage" was also applied quite generally to any marriage made under Hindu or Muslim ritual authority, as when a Legislative Council member argued in the 1918 debate against the protection for marriage by Indian custom. "I thought we had arrived at an agreement that once we got this statute passed we would have the proper marriage, law, in other words, we would have State marriages and not recognize what may be termed the 'religious' form of marriage." In the spirit of this member's argument, the Legislative Council began in 1918 to debate amendments to the bill, supposing that they would pass it without the proviso protecting marriage by Indian custom. One member offered a new clause, which would instead allow Indians a twelve-month period to register extant marriages by "Indian custom" but require all future marriages to follow the terms of the ordinance, including registration with the state. He argued:

These people have been living together for many years as husband and wife, and we say, "We will make up to you as far as we can the defects in our old laws, we will put you in the same position as your fellow countrymen are to occupy in the future." . . . We give people the opportunity of rectifying the wrong which was done in the past; the wrong as far as the Indian was concerned was owing to lack of opportunity. The machinery did not exist for legalizing the marriages according to their own customs and by their own priests, and they lived according to their own consciences, took advantage of the marriage customs of their own religions and were regardless of any law of the State regarding marriage. We are not party to any wrong system, we are simply suggesting that we should for twelve months give people the right of regularizing unions which in the past have been regular according to their own consciences, but have been irregular according to the laws of the State.

The Attorney General spoke against the suggested clause: "I take it that the greater part of the so-called marriages according to Indian custom would, under the provisions of this very wide Bill, be still what I term 'irregular marriages'; they would have no existence in law at all." He called it "illogical" to pass a bill not recognizing such marriages as "valid" and then include "a section that validates marriages of a similar class that have taken place in the past."

Two different notions of the problem with Indian marriages were here in confrontation, a confrontation to recur in marriage law debates between 1928 and 1931. The proponent of the clause sought to "rectify" a situation in which "the machinery did not exist to legalize"

Indian customary marriages. The Attorney General sought to abolish "the so-called marriages according to Indian custom," and to replace them with valid marriages in law. Behind this confrontation lay the problem of interpreting Indian custom, a problem to which the debate then turned.

The council never voted on the proposed clause, because the Governor made clear that "positive instructions from the Secretary of State" bound them to retain the portion protecting Indian customary marriages more generally. Then Badri Maharaj proposed his own amendments to the ordinance, concerning minimum legal ages. He wanted to raise the legal ages for marriage but retain lower age limits, thirteen for girls and sixteen for boys, for legal "betrothal ceremonies." "According to Hindu and Mohammadan religions" he argued, girls and boys of these ages were still "children, immature adults." "Their brain and body will be underdeveloped at that age." Children born to parents so young "will naturally be very weak," he argued:

These children when grown up will not be very useful to the Government nor to the family itself, and it will tell upon their own generation gradually. It is on account of such privileges granted in this Colony that we hear of so many evils and vices. . . . If marriages are allowed to be legalised at that tender age it will tell upon their generation in course of time.

The council was confronted by its own chosen Indian "representative," arguing eugenics and claiming his argument as Indian religious principle. Was he, with his theory that the "evils and vice" among Fiji Indians sprang from parents of "tender age," whose offspring were "naturally weak," to be accepted as the voice of authority? The Colonial Secretary replied that

while the honourable member voices probably the opinion of certain Indian members of this community, his views are not shared by other Indians in this Colony who perhaps do not adhere to the same religious tenets as he does. I should like the Acting Agent-General of Immigration to address the Council on this subject.

The Indian member could only speak for his own subsection of the Indian community, no matter his status as the sole representative of all. For objective, nonpartisan opinions, the European experts on the Indian community were to be the voices of authority. This voice of authority then spoke, and it raised further problems.

ACTING AGENT-GEN OF IMMIGRATION: With regard to this matter we have to remember that in the Indian marriage customs they have three ceremonies. I should like to know which ceremony this [the legal marriage age] refers to. . . .

MR. HEDSTROM [an elected member]: I take it this refers to the marriage by the State, the legalised marriage.

COLONIAL SECRETARY: What is the legal marriage? The Indian recognises the betrothal as the marriage.

THE ATTORNEY-GENERAL: The marriage recognized by the State will be the marriage consequent upon the filing of the declaration and the giving of the notice.

* * *

ACTING AGENT-GEN OF IMMIGRATION: I am not attempting to criticise the Bill, but I must admit I was very disappointed to find the Hindu customs recognised so little. . . . I cannot see how the Indians can fulfill the conditions of this Bill and keep to their Hindu customs. [Proposes amendments calling for a marriage officer to "observe and fulfill all religious rites."] I feel it would be a very big and important concession to have that amendment inserted. It is generally recognised that the Hindu customs in regard to marriage ceremonies not being considered legal in Fiji is the root of a tremendous amount of crime and evil at the present time. When this betrothal takes place a certain amount of jewellry and money passes from the proposed bridegroom to the parents, and then the difficulty arises when the parents have the daughter betrothed to someone else. If we had recognised the betrothal and had it registered as part of the marriage ceremony . . . the Ordinance would have been of more use to this Colony of Fiji. . . . As a small concession I wish to have the amendment made as stated.

HIS EXCELLENCY [the Governor]: Can the honourable member kindly inform the Council what are the formalities known as the betrothal?

ACTING AGI: I would sooner refer to the Honourable Badri Mahraj [*sic*], who would have more information than I have.

HIS EXCELLENCY: Does the honourable member intend that this should apply to the Hindus?

ACTING AGI: To the Hindus only.

MR. BADRI MAHRAJ: The betrothal ceremony would take place at the thirteenth year and may be registered if those parties are allowed to remain as husband and wife in their fifteenth year.

HIS EXCELLENCY: In view of the ignorance of what constitutes the ceremony I doubt whether the Government should accept the proposed amendment. I am entirely ignorant on the subject and the Government must oppose the amendment.

In view of the preceding, we cannot accept the Governor's last remark, the claim that Fiji's colonial authorities were simply ignorant of Indian custom as they resisted enshrining it as law. Rather, they were willfully ignorant. As the first exchange suggests, the government resisted allowing Indian-defined forms or terms to enter its discourse. The problem of choosing which of three rituals constituting an Indian marriage was to be the "legal" marriage was not solved by specifying one of the three, though it would have been simple enough to designate the third. Instead, the "state" marriage would be known by the marks of the state marriage, pure and simple: filing of the declaration and giving of notice. The question of how this state marriage was to articulate with Indian custom was explicitly avoided—in this, the ordinance intended to "legalise" marriages conducted by Indian custom. Next, an explicit contradiction in scheduling was raised, occasioned by the alleged requirements of custom on the one hand and the terms of law on the other. Further, a problem in social practice was shown to exist, created by the lack of legal protection for the arrangements of the earlier, betrothal state. Here again the government refused involvement in Indian custom. The clarity and control provided by laws based on colonial forms were to be maintained.

There was also the problem of licensing Indian religious authority.

MR. HEDSTROM: I suggest that the words after "any" in the second line to "priest" in the fifth line be deleted and the following words inserted: "person professing any Oriental religion to be a marriage officer for the solemnization of marriage between immigrants who are of the same religion as such person." We may have other Orientals here who are not either Hindus or Mohammedans. . . . A name might be adopted—"Oriental Marriage Officer" or "Indian Marriage Officer" as the case may be.

HIS EXCELLENCY: Will the honourable member accept, instead of his proposed amendment the insertion, after the word "priest" in the second line, of the words: "or such other Indian priest professing any recognized religion." . . .

THE ATTORNEY-GENERAL: The reason why I proposed to insert the words that His Excellency has just read out in place of the words suggested by the honourable member is that I do not know what an "Oriental" religion is, how far it extends. . . .

MR. HEDSTROM: The difficulty, to my mind, lies as to the word "priest." There are numbers of Indians in the Colony who would be acceptable to the people as marriage officers, but who may not be properly classed as priests, and I am afraid that by retaining the word "priest" you are limiting the application of the section. . . . Could we say "such other person whom the Governor may appoint"?

COLONIAL SECRETARY: Instead of "Mohammedan or Hindu priest" we might say: "any person of Indian nationality and race." There are a good many Buddhists in this Colony [unlikely, unless a reference to Chinese], and if this Ordinance were passed I do not know what the Buddhists would do.

HIS EXCELLENCY: The object of this clause is to provide some form of religious marriage amongst Indians. There would be no objection to the insertion of the words "or such other Indian priest professing any recognized religion." I have no doubt that a Governor will not be too exacting if the Agent-General of Immigration recommends somebody for appointment as a marriage officer, and will be prepared to accept the Agent-General's recommendation. There is no laying on of hands specially required in regard to the appointment of a priest of an

Indian religion. I imagine that the Agent-General of Immigration, if he were approached by any responsible person who had been accustomed to solemnise such marriages in the past, would recommend to the Governor that such person should be recognised for the purposes of this clause.

ACTING AGI: After due enquiry, if the man were found to be regarded as a priest he would be recognized by the Agent-General.

The same Governor who professed ignorance of matters of Indian custom was here certain that "there is no laying on of hands specially required in regard to the appointment of a priest of an Indian religion." Niceties of theology did not detain him, because in the end it would be his government that would recognize the priests and the religions. Not only the Governor but all parties to the exchange sought to formulate smoothly the mode in which colonial authority would designate Indian religious authority, from the proposed coining of a new social agent, the "Oriental Marriage Officer," to the idea of government authority to designate "any person of Indian nationality or race" it deemed fit to hold the position. To the Governor, all of this was already included in the very concept of "Indian priest."

As the Governor made quite clear, the purpose of the ordinance was not to articulate existing Indian practice with existing law, not to construct the "machinery" by which the marriages conducted according to Indian "conscience" or custom could be legal, as one member had sought. It was instead the other project, to create obligatory legal forms and "state" marriage. The state marriage was simply to be given a religious idiom; the ordinance need not enshrine custom but only "provide some form of religious marriage amongst Indians."

This second project was opposed by the government of India. The first change it imposed on Fiji simply removed the obligation, forcing Fiji to accept the "irregular marriages" conducted outside the new ordinance. But India was still not satisfied, because Fiji still was not articulating its law with custom. Following the 1857 revolt in India, known to the colonial Europeans as "the Mutiny," the British Raj made respect for "customary law" or "personal law" of the multiple communities of India a foundation of law and policy. In India legal authorities were considerably more adept than Badri Maharaj in welding European legal form and the authority of religion and custom. In the new instructions of 1919 they tried to force Fiji to accept the same project, to accept in law the authority of "the personal law" of the individual Indians.

Still hoping to import more "coolies," the Fiji authorities knew they had to accept the second set of amendments also. But they were more than unhappy about it. One member called a provision allowing cross-cousin marriage "the height of absurdity" and protested "having legislation of this kind forced on us by somebody who may understand the Indian in India, but who has not the faintest knowledge of the Indian in Fiji." But what was the Indian in Fiji? For most of the rest of their debate, the members, including Badri Maharaj, debated whether the Indians in Fiji had caste. The debate was heated because the real question was the administration of personal law:

MR. HEDSTROM: Will the learned mover explain what, in his opinion, . . . does the "personal law" mean?

THE ACTING ATTORNEY-GENERAL: The meaning of the words "personal law" is as I understand them, the law of caste and caste-customs. I should like to refer to two text-books on the subject. I will first read an extract from page 302 of Eversley and Craies "Marriage Laws of the British Empire":—"In British India, as in the Ottoman Empire, marriage is in the main treated as part of the personal law of the parties considered by reference to the religious faith which they possess." That is, as I have said before (and I think the Agent-General of Immigration will support me here), the personal law in India—the law of caste and caste-customs. I will next refer to page 65 of Renton and Phillimore's work "The Comparative Law of Marriage and Divorce" under the heading of "Law of India":—"The marriage law of India is purely personal. It varies generally according to the religion, and sometimes according to the tribe or caste of the persons concerned. Occasionally a family custom may, amongst Hindus, have a binding effect."

MR. CROMPTON: Will the learned Acting Attorney-General tell us how he thinks anybody can carry that into effect in this Colony? Take the definition he has just read of "the personal law." That might be interpreted as the law of particular families. Are we supposed to be incorporating all of that? How one can talk of the "personal law" of people in this Colony, I cannot see. I do not know how anyone is going to define it.

ACTING AG: I would point out that it is surely a matter of fact we have to ascertain.

MR. CROMPTON: How can you ascertain it?

MR. SCOTT: The learned Acting Attorney-General says he is going to do it.

MR. CROMPTON: How can you ascertain the different marital customs of certain families? I do not know how anybody here is going to deal with these people if they offend the Marriage Laws, for they may say "Whatever I have done is according to the custom of my family." Who on earth is going to decide it?

MR. SCOTT: The honourable the Acting Agent-General of Immigration seems to think that it would be quite an easy matter to administer this provision. He says that caste is recognised in Fiji. To what extent it is recognised of course he perhaps knows more than I do, but I have discussed this question with very many leading Indians both on this and on the other side of the island, and I will put this case to him: An Indian comes to Fiji a very poor man, and is so for some years presumably; but he obtains wealth and station and comes forward as a Brahmin. Under the "personal law" is the honourable the Acting Agent-

General of Immigration going to decide, after inquiry into this man's case, as to whether he is a Brahmin, a Hindu, or some other caste? What decision is he going to come to?—because this is the most difficult thing. As has been pointed out, in the majority of the cases there is, strictly speaking, no caste, and I still assert that Mr. Andrews (who at all events is still an authority on the question of caste), has said that in his first report that, strictly speaking, there is no caste in Fiji as it is understood in India. I would like to know how the honourable the Acting Agent-General of Immigration is going to construe the words "under the personal law"?

MR. BADRI MAHRAJ: If I am not interrupting, I might say that "caste" means, amongst Indians, different classes of men. There are four main divisions amongst the Hindus—Brahmana, Kshatriyas, Vaisyas, and Sudras—and even amongst Brahmins there are class distinctions such as Gaur, Maharastra, Draviia, Kanyakubja. Men of different classes may not intermingle socially. The Indians follow the same course as to caste marriages. According to the Vedas and Shastras, a Brahmin cannot marry a Mussulman; he can only enjoy the privilege of inter-marriage and social intercourse in the community to which he belongs, i.e. the twenty Rishis who were the progenitors of "Gotrya."

THE ACTING AGENT-GENERAL OF IMMIGRATION: In answer to the question asked, may I say that these people are given the caste they are born into. If a man is born of Brahmin caste, if he comes to Fiji he retains that caste. If a man who is not a Brahmin passes himself off as such he is an impostor, and I take it that no decent Brahmin would give him his daughter to marry. That man would have to prove that he was a Brahmin.

MR. SCOTT: Does the honourable the Acting Agent-General of Immigration realise that he will have to enquire into all that, under this amendment? That is the point I am putting.

ACTING AG: It is perfectly true that certain inquiries will have to be made by the Agent-General of Immigration under these clauses, but I understand the practice has been that, when a ship arrives from India, the Inspector of Immigrants goes to the island where the ship is quarantined and makes all inquiries in regard to the parties coming to him and asking to be married under the provisions of the Marriage Ordinance.

ACTING AGI: In regard to every Indian who leaves India and comes to Fiji, all particulars are taken of him—particulars of his caste and the village he comes from, and by turning up the name of any Indian introduced into the Colony under any Immigration Law, all particulars as to his caste, &c., are to be found in the records of the Immigration Department.

MR. SCOTT: What about those Indians who come to Fiji and who are not introduced as immigrants?

MR. HEDSTROM: . . . In a recent report it is stated that one of the evils found in Fiji was the fact that the caste system was so repeatedly broken, and the view is expressed that the son of a Brahmin should only marry the daughter of a Brahmin. . . . I do not know what personal law low-caste girls would be subject to. According to this Ordinance they will not be subject to the law of England.

The matter is very complicated when you get marriages between people of different castes, which, as we have been told before, happens not infrequently in Fiji.

The debate went on to aspects of personal law apart from caste, but the basic lines had all been drawn. Again different conceptions of the Indians in Fiji competed with each other, and different diagnoses of their past and present order were offered. Did caste exist for some? For all? The Acting Agent-General of Immigration foresaw relying on the indenture records and offered the theory that birth would simply rule. Others cited mixed marriages and (elsewhere in the debate) other signs of caste loss and pollution, concluding that caste was "broken" for many of the Indians. What was their law, then? To the Fiji authorities the key point was probably Hedstrom's at the end: according to this ordinance, it was not to be the law of England.

This debate reflects in sharper outline the same themes as the other. The council simply ignored Badri Maharaj when he offered definitions of custom, and never considered the possibility of granting the Indians authority to define their law. Acceptable forms of authority, including authority on caste and India, were Western sources: British lawbooks, even their enemy C. F. Andrews. But what was the answer to their question? What was the personal law of the Fiji Indians on marriage near the end of indenture?

Their perception was that there was none, and would be none until the government established it. Reflecting their missionary and plantation sources, what they considered novel about Fiji Indian social life might be summed up in the terms "vice" and "evil." This attitude affected the patterns of order in Fiji Indian communities in a most peculiar way. On the one hand, it facilitated the Indian withdrawal; just as most of their money was not in European banks, under the amended marriage ordinance most of their marriages were not registered. But on the other hand, the Indians' ability to organize their separated lives was limited, not by the forms they could choose, but by their inability to impose them on each other. They were limited by the absence of authority in their own ranks. Let us complete our discussion of marriage and law, then, by considering the class of legal experts to whom the Indians did turn in the breach, the influential but marginal figures who mediated between the Indian world and colonial officials: the Indian clerks.

The importance of Indian clerks is clear in any careful examination of the mechanisms of colonial life. They were subordinate, almost invisible within the workings of colonial society from the European point of view. The official Europeans were comfortable taking their presence and performances for granted, as when Indian depositions and testimony in Fiji Hindi were recorded by the European officers of the court in a clerk's English translation. The witnesses' name and the name of the officer before whom the account was taken and sworn were always recorded, but the translator's name was generally not unless special problems arose in the translating. Similarly, attention to the proper role of clerks arose mainly when problems were perceived.

The clerks received Indians visiting government offices and led them through whatever business was at issue. They also were the colonial officials' principal resort when information about Indian affairs was required, even before they began at government insistence to write confidential reports in 1931. Occasionally this role was recognized explicitly, as when the District Commissioner of Labasa, A. A. Wright, submitted a fourteen-paragraph plan to the Indian Franchise Commission of 1921, detailing eight classes of Indian voters he would recognize and the complex voting and selecting procedures he would advocate (CSO 718/21). He concluded,

I have discussed the above scheme with Mr. Bere Singh, Clerk and Interpreter here, who has an extensive acquaintance with Indian political thought in Fiji, and he is of the opinion that such a scheme would be unobjectionable from the Indian point of view.

More often, however, the clerks came up not when praised but when criticized. By 1929, as Europeans grew increasingly concerned about the new "Indian problem" (chapter 6), such criticism was more frequent. After the election of Vishnu Deo and his colleagues, but before the walkout, J. R. Pearson's own clerks were attacked by another government officer for their participation in sectional societies (principally the Indian Reform League, which the critic did not distinguish from less "moderate" groups), and Pearson was attacked for giving them access to confidential papers. "It is not surprising, if this is the practice in the office of the Secretary for Indian Affairs, that Indian Societies appear often well informed of the Government's intentions and decisions" (CSO 4579/29)—an undesirable state of affairs, in the mainstream view of official Fiji. In reply Pearson made some illuminating comments about the role of Indian clerks in general. He praised one of his clerks, M. S. Buksh, for the role he played in Indian political affairs: "He has almost invariably acted with discretion and his participation has been to advantage. He has several times consulted me as to whether he should or should not take part in some particular meeting. I am almost inclined to say that it is ungenerous to speak of his activities in these terms after the successful way in which he handled matters over the Indian Jubilee Celebrations."[5] Pearson criticized his other clerk, "a staunch member of the Presbyterian Church," because, "if anything, his tendency is to hold himself too much aloof from the general body of Indians in Suva, and on this account to be unable to supply the S.I.A. with information." "I presume that it is my duty to control my Indian staff and to watch over their connection with Indian societies," Pearson wrote, and concluded:

The administration will not get good and responsible work out of its Indian staff unless it imposes some trust in them, and as the matter has been raised I will record my impression that over some classes of work such as leases, accounts and interpretation in Court, too much responsibility is put on them and too little on their immediate supervisors, while over other matters their sense of responsibility is stunted by mistrust.

By 1929 relations between clerks and officials, as between Fiji Indians and Europeans, had become increasingly tense as they were contested. But perhaps the first crisis in the organization of Fiji's legal operations came in 1912, when the first properly accredited Indian barrister, Manilal arrived in Fiji and began to practice law. Manilal was a highly popular figure in the Indian community, but he was also openly anticolonial. Manilal broke the rules. A description of a single, mundane court action will be sufficient to describe his impact.

In early April 1913 Manilal came to Suva Police Court and withdrew a divorce petition on behalf of the plaintiff. The matter, he said, had been settled out of court, and he moved that the court award no costs. The defense lawyer was outraged. He accused Manilal of professional misconduct—consulting his client behind his back and approaching his client to settle without consent. Manilal explained that he had not approached anyone. The defense counsel's client had come to him, and in Manilal's chambers the settlement had been arranged. The defense counsel's office had even been represented: Manilal had called in the defense counsel's Hindi-speaking clerk-translator. The defense attorney became abusive in court, attacking not only Manilal but Manilal's client, who he said was a known adulterer. "His Worship told Mr. Berkeley that he should not say that" (*Fiji Times,* 5 April 1913). The defense counsel, Mr. Berkeley, was awarded costs simply because he had been retained. But in such cases the monopoly of the colonial European barristers over legal authority in the colony was, temporarily at least, broken.

The stormy career and anticolonial politics of Manilal contrast sharply with the average profile of the clerks. Fiji was neither the first nor the last British colony in which Manilal worked as a barrister to fight social and political battles for overseas Indians. Most clerks, on the other hand,

5. On the Indian Jubilee celebrations, see the introduction to chapter 6.

were recruited and hired by Europeans. They were disproportionately Christian in an Indian community with a very small Christian population. Most had a formal, Western education, and most were products of mission schools in Fiji or India. To discuss them and their Indian Reform League, we will place both in their proper context and consider religion and education in the 1910s and 1920s.

Religion and Education

The 1922 census found a total Indian population of 60,619, of which only 708 professed to be Christians. The expensive Methodist mission efforts to organize a Christian Indian church (see Thornley 1973) were a near total failure. Two stories from J. W. Burton (1910: 298–301, 341–42), one of the leaders of the Methodist mission to the Fiji Indians, present an interpretation of the problem. The first concerns the scene in the Indian bazaars, the second concludes his chapter on Fiji's religious destiny:

Religion is offered for sale in the bazar also. Here is a Muhammadan *faqir* offering charms guaranteed, by the beard of the Prophet, to cure rheumatism, colic, and the itch, which are all very common diseases among the coolies. They are tiny bits of paper upon which is written a verse of the *Quran*. . . .

Sitting on a box is a Hindu *sadhu,* or saint. . . . Fifth and droppings of milk mat the beard; and the hair is in much the same state. . . . His clothes are vile in the extreme and smell rankly. . . . Scores of Hindus come up to him, reverently prostrate themselves before him, and . . . usually leave a small coin on the ground. . . .

A Christian teacher, nearby, is trying to sell Bibles and Testaments. . . . He does not seem to be doing much business, however. . . .

At the very end of the bazar a Muhammadan *moulvi* . . . reads from a paper, printed in the vernacular, in which the statement is made that the English are giving up Christianity; and that "Professor Campbell sahib, of the City of London Temple, is now earnestly studying the *Quran*." He reads this with the authority we would give a Reuter's cable. A Hindu interrupts, and caustically remarks that if it is a religion the English are taking up, it is clearly a shallow one. Whereupon numbers of the company nod enthusiastically, and exclaim—"*Sach! Sach! Bhai!*" (That's true, brother, true!)

A few yards distant a Christian missionary, in spotless white suit and broad-brimmed helmet, is preaching eloquently in Hindustani. His accent sounds a trifle English; but the faces of his audience show that his words are understood. He is pointing out that Christ is the fulfilment of the yearnings of all good men throughout the ages. He seems to be making an impression, for the people smile at his thrusts, and call out *sach! sach!* at his pauses. A subtle-faced pandit takes advantage of a longer pause than usual, and says—

"The words of the sahib are true—very true. There is only one religion in the world—it is the religion of all good men, no matter whether they are Christian, Hindu, or Mussulman. There are many paths: they all lead to the same place. The circumference has a million points: the center one."

The missionary hastens to explain; but the crowd now moves off, saying, 'Sach! Sach! bahut Sach!' The pandit smiles with his eyes.

* * *

A messenger came to the church saying that the old woman was dying and wanted to see the padri. He went to her thatched hut and stooped himself in. On a bed of bamboo, with a few filthy rags thrown over them, lay the old widow. . . .

The missionary took her hand. The pulse beat feebly. She whispered and tried to make herself audible. He bent down to her and in gasps she said this—

"Sahib, I've gone to your church since many days and have listened to the words there. They have been good words—my heart told me so. Sometimes I carried them home and thought about them. Then I tried to believe them. But, Sahib, *I can't.* I'm too old to change now. *My mind is bent.*" She sank back, exhausted, and after a while broke out in a wail almost supernatural in its intensity—

"Oh, Sahib, sahib, why didn't you come *sooner?*"

The missionary had no chance to answer that question. She swooned, and in a few minutes was dead.

The saddest thing one can say is that for hundreds in Fiji to-day it is *too late.* The Christian Church, though she had the chance, did not come *soon* enough. Their minds are bent, and no power on earth can unbend them. . . .

But there are thousands for whom it is not too late. Their minds are still flexible. They are the responsibility of the Church of God. What shall be the future of Fiji? Shall Muhammad, Krishna, or Christ reign? Let the Christian Church reply. God has given her the answer in her own breast. [emphases in original]

The church's reply was to devote the mission to orphanage and Indian education, to pursue the Indian children and thereby get them before it was too late. These texts reveal more reliable information about points of view than about particular events; one might doubt whether these events happened, certainly whether they happened as Burton describes them. However, they tell us a great deal about how Burton and the other Christian missionaries to the Fiji Indians saw themselves, a point of view that guided the mission as a project.

The Christian missionaries saw themselves in a market competition, a competition in which they were actively opposed by contentious Muslim *maulvis* and scheming Hindu *pandits*. There was no question, however, about the actual comparability of the Indian religions. It was a market competition, but also a competition they had lowered themselves to enter into. More fundamentally it was a contest between light and darkness. The Indians were not only, like indigenous Fijians, black, physically inferior (the missionary has to "stoop" to enter their houses), and mentally inferior (their minds "bent"; see Burton's testimony before the 1909 Education Commission), they were also physically dirty. The contrast between filthy Indians and missionaries in spotless white corresponds neatly with the competition between the rhetorical tricks of the devious *pandits* and the earnest efforts of the servants of the true God, all part of bringing Christ's universal message into the marketplace and waging its war against darkness.

It is unlikely that the Indians saw their religious situation as a market competition. The same people were likely to give donations to the *sadhus,* seek charms from the *faqirs,* and go to recitals of a wide range of sacred texts. In the breakdown of caste and other communal boundaries with the pollution of indenture, the Indians were aware of differing religious identities, and some did practice rituals specific to their religion. For example, some Muslims did pray and fast during Ramadan. However, by most accounts (for example, Sanadhya 1914; Ali 1979) there was little communal antagonism. The Christian missionaries mounted the first major effort to establish a field of religious antagonism, and they seem in the first place to have united the Indian community collectively against them. However, their efforts also established a rhetorical field and a set of images and issues related to religion.

According to Sanadhya (1914), in the 1910s some *pandits, maulvis,* and also *sadhus* of the Kabir Panth undertook to reconvert—*shuddh karna,* "to purify"—Indian Christian converts. The Hindi idiom is revealing, uniting the purity concerns of Hinduism with the Christian themes, signs reversed, of cleanliness and filth, light and darkness. As we have seen, the Christian missionaries were virulent critics of the morality as well as the hygiene and religion of the Indians. "Religion" came to concern group moral standing; religious authorities set out to secure and defend the moral characters of adherents. Opponents were portrayed as corruptors both ignorant themselves and dangerous to others.

Indian sources on indenture times (Sanadhya 1914; Ali 1979) agree with Burton that even in indenture days the Fiji Indians were interested importers of religious texts. They imported not only sacred texts but polemical material, newspapers and pamphlets concerning religious as well as political controversies. The 1922 census included an inquiry into literacy and found 16 percent of Fiji Indians able to read and write, and 45 percent unable to do so; and 39 percent to be under the age of fifteen. The very categories presumed that Indian children were illiterate, since schools were available for only a small fraction of them. These statistics show—though their standards are unclear—that at least some Fiji Indian adults were capable of reading. Of these the overwhelming majority must have been literate not in English but in "vernacular" Indian languages, which principally meant Tamil, Telagu, or Malayalam for the South Indians, Hindi and Urdu for the North Indians. Among Fiji Indians this situation is well remembered, now part of their historical lore: people would gather around a literate person who would read, and if necessary translate and explain, imported newspapers and pamphlets.

Through such vehicles, the Fiji Indians became aware of the rhetoric being developed in India to counter both the Christian mission in particular and colonial society more generally. Controversies over the definition of Hindu and Muslim religious traditions had long been raging in India. Multiple efforts had been launched to capture the rhetoric of the Christian mission—themes of social progress, light, superiority of scripture, hygiene, and moral and intellectual character—but to reverse the signs, making the Indian religious civilization the superior one, and to synthesize these themes with principles found in traditional texts and teachings. The Arya Samaj itself might be seen as a project of this type (see Jones 1976 and chapter 5), and many Fiji Indian "Hindu" leaders turned to it for help in the 1910s and 1920s, notably Sanadhya and Chaturvedi, who called upon the Arya Samaj to send missionaries to Fiji. As we have seen, Manoharanand Saraswati, the first Arya Samaj missionary to Fiji, came in 1912, and several others followed in later years.

A stated aim of most of the Hindu and Muslim missions to Fiji was the "uplift" of the Fiji Indian community generally. Almost all became involved in a battle with the missions for control of the Fiji Indian schools. Saraswati (who wrote to India about Kunti and testified before the Franchise Commission) became famous in Fiji in particular for his educational efforts, as did C. F. Andrews and, in 1921, the strike leader *sadhu* Bashishth Muni. In educational policy Andrews parted company from the other Christian missionaries and joined the Indians to protest Methodist domination of Indian educational facilities. The Indians feared the impact of an equation between education and Christianity and fought to found schools of their own.

Literacy and education were for the Indians a twofold matter—on the one hand literacy in Indian languages and knowledge of such texts as the Koran and the Ramayan, and on the other hand training in English and Western cultural forms. When writing to Gandhi during indenture seeking a political and legal champion, Fiji Indians specifically asked for a man educated in law and English; when a newly established Sanatan Dharm Sabha wrote to Hindu leaders in Allahabad in 1928, they requested "a Pandit-Teacher (Vaishnav) who should be a graduate in English and a thorough scholar in Allahabad Hindustani languages."

This inequality—legal experts trained in English, religious experts trained in Hindi and English—reflects a general principle underlying the Indian education projects. The Fiji Indians wanted their own institutions and experts and knew they needed competence in English as well as Indian languages and forms.

The Christian mission developed schools for Indians faster than the Indians could establish and arrange government support for schools of their own. As early as 1900 the Methodist mission (of Hannah Dudley) ran a school for Indians in Suva. By 1911 six Methodist schools taught 414 students (Thornley 1973: 83). In 1917 the Fiji colonial government finally began its grant-in-aid program for Indian schools. By 1919 there were one government-established-and-run Indian school and seventeen assisted schools: twelve run by the Methodists, one by the Catholics, and four by Indian school committees. By 1921 there were twenty assisted schools, thirteen run by the Methodists, one by the Catholics, and six by Indian committees. Not only did the missions run the large majority of the early schools; they ran the prestigious ones, notably Marist Brothers College, the Suva Catholic school regarded to this day as one of the best in Fiji.

Not all of the students who went to these schools converted. As a project in conversion the Christian mission fared little better in its child-oriented strategy than it had when trying to convert adults. However, the broader influence on their students was considerable. The "Memorandum on Educational Policy" of the 1917 Methodist Conference in Fiji argued that in its Indian schools "we have the supreme opportunity of influencing boys for Christianity by personal contact in a good clean environment" (Thornley, 1973: 112). These schools may have failed to make students Christian, but no doubt they influenced opinion about what "a good clean environment" was and why it was important.

By 1918, according to Thornley (1973: 133), the Methodist mission was "struggling against the tide." The Indian community, and especially the Arya Samaj, was actively organizing alternative schools to compete with the Methodist institutions. Rev. Richard Piper (who had testified in 1909 on the dangers in Indian education) was already certain in 1918 that "we shall have strong opposition from the Arya Samajists." By 1929 Piper bitterly observed that every Indian center was producing a "crop of nationalistic schools" (Thornley 1973: 133, 129).

The future would be different. But for the 1910s and 1920s, the core of the English-educated minority of the Fiji Indian community was the product of the mission schools. They were the Indians available to mediate between the European society and the Indians at their remove. Some of these graduates-become-clerks also became Indian "radicals" and nationalists. Vishnu Deo was a graduate of Marist Brothers College whose career began as a government clerk; he went on to become leader of Fiji's Arya Samaj and for the key period 1929–1932 was the leader of the Fiji Indians generally. However, the majority of clerks were far more conservative and colonial in their attitudes than Vishnu Deo. Consider, for an extreme in this direction, the following comments by V. J. Christian, the Indian clerk and interpreter in Taveuni. In his first monthly confidential clerk's report on Indian affairs in Taveuni, in February 1931, he wrote about the implementation of another new marriage ordinance:

> Marriage Ordinance is being well regarded as a sacred weapon of unity and Indian people are realizing the benefit of the marriage under the ordinance. . . . The Indians are forgetting their priests who were only a menace to them in those days of ignorance, and they directly appear in D.C.'s [District Commissioner's] office and say to Baboo, Baboo we want "Marrit"—which is then fixed at once and without any delay etc. They leave the office with smiles over them.
>
> When education is enforced and mothers are educated they will surely teach their children the true path of civilization and make their children useful to the country.

In the 1920s the intermediary class of Indians made their social and political organization more formal. In 1924 missionary A. W. McMillan and "a number of modern-minded Indians" founded the Indian Reform League because the Suva YMCA refused to admit Indians, "even Indian Christians" (Gillion 1977: 105). Government clerks and interpreters were prominent in the society from its outset, and according to Gillion the majority of its members were Indian Christians (of a population of only 708 Christians in total). On 10 August 1925 the league began its first important political action, an effort to reform the Marriage Ordinance of 1918. In a letter to the Colonial Secretary (CSO 2845/25), the league called for repeal of the clause exempting Indian customary marriages from required registration.[6] The league's letter made reference to India's insistence on this clause and then argued that

> the existence of the said proviso has defeated the object of the Marriage Ordinance, in respect of marriages amongst Indians, viz., "establishment of marriages registered and sanctioned by the State", and has had the effect of perpetuating the irregular unions which have existed in the past amongst Indians. It is needless for me to state that such unions have done considerable harm to, and caused trouble amongst, Indians resident in Fiji.

6. This letter and the other quoted texts to the end of this section are from CSO 2845/25.

The league was familiar with the history of the ordinance, and its rhetoric mirrored that of the European legislators themselves. Fiji's last Agent-General of Immigration, J. S. Neill, was encouraged by the letter, minuting that "the fact of the failure of the Ordinance has to be faced, and when the demand is made for revision of the law by Indians themselves, the argument for revision is, I submit, strengthened." Thus in a year the league had become the voice of the "Indians themselves." Neill suggested that a committee be formed to consider the question of reforming the ordinance and that the Reform League be delegated to appoint the two Indian members of the committee. The Governor agreed to appoint the committee, with Neill as chair, but resisted the idea of asking the Reform League to make appointments, "a dangerous procedure to adopt." Instead, therefore, Neill himself put up two Indians for appointment to the committee: one a Hindu, one a "Mohammedan"; one North Indian, one South Indian; both government clerks; both leading league members. The committee met, and it presented its report in August 1926, calling for repeal of the provision in question. It even managed to solicit letters from religious committees supporting this conclusion. A letter from the Sikh Church Committee argued that the repeal "will be a great boon to the Indian community and will lead to their social and moral uplift." A letter from the Anjuman Hidayat-ul-Islam of Nausori argued that "in Fiji they do not abide by their customary laws" and that "the welfare and improvement of the Indian community, socially and morally, depend on the local marriage law being placed on a sound footing." A letter from the "Sanatan Hindu Dharma, Nausori" argued that "in Fiji the Hindus generally do not govern themselves in accordance with either the Hindu or the customary law" and that "it would bring numerous advantages to the Indian community and improve the social life of the Indians" for the ordinance to be "placed on sound footing." This letter also, in an extraordinary mixture of rhetorical forms, combined a trope of radical Indian literature—the idea of the selfless communal activist facing selfish opposition—with a powerful Western model of authority:

Some self-interested individuals may be against our aspirations for social progress, but to such people the law should be administered in the same way as a doctor administers bitter and unpalatable medicine to a patient.

It thereby admitted that it did not represent a consensus opinion in fact.

The league's request and the committee's report led to formulation of a new ordinance. Again an Attorney General led a faction against allowing past marriages to be registered under the new bill, minuting: "You say, in effect, 'We are going to have you marry and register or suffer the consequences. . . . We will have you married, not wink at your customary ceremonies.'" However, the Secretary of State again defended the Indians' interests, preferring a version of the ordinance allowing past marriages to be registered. The new amending ordinance was to be drafted and passed in 1928.

In these episodes we are presented with the tableau of agencies related to Indian custom and its protection in 1926. An Indian Reform League worked, indeed, for reform. An Agent-General of Immigration was in close alliance with them, regarding them as the representatives of the "Indians themselves." The government was more interested in imposing its own forms of order onto Indian social organization. The Colonial Office in London requested consultations with the government of India and otherwise pressured for respect for Indian custom. This pattern of order was about to shift significantly. As the school openings show, there was already growing a new group of well-organized, articulate, educated Indians, ready to challenge the Indian Reform League for the right to speak for the Indian community: a very different type of "reform" organization, the Arya Samaj. Further, the organization of authority within the colonial government was about to change. In the 1920s, nationalist spokesmen in India provoked the Indian government to call for the appointment of an Indian Agent, an officer of the government of India in Fiji. Official Fiji resisted, and the Colonial Office arranged a compromise. A retiring member of the Indian Civil Service, J. R. Pearson, accepted appointment under Fiji's Governor and in 1927 became Fiji's first Secretary for Indian Affairs. The sympathetic meddling of the colonial government of India was now personified.

Did the colonial Europeans of Fiji desire an Indian social withdrawal? In many ways, yes, because they certainly were not prepared to offer them any place outside of "labor" within colonial society. Was the withdrawal a consequence of policy? In some ways, yes. The Indians were consistently thwarted in efforts to establish recognized political institutions. The colonizers in Fiji created as little space as possible for what Gramsci (e.g., 1957: 174) would call the normal politics and "traditional parties" of the colonized Indians. A hegemonic order, as Gramsci imagined it, would include controlled arenas for political contests into which the political challenges of the unprivileged could be directed and balanced against other contending forces. In Fiji, for the Indians, there were few such arenas, and opportunities to create more, such as the *panchayat* scheme, were resisted by an apprehensive colonial leadership. The Indian Reform League did its best to work with colonial authority and received some limited recognition in return. But little beyond Badri Maharaj's appointment was official, and instead Indian political projects were virtually forced to be "disloyal" and "disaffected," forced outside of the almost nonexistent normal channels. In other ways the colonial government did try to prevent the Indian withdrawal. They sought legal means to maintain, over free Indians, basic governmental control without political institutions that would grant Indians intermediate authority. They could not manage it, not only because they were thwarted by the interference from above, but also because they sought at the same time to maintain their own distance from what they called Indian "custom." Though they were not yet willing to admit it, Indian culture had already become an irreducible part of the social field of Fiji.

The Mission of the Arya Samaj

In the late 1920s Fiji's Arya Samaj was dynamic, aggressive, accomplished, and promising. It was an effective organizer of counter-Christian school-building projects. Under its aegis gathered an alliance of wealthy and educated Fiji Indians, and teachers and missionaries recruited from India. The Samaj members were articulate in vernacular discourse and had by far the largest membership of any Indian organization, other than the Indian Reform League, that was articulate in English and effective in colonial legal and social speech genres. When in 1929 the Fiji Indians first elected their representatives to Legislative Council, and 1,404 of the 75,000 Indians managed to meet the qualifications and register to vote, two of the three candidates they elected were Arya Samaj leaders. The third was a onetime Arya Samaji who had become a Christian upon his marriage into a prominent Indian Christian family (Ali 1980: 115). Arya Samaj Vishnu Deo led these representatives and was also the editor of *Fiji Samachar*, Fiji's leading Hindi-language newspaper, published by Arya Samajis; he easily defeated John Grant, a leader of the Indian Reform League, to win the Suva-area Indian seat on the council.

Vishnu Deo's actions as a leader of the Fiji Arya Samaj, from this election victory to his conviction for publishing obscene materials in 1932, will be a focal concern in chapters 6, 7, and 8. However, we begin our examination of the role and fate of the Arya Samaj in the events of 1929 to 1932 with an inquiry into his history of the project of the organization itself, in India and elsewhere as well as in Fiji. Up to now our discussion has mainly entailed dialogues in Fiji and about Fiji in India. But to understand the Arya Samaj we have to understand a project launched in nineteenth-century India, with far more than the problems of oversees Indians in mind.

Self-Representations

On more than one occasion during my field research in 1984 and 1985, Arya Samaj leaders in Fiji gave me copies of an English-language pamphlet published by the Arya Samaj in South Africa in 1975, entitled *Arya Samaj—Its Ideals and Achievements*. The following is from the introduction:

On the 10th April, 1875, a few public-spirited persons imbued with religious fervour met in Bombay, India, under the guidance of a dynamic and illustrious sannyasi. On this day they gave birth to a new movement with the prime object of doing good to the world, i.e. to make physical, spiritual and social improvement of all men. This movement focussed a new light and, like a flame, began to burn to ashes the ignorance, blind faith and superstitious customs that had polluted the very vitals of Hindu society. It began to lay anew the true foundations of religion and divine knowledge. This spark brought about revolutionary changes in the religious, social, and educational spheres. It reawakened people from mental lethargy and removed ignorance from the rust-laden intellect of men who had slavishly accepted the evil traditions and customs for many centuries. This movement not only brought about enlightenment in India alone but also in places beyond the shores of India. It created a religious reawakening among the people. The movement was called THE ARYA SAMAJ, and its founder was the illustrious sannyasi Swami Dayanand Saraswati.

The Arya Samaj has been called revivalist and reformist, fundamentalist and modernizing. While these and other depictions fit, I find it most illuminating to look at Arya Samaj discourse in a more specific set of historical relationships—as counter-Christian and countercolonial. Such a perspective unravels the paradoxes in the Vedic-fundamentalist, Western-scientific commitments of the Samaj. The Samaj reformed Hinduism and fought European influence by seeking a lost, more respectable, Vedic faith. They found, and founded, a Vedic Hinduism consistent with Western forms of knowledge and practice as their bulwark against them. The two signal features of their discourses can be understood in this light: the reflection in their own formulations of Christian and colonial evaluations of Hindu religious practices, and the intensity of their commitment to social and political action, both in practice and as matters of "Vedic" principle.

In this light reconsider the passage above. Before the Arya Samaj the

Indian people were ignorant and superstitious, lethargic and slavish, bound to evil traditions and customs for many centuries. The Arya Samaj was a Hindu enlightenment, a great awakening. But while its basis was "the true foundations of religion and divine knowledge," its goals were decidedly worldly, concerned with the social and educational as well as the religious spheres. Its "prime object" was "doing good to the world, i.e. to make physical, spiritual and social improvement of all men." The very concept of society employed by the Samaj, dependent on a nature/culture, physical/spiritual distinction, resonates more with colonial than Indian discourses. But the intention expressed is in other ways quite opposite to the social reforms sought by such westernizing agencies as Fiji's Indian Reform League. A purified, respectable, modern, scientific, and self-sufficient Hinduism was sought, the basis for a Hindu nation that could be modern, respectable, self-sufficient, and, the Samajis were among the first to hope, independent.

The Arya Samaj propounded an ontology quite far from that of the *bhakti* movements. *Bhakti* movements gave God absolute priority as the source and foundation of everything real and gave the project of "God-realization" through devotion an absolute priority among the actions of man. A version of the project of God-realization is present in some Arya Samaj literature, no doubt partly in an effort to encompass the concerns of other South Asian religious discourses. The pamphlet (Nardev 1975: 9) argues: "The goal of life is to know oneself and by the acquisition of that Truth of oneself to realise God. Having attained communion with God, man experiences immense joy and peace." However, devotion is not the sole or even the principle means for realizing God: the pamphlet cites a "combination of the three media—deed, knowledge, and devotion," and for the Arya Samaj the supreme vehicle is knowledge (*jnana*). Further, God-realization is not a disintegration of the world, nor of the self:

The Arya Samaj also believes that any individual, however much learned or religious or pious he may be, is not God, nor can he become God. An individual can realize God but he does not lose his identity in God. . . . Both God and the individual are absolutely distinct in their qualities, deed and nature (Nardev 1975: 9–10).

Finally, the goal of God-realization is highly ambiguous, an adjunct of another goal of life: to know oneself. Although "a gradual movement from worldly objects towards the realization of God" (p. 13) should be part of the final stages of life, the pamphlet advocates overall a "well-balanced life" combining "the path of pleasures" and "the path of renunciation." Consider in this light the generalization of the president of the South African Arya Pratinidhi Sabha, in the preface to the pamphlet:

> The attention of the reader is focussed on the ultimate purpose of life. The maintenance of an equilibrium between the path of pleasure and the path of renunciation will bring about a realisation of true happiness and peace.

The ultimate purpose of life moves from God-realization to self-realization to the "realisation of true happiness and peace"—effectively, from devotion to the pursuit of happiness.

It may seem unwise to use a 1975 South African publication to define the outlook of the Arya Samaj in India and Fiji early this century. However, the principles here adduced are quite consistent with the more philosophically and Sanskritically propounded principles of the founder of the Arya Samaj, Swami Dayananda Saraswati, in the late nineteenth century.[1] Let us consider a few of his own arguments, then, from his *Svamantavyamantavya*, "My Beliefs and Disbeliefs," a summary written in 1875 (Dayananda 1976: 54–65). Rejecting Vedantic and devotional ontologies, which regard the material world and the souls of all beings as productions or emanations from a divine source, Dayananda argues for a threefold ontology:

> 5. God and souls are distinct entities, being different in nature and characteristics: they are, however, inseparable being related as the pervader and the pervaded, and having certain attributes in common. . . .
>
> 6. There are three things beginningless: namely, God, Souls, and *Prakrti* or the material cause of the universe. . . .
>
> 10. The world is a creation, and its Creator is the afore-said God. Form the display of design in the universe and the fact that dead inert matter is incapable of moulding itself into seeds and other various requisite forms, it follows that the world must have a Creator.

Dayananda's scheme shares some attributes with the Samkhya philosophical system—notably the primordial *prakrti* and emphasis on knowledge as a vehicle—and also with other Indian systems. But as fundamentally it reflects Christian cosmological principles, defense of the fact of a Creator by an argument from design, and a theory of an inert separate world of matter to which the Creator gives form and order.

Dayananda formulates principles concerning another standard Hindu philosophical topic, the *purusharthas* or ends of action. First discussed is *moksha*, i.e., liberation, final salvation, release. *Moksha* is described in a way that is indeed Vedic—as an achievement of a tempo-

---

1. For a biography of Dayananda see Jordens 1978.

rary state of heavenly pleasure, "a life of liberty and free movement . . . a fixed period of enjoying salvation." After discussing the means for attaining *moksha,* which amount basically to knowledge and virtuous deeds, Dayananda addresses the other three ends of action: *kama,* "passion," "desire," orientation by an affective attachment; *artha,* "gain," "goal," orientation to an interest in an object; and *dharma,* "righteousness," "duty," orientation to natural-moral law. Like many writers, Dayananda establishes a hierarchy among the three goals—but the hierarchy he creates is unusual.[2] Rather than relating *kama* to *tamas,* the lowest *guna* or quality, and thus to ignorance and sloth, *artha* to the middle *guna* (*rajas*) and thus to activity and restlessness, and *dharma* to the highest (*sattva*) and thus to goodness, Dayananda relates the ends of action in means-ends hierarchy and makes *kama* the final end. *Dharma* is reduced to a means to *artha* and then, through *artha,* to *kama:* "*Artha* or true wealth is that which is righteously acquired. . . . *Kama* or enjoyment of legitimate desires is that which is achieved by righteousness or *dharma* and honestly acquired wealth or *artha.*" In short, Dayananda's treatment of the ends of action makes the move observed in the pamphlet: from an ambiguous interest in God and liberation from worldly forms, to the pursuit of pleasure and happiness. In a world where material nature and the selves of agents are real and separate from God, the ends truly preached by the Arya Samaj are decidedly worldly.

Dayananda grounds his social and political objectives in Sanskrit sources. Before he enumerates his particular beliefs in the *Svamantavya-mantavya,* he cites verses from Bhartrhari, Manu, and an Upanishad on the eternality and power of *satya* and *dharma,* "truth" and "righteousness, duty." "Everyone should hold convictions in accordance with the teachings of the above verses," he writes. He also propounds in detail his interpretation:

He alone is entitled to be called a human being who, keeping his mind cool, feels for the happiness and unhappiness, profit and loss, of others, in the same way as he does for his own self, who does not fear the unjust, however powerful he may be, but fears the virtuous though weak. And not only this: he should always exert himself to his utmost to protect and promote the cause of the virtuous people even if they are extremely poor and weak and to discourage, suppress and destroy those who are wicked and unrighteous, even though they be the mightiest sovereigns of the whole world. In other words, a man should, as far as it lies in his power, constantly endeavor to undermine the power of the

2. It is unusual, but not unique. One also sees it, for example, in Yasodhara's *Jayamangala,* a commentary on the Kamasutra.

125

unjust and to strengthen the power of the just, even at the cost of great suffering. He should perform this duty which devolves on him as a man, and which he should never shirk, even if he has to sacrifice his life.

It is significant, I think, that this overarching political metaphysic is not among the enumerated beliefs, but stands as a charter for the project of enumerating, propagating, and defending a list of true beliefs. In his system *kama*, pleasure, appears to become the ultimate end of life, with even *moksha*, release, itself considered a sort of temporary pleasure. But the potential for hedonism is contradicted at the outset. *Kama* must be attained by means of *dharma*, righteous conduct, and this *dharma* includes, he asserts from the beginning, political struggle against the unrighteous and concern for the wealth and happiness of others before concern for the wealth and happiness of self.

The Arya Samaj in India

In both India and Fiji, these founding principles were used to justify Arya Samaj projects of social and political action. Particular circumstances, opportunities and obstacles, past successes, and confrontations with new challenges and challengers all changed the shape of the Arya Samaj mission and its ongoing discourse in India. The Arya Samaj project in Fiji was influenced by its history in India, an influence mediated by Samaj literature, press reports, and the experiences and teaching of the Indian Arya Samaj missionaries who came to Fiji in the 1920s.

From its beginning the basic mission of the Arya Samaj was to teach its Vedic religion. As many scholars have pointed out (e.g., Thursby 1975; Jones 1976), the Samaj borrowed its missionizing project and style from Islam and Christianity. Its goal was to defend and advance the one true religion, a religion universal in nature and value. Absent then was a more typical Indian epistemic sense of a hierarchy of truths, or theologically a hierarchy of divine forms. Instead, its model of religious and philosophical truths was "bi-polar" (Thursby 1975: 3), one system true, all others simply false. The world was not seen as a field in which low people worshipped lesser forms of God through less demanding methods, and so on up a hierarchy of method and insight. Instead all were capable of the proper faith, belief, and practice, which was to say, all were capable of becoming *arya*. The notion of an *arya* race, then, played a double role in the system. First, all Indians were descendants of the great Aryan race, deserving to be proud as descendants of the first practitioners of the Vedic religion and shamed that their own religious practice had fallen into corruption. But second, *arya* status became something to which anyone could aspire. Only in corrupted Hinduism was birth regarded as fixing nature and destiny. Instead, the *varnas* (caste groupings) of *arya* society were matters of social achievement. The regeneration and uplift of society would consist in raising people to higher stations, making people *arya* by teaching them the truth.

To carry out its mission program, the Arya Samaj developed in India an agenda of concrete goals and means. As we discuss these means, we are also reviewing, in brief, the transformations of the Arya Samaj project in India.

First, the Vedic religion had to be propagated and defended. This was the business of *upadeshaks*, "preachers," "teachers," or "missionaries," who traveled widely and spoke out in public. Forms of weekly worship were developed involving a Vedic fire sacrifice, and also hymns and sermons on a Christian model (Jones 1976: 44) by which *upadeshaks* could propound doctrine. But the *upadeshaks* gained more notoriety in public debates (*shastrarth*) in which they confronted expert authorities from other faiths and aggressively sought to prove the illegitimacy of all other religious practice, especially Christian, Muslim, and "orthodox Hindu." The Samaj orators developed a witty, uncompromising, even savage style. Thursby (1975: 17–18) provides a good example from lectures given at anniversary celebrations of the Arya Samaj in Uttar Pradesh in 1915, lectures that were followed by Hindu-Muslim violence:

He claimed that authoritative Muslim literature represents God as an embodied person who is stark naked (*nang dharang*) and lies upon a heavenly throne face downwards (. . .). Further, if God is embodied and yet sees everything, then he must have eyes even in his buttocks. The conclusion which Dharam Bir drew for his audience was . . . that for attracting adherents the religion of Islam is dependent upon promises of youthful consorts and cool drinks in Paradise.

Many Christian and Muslim organizations were ready to engage in debate and controversy. Both religious communities could draw on missionary traditions and rhetorics just as uncompromising, if not so brash, as that of the Arya Samaj. But "orthodox Hinduism" was not as well prepared for such self-representation and self-defense. Largely in response to the Arya Samaj challenge, new organizations sprang up to defend "orthodoxy," choosing by the end of the nineteenth century to call their "orthodox Hinduism" the Sanatan Dharm, the eternal *dharma*. From this usage and under other pressures, *dharma* itself gained a new meaning, "faith" or "religion"; "Sanatan Dharm" is thereafter glossed often as "eternal religion." Under Arya Samaj pressure, "orthodox Hinduism," a vast and internally inconsistent set of ritual forms and practices, became represented by self-proclaimed defenders as another religion in a competitive religious marketplace.

Second, the Arya Samajis quickly adopted mass media as a means to promote and defend their Vedic faith. Though public oratory was his primary vehicle, Dayananda himself not only wrote texts—most importantly the "bible" of the Arya Samaj, *Satyarth Prakash*, "the Light of the Truth"—but also tried to found a journal. By the 1880s his followers were more successful with newspapers and journals, and shortly thereafter they owned their own presses. Centers for publication of Arya Samaj discourse preceded the creation of a centralized umbrella-organization for all the individual Dayananda-inspired Arya Samajs (Jones 1976: 121). In Fiji a central body for Arya Samajs, an Arya Pratinidhi Sabha, is said to have been founded in 1917 (*Souvenir Magazine of the Golden Jubilee of the Arya Samaj Primary School*, 1981). Still, the publishing center was vital, and its mass-produced discourse spoke for the Samaj in public, tending to overshadow the other forms of organization and authority.

Education was a third major vehicle of Arya Samaj discursive practice, dating back to the days of Dayananda Saraswati himself. The Samaj emphasis on the primacy of truth and knowledge for religious practice entailed an emphasis on proper learning, and the educational efforts also had a social agenda. "The vision of young Hindu boys submitting to daily Christian indoctrination haunted Aryas," writes Jones (1976: 48). The Arya Samaj schools of Fiji followed a charter for competition with Christian schools developed long before in India.

By the time the Fiji schools were opened, a key issue of early, internal Samaj controversy had largely been settled. What was to be taught in the Samaj schools? All could agree on a curriculum stressing pride in Aryan tradition. But should the lessons be about Sanskrit, the focus Vedic, or should the emphasis be on English education and the preparation of young Aryas for participation and struggle in colonial arenas? Dayananda himself was committed to Sanskrit studies as essential to a proper Aryan education. He backed his commitment with his own extensive writings on various Vedic texts and Paninian Sanskrit grammar, intended as primers on the Vedic religion. However, Samaj educational policy drifted over time away from Sanskritic curriculum toward the education that was "key to worldly success" (Jones 1976: 48), education in English covering the standard subjects of European curriculum. As with the matter of God-realization and pursuit of happiness, a tension had developed between religious and social orientations in the definition of priorities. Again the tension and resolved in favor of the social, in keeping with the overriding commitment of the Samaj to a *satya,* "truth," of political conflict and a *dharma,* "duty," of political struggle. For education in Fiji, Sanskrit was never an issue, and when the question of education in English as against education in Indian vernacular languages was raised, the Samaj was firmly in favor of English education. It was generally spokesmen for Fiji's Muslims, seeking support for the teaching of proper Urdu, and for Fiji's Sanatan Dharm, seeking support for teaching of proper Hindi, who objected to English as the lingua franca of education. For Fiji's Arya Samaj, while proper Hindi was and is still taught in their schools, the desired emphasis was on education in an English and colonial curriculum.[3]

A fourth major arena of Arya Samaj efforts, again from quite early days, was *shuddhi,* purification or "conversion" of others to proper *arya* standing. This was the Samaj answer to Christian baptism or a Muslim vow of faith, in the mission competition for formal public allegiences. Rituals for *shuddhi* or purification were not invented whole; Hindu procedures for removal or negation of impure states were adapted to the new purpose. The Arya Samaj was not the only group conducting *shuddhi* rituals for conversion or reconversion to a form of Hinduism. However, they came to be closely identified with it when they made *shuddhi* an integral part of their project. *Shuddhi* rituals played two major roles for the Samaj (Thursby 1975: 136ff; Jones 1976: 129ff., 202ff.). At first they were a vehicle for transforming those who had accepted Christianity or Islam into proper Aryans and, more especially, to bring those who had once been "Hindu" back into the Aryan fold.

---

3. Constructions such as "English education," "proper Urdu," and "proper Hindi" all require historical and critical clarification. In worlds of social complexity, interconnections, and creole-speaking competences of variant composition—any colonial or postcolonial social field—assertions of language boundaries and proprieties are assertions of authority, acts of power. Fabian 1986 discusses the matter in detail. Rejecting naturalist and evolutionary models of language spread and change, Fabian demonstrates that the codification of Swahili as a colonial "vehicular language" followed a series of policy contests between economic, political, and religious interests in Belgium, the Belgian Congo, and elsewhere. For South Asian languages, Cohn 1985 describes the early British efforts to define the language field of their colony, find usable sources of authority in Persian and Sanskrit law books, and shape a "language of command" of their own, Hindustani. To make Hindustani, the British mixed Mughal court language and the pidgins spoken between various masters and servants, then taught other British how to use the new language to control interactions with Indians. Hindi and Urdu are outside of Cohn's purview, since they emerge with insistence that Hindi and Muslims' Urdu are languages with their own literatures and, according to some authorities, are not alike. Finally, Viswanathan 1989 suggests that the codification of English language and more particularly of an English literary canon is itself enmeshed in colonial history and problems of colonial authority. The question of the language of instruction for Fiji Indians is discussed in greater detail in the second section of chapter 7.

Later, by 1900, they became in addition a vehicle for uplifting untouchables into *arya* status. To the Samaj, the outcaste status of
untouchables was a symptom of the corruption of "orthodox Hinduism." Even the untouchables could be made *arya* by the proper rituals
and commitments on their part. Furthermore, the low castes and out-
castes were the groups in which conversion to Christianity or Islam was
most common. At first together with Sikhs, at times together with other
Hindus in Shuddhi Sabhas, and often on their own, Arya Samaj
groups undertook *shuddhi* reconversion campaigns among low-caste and
outcaste groups and celebrated mass reconversions to Vedic Hinduism.

Even in Dayananda's day, his Arya *dharm* was highly controversial and
publicly contested. By 1887 a formal organization emerged to challenge
the Arya Samaj. In Punjab, and by the turn of the century a network of
Sanatan Dharm Sabhas was organizing to oppose the Arya Samaj
throughout Punjab. In the late nineteenth and early twentieth centuries
the public performances of *shuddhi* rituals became a focus of controversy
in Punjab and elsewhere. The public, even mass, rituals of conversion
were major occasions for the promulgation of Arya doctrine. In social
profile the Arya Samaj developed a curious dual structure, on the one
side a privileged, formally educated, largely urban elite, and on the other
side growing numbers of converts of low caste and few means.

Then in the early twentieth century, this social reform project was further radicalized by a new and more controversial institution. *Shuddhi*
efforts by themselves could not really transform society into an *arya*
mode without the institution of some type of proper *arya* caste system,
some kind of society based on Vedic principles of order: personal virtue
and merit, not birth, determining one's place. But articulation with caste
was a great stumbling block for *shuddhi*. Untouchables may have been
declared purified and *arya*, but even within the Arya Samaj community
this did not lead to social equality with high-caste folk. Dayananda had
hoped for a simple and direct rejection of caste and the substitution of an
Arya *varna* system based on merit. But by the turn of the century this
plan was dead in practice, having foundered on the difficulty of specifying the marriage and other social rules for the Arya *varnas* in the face of
the elaborate and rigorous systems surrounding it. In the first decades of
this century, the problem was related to the problem of the disorder and
weakness of Hindu society in its political context, and a new organization plan, explicitly political, was suggested: a drive to create a national
network of Hindu political societies, the *sangathan* or "consolidation"
movement.

The *sangathan* movement also became an effort to bring Arya Samaj,
Sanatan Dharm, and other Hindu organizations together into one ef-

fective political body, in order to compete effectively with increasingly militant Islamic political agencies. As Thursby (1975: 159) summarizes it, the *sangathan* movement

was a rhetorical and an imaginative phenomenon as much as it was a proto-political organization. It sought to efface the image of the Hindu as a *dhoti*-wearing coward and to replace it with the image of the Hindu as a militant who would be willing to use whatever means might be necessary to maintain his honor and that of his community.

By 1909, Hindu advocates for the *sangathan* movement were expressing themselves with explicit Social Darwinist rhetoric (Thursby 1975: 159), describing communal struggles as governed by a universal law of the "survival of the fittest." In the early years of the *sangathan* movement, an All-India Hindu Maha Sabha was created, with Sanatani and Samaji members. By the mid-1920s the divergence of its plans with the Arya Samaj mission became clear, and the agenda of the *sangathan* movement varied according to who was describing it. The general idea was for a national Hindu political society to exist as the coordinating body of a network of local Hindu *sabhas* ("organizations"), which together would function politically to defend Hindu interests at the various political levels from locality to nation. Other versions of the *sangathan* movement were more radical socially, especially that preached by the Arya Samaj leader Shraddhanand in the mid-1920s until his assassination in 1926. Shraddhanand advocated the coordination of *shuddhi* ("conversion") and *sangathan* ("consolidation") and sought a reincorporation of society as a whole in the Hindu Maha Sabha. Where he was effective, the local untouchables were given access to public institutions—water wells, schools, public meetings—as part of the constitution of local Hindu *sabhas*. But overall, the Arya Samaj did not transform Indian society, even in Punjab. Its social and political efforts were superseded by the other social and political projects of Indian nationalism; the Arya Samaj remained a minority organization in India, with a strangely split elite and low-caste membership.

Let us return to Fiji and the late 1920s to consider the developing project of the Fiji Arya Samaj.

The Arya Samaj Project in Fiji

Because of its advanced schools and trained *upadeshaks* ("preachers," "missionaries"), the Arya Samaj was in a better position to help overseas Indian communities than other Hindu organizations, especially when the demand was for leaders educated in both *shastra* and English. In the anti-indenture polemic *My Twenty-one Years in the Fiji Islands* (1914), Sanadhya and Chaturvedi called it "the duty of all the great organizations for Indian religion to send a good religious instructor to Fiji." They praised Manoharanand Saraswati, the Samaji teacher and preacher already in Fiji, and singled out the Arya Samaj in a request for further assistance:[4]

There is a very great need for this sort of religious instructor there, who knows Vedic principles and knows English as well. . . . We know that quite a burden is put on the Arya Samaj, and that the Arya Samaj is doing a lot of work, but aren't these givers of aid to the world, the Arya Samaj, able to send one more religious instructor to Fiji, for the benefit of our foreign-dwelling brothers?

The Arya Samaj, more than any other group, managed to send teachers and preachers to Fiji in the 1910s and 1920s. While founding schools was on the agenda of all the Fiji Indian religious and other sectional societies as they organized themselves, the Arya Samaj got the most schools organized. The Christian missions, especially the Methodist mission, tried to monopolize Indian education in the 1910s, but were thwarted in a test case in Lautoka, where the government turned down a Methodist bid for a grant to open a second Indian school. Observing the Arya Samaj opening its *Gurukul* school there, the government opened a nonreligious government school for Indians in order, the Superintendent of Schools told one of the missionaries, to check the trend of Christian-Hindu school polarization and "to limit the establishment of Arya Samaj schools" (Thornley 1973: 133). But the government opened few such Indian schools of its own; Indian fundraising committees opened many more, some affiliated to a religious society, some "general" Indian schools. As the Indian sectional societies developed, struggles for control of the school boards of Indian "general" schools sometimes led to schisms and new school-building. By the early 1930s the other societies were starting to catch up to the Arya Samaj in school organizing, and together they outpaced the Christian missions. By 1931 the schools run by Indian committees and Indian societies had more

---

4. Sanadhya and Chaturvedi also wrote with pride about "the germ" of *sangathan-sabha,* organization and consolidation, that had begun in Fiji, in apparent approving reference to the *sangathan* organizing projects in 1910s India. The organizing in Fiji they described was a developing ability to raise money for public projects, the foundation of a British Indian Association led by Manilal, and Manoharanand Saraswati's efforts to found a school. Another sign of approval for the Arya Samaj and its agenda was their endorsement of widow remarriage for Fiji, in the context of the violence and adultery of Fiji's indenture system. On the other hand, in their section on *sangathan-sabha,* Sanadhya and Chaturvedi specifically praised the way Fiji Hindus and Muslims mixed socially, "a pleasure" that was "no ordinary thing."

children enrolled than did the Christian mission schools (Gillion 1977: 120), this leaving out the Indian schools run informally or without government aid.

The Arya Samaj project in Fiji, as in India, began with preachers, teachers, and schools and then created new conditions of possibility with establishment of its newspapers, especially *Fiji Samachar* in 1923. Before this time, imported newspapers and books from India described the controversies there, and such local Fiji Indian leaders as Badri Maharaj identified themselves as Arya Samaji in the 1910s. But the newspaper brought a new kind of power to the local Samajis, especially since *Fiji Samachar,* "Fiji News," aspired to be the general newspaper of the Fiji Indian community.[5] Then in 1927 an *upadeshak* named Shri Krishna Sharma arrived and became Fiji's first major Samaji controversialist.

In the standard Samaji *upadeshak* style, Shri Krishna Sharma toured Fiji and held public meetings. In his *History of the Arya Samaj in Fiji* (1966: 27), Sharma described the *bhajans* (religious songs) and speeches at the public meetings of Samaj leaders as publicity (*prachar*) for Vedic dharma: "This publicity planted the seed of Indian tradition [*samskrta*] in a modern [*naya*] form in the hearts of Indians." He viewed himself as a modernizer, a dispeller of darkness, and a planter of seeds. Other depictions of his mission and his character vary as widely as the depictions of Kunti's "virtue." According to an official Arya Samaj source—a centenary publication called *Arya Samaj and Indians Abroad* (Nardev and Somera 1975: 123)—written in South Africa, its Fiji chapter from accounts sent by Fiji Samaj leaders—Sharma in Fiji

gave a new direction to the Arya Samaj and increased its influence and popularity. He was young, energetic and full of life. He endeared himself both to the young and old alike. He was a fluent speaker with a charming personality. The listeners were ever fascinated by his selection of inspiring songs.

A vision of Sharma somewhat different from this one comes from a confidential account by J. R. Pearson, the Secretary for Indian Affairs,

---

5. Fiji Sanatanis later tried, and failed, to launch their own newspapers in competition with *Fiji Samachar*. Through the period of controversy, 1929 to 1932, *Fiji Samachar's* main competitors in purveying news to Fiji Indians were newspapers imported from India, the *Fiji Times and Herald* (the colonial, English-language newspaper), and *Vriddhi* and the *Pacific Press,* the former a journal, the latter a short-lived 1930 newspaper, both published by Dr. I. Hamilton Beattie, a European sympathetic to the Indian Reform League. *Vriddhi* was bilingual in Hindi and English but published especially in English; *Pacific Press* was trilingual, publishing in English, Hindi, and Fijian; *Fiji Samachar* published articles in Hindi and English, but especially Hindi.

who "arranged to be present" at one of Sharma's meetings after they had become controversial:

> The Pandit is a well nourished Hindu youth, about 25 years of age I should say. He was dressed in white clothes, a coat and a loincloth. . . . he talks extremely fast in rather difficult Hindi and is extremely verbose. When he runs dry on one topic, he pulls out a paper copy of some poem in Sanskrit verse, and chants a passage accompanying himself on the harmonium. Like many of these preachers he gets worked up into his own eloquence and from the look in his eyes one would imagine he was intoxicated.

> He spoke for nearly three hours I fancy altogether. . . . There was nothing so far as I could make in the address to which any exception could be taken, though I am bound to confess that I had great difficulty following at times, and most officials present stated that they thought it doubtful whether a good deal of the speech was really intelligible to the audience. An audience of the class present would not resent this. They like to listen to Sanskrit and highflown Hindi being rolled out.

Sharma also had much more severe critics. Indian Muslim and Christian leaders complained about his preaching within months of his arrival in Fiji; in a confidential letter the Vice-President of the Muslim League called him "very repugnant and possessed of a repulsive temperament." Official Fiji despatched non-Muslim clerk-interpreters and European missionaries and policemen to report on his meetings; a police report described him as "an poorly dressed, untidy, and inoffensive looking young Indian" (but whose mission was religious and educational, unlikely to affect politics unless redirected by "local malcontents and hotheads"). Hindi-speaking missionary A. W. McMillan also reported on one of Sharma's meetings: "There was an entire absence of friendliness toward anyone, and the whole tone was belligerent and inclined to be provocative."

Noting this gap in perceptions, we can still get a sense from McMillan's, Pearson's, and Pearson's clerk's confidential accounts, the most detailed sources from the time, of the style and substance of this *upadeshak*'s mission to Fiji Hindus. Pearson was the observer most interested in the audience. Of 150 people, "I doubt if there were more than 100 at the outside really listening," and many of these were not local people of Nausori, site of the meeting, but "officials and visitors from Suva. . . . I do not think there can have been more than 60 or 70 real residents of Nausori and these did not stay the whole time." Pearson concluded that "there was an entire absence of excitement or even enthusiasm about the meeting." However, as he also noted, his own presence had affected it.

Persons's most interesting comment on the substance of Sharma's remarks was that Sharma "deplored the decadence of modern Hinduism, but claimed that the signs were encouraging and India was producing famous men, some of whom he mentioned (including Mr. Gandhi)." Pearson was accompanied to the meeting by his Presbyterian clerk W. M. Caldwell, who understood better the substance of Sharma's remarks. Pearson had Caldwell write his own account. According to Caldwell, Sharma emphasized the need for rituals to purify the air (no doubt, Arya Samaj *havan* rituals); criticized the Darwinian allegation that men descended from monkeys and these from "lower forms," because "according to the Vedas God has aeons before evolved the world out of His attributes and promulgated the Vedas to Rishis"; and told the story of King Bhoj: "There seemed to be moral teaching in it regarding right-living, unselfishness, and the avoidance of fear of death for noble ends." Caldwell also noted remarks by Sharma about two Europeans. Sharma "expressed pleasure at seeing Mr. Pearson S.I.A. there and exhorted his hearers not to lose the 'golden opportunity' of going to him for redress of grievances if they had any." He also criticized "the statements of people like Mr. McMillan who speak of beef-eating and animal sacrifice as having been in vogue in Aryan times. . . . The texts they quote from are interpolations of interested people."

Sharma's reference to McMillan concerned a letter from the missionary printed in the *Fiji Times,* to which Sharma also published a reply. Pearson noted in his account that McMillan was not "well advised to raise this controversy," that there was "no hope of his arguments carrying conviction to Hindus, and they are likely to raise annoyance," and that he would write to McMillan about it. In 1927 McMillan's correspondence with Pearson was formal and solicitous; within a few years McMillan's mission and Reform League work was superseded by employment as Fiji's Inspector of Indian Schools, and after Pearson's departure McMillan was influential as a foremost Indian expert for official Fiji. All of this noted, let us consider McMillan's account. "The speaker commenced by insisting upon the existence of God. . . . He then proceeded to show that European scholars are wrong in asserting that Aryans in Vedic times were worshippers of Fire, Wind etc., that these were expressions of Deity." From challenge to this form of European authority Sharma turned to a social agenda, first criticizing meat-eating ("He who eats any kind of meat makes a cemetery of his stomach") and use of alcohol ("he told a story of a drunken man which according to Western standards was scarcely decent though not so offensive to Indian ears"). "A considerable time was given to warning hearers against embracing Christianity." Sharma "dealt flippantly with the Bible," arguing that the Vedas were much older and that "the writers of the Bible have taken Vedic material and made it serve their own purposes." He argued that Christian Indians "become unpatriotic" and are "destroyers of" *dharma*. "These people have taken our Krishna and called him Christ. . . . Notice also the story of Abraham and how he called his wife his sister."

This last comment exemplifies not only an anti-Christian agenda but also an interest in sexual morality. Sharma went on to criticize in song "all the tendencies in Fiji towards the adoption of foreign fashions and different standards," including Western-style clothes, cutlery, houses, and food. More particularly, he turned his attention to what was appropriate behavior for Indian women. He criticized women "for wanting to learn English," for their desire for luxuries such as motorcar rides, "petticoats instead of saris," and servants to help with cooking, and most generally "for their spirit of independence." Sharma, McMillan reports, was followed by another itinerant Arya Samaji preacher from India, Ramnarayan. "I listened for half an hour and then came away. He did little else than challenge anyone to show that the Vedas allow beef-eating or the sacrifice of cows." It was Sharma who stirred people, including McMillan, and helped set the agenda for Fiji's Arya Samaj.

Shri Krishna Sharma left Fiji after making a short but vivid impression in the late 1920s. A sharp critic of westernized habits and of Christianity, he apparently grew cautious about anti-Muslim remarks at roughly the time that Fiji's new Muslim League protested and government "reporters" began appearing at his meetings. But he was by many reports (including Nardev and Somera 1975: 125) an advocate of *shuddhi*. He propounded an Arya Samaj view of Hinduism, sexuality, and colonial relations, from concern about the "decadence of modern Hinduism" to a call for selfless bravery in conflict with selfish people and a reform of habits to make people stronger. He shared the brashness of other *upadeshaks*—a Fiji Arya Samaji who had personally heard him speak told me that Sharma was "very aggressive"—and also their tendency to seek evidence of sexual misconduct in opposing religious traditions.

A Hindu Maha Sabha, a Fiji-wide Hindu society, was founded in 1926, the year of Shraddhanand's assassination in India. The Fiji Muslim League, founded in the same year, alleged when complaining about Shri Krishna Sharma that the Hindu Maha Sabha was formed "to commemorate" the death of Shraddhanand, the aggressive Indian Samaj and *sangathan* leader. Whether or not this was true, another Indian Samaji, Thakur Kundan Singh Kush, arrived in Fiji in 1928 and was soon thereafter both a schoolmaster and a principal force behind Arya Samaj *shuddhi* and *sangathan* efforts.[6]

Both the Hindu Maha Sabha and the Fiji Muslim League quickly contested with the Indian Reform League for the right to represent Indian opinion. The Hindu Maha Sabha claimed, in its correspondence with the government, to represent the colony's "60,000 Hindus," while the Muslim League claimed to speak for the Muslims. The Samaj polemicists criticized the Indian Reform League as the advocate of Indian westernization in dress and eating and drinking habits; the loyal Indian Reform League fought back covertly as well as overtly.

One covert method of fighting back was informing the government about disloyal activities. For a time some government clerks were members of the Reform League, the Arya Samaj, and the Hindu Maha Sabha. They attempted from within the Reform League to prevent it from presuming to represent the whole Indian community. Their obstructionism was reported secretly to the government by other Reform League members. One such informer was John F. Grant, an Indian Christian leader. In 1927 Grant wrote confidentially to the Inspector-General of the Constabulary about Raghvanand, an Arya Samaj leader, government clerk, and son of Badri Maharaj. At issue was an impending visit by royalty, for whom the Indian Reform League wished to orchestrate the presentation of an address of welcome on behalf of the Fiji Indian community.

> I beg to inform you that a meeting to which representatives of all sections of the Indian community were invited, was held in the rooms of the Indian Reform League and under the Chairmanship of W. M. Caldwell [Pearson's clerk and a Reform League member].
>
> At this meeting the question of presenting an address of welcome to their Royal Highnesses, the Duke and Duchess of York was discussed.
>
> Mr. Raghbanand opposed the presentation of the address and in doing so asked in what capacity their Royal Highnesses were visiting Fiji; what good their visit would do to the Indians resident in the Colony, and why the

6. On his "character," Nardev and Somera (1975: 125) noted that he "served the Arya Samaj with distinction. He conducted debates and lectured very ably. His logic and methods of presentation were really very marvellous and worthy of remark." The Fiji government, on the other hand, was sufficiently worried about his "character" that it repeatedly inquired into his fitness to teach schoolchildren, removed him from control of one school, temporarily suspended his teaching license, and made a special effort to censor his mail, especially his literature imports.

Indian community should present an address of welcome.
He further asked what the Fiji Government had done for
the Indians in the Colony to justify the inclusion in the
address of the expression "the Indians were living
peacefully etc., etc., under the regime of His Excellency, Sir
Eyre Hutson".

Mr. Gopendia Narain supported Mr. Raghbanand and
suggested that the address if presented at all, should be on
behalf of The Indian Reform League and not on behalf of
the Indian Community.

Requesting that you would be so good as to forward this
letter to His Excellency,

> I beg to remain,
> Sir,
> Your Obedient Servant,
> John F. Grant

Reacting to this and other reports, the Governor minuted days later, "I
gave a warning to [Raghvanand] and, indirectly, to his father Badri
Maraj [*sic*], who was present." By 1931, the Fiji government acted more
formally, forbidding clerk-interpreters from joining any Indian communal or political organizations and requiring them to submit to the
government confidential official reports on communal affairs. The Indian Reform League was excepted from the proscription on societal
memberships, because it was considered simply a cultural and recre-
ational organization.

However, if the Reform League could win battles in the manipulation
of official channels, and if the government could shed itself of clerks with
divided loyalties, the distance of both from the larger Indian community was apparent in the 1929 election with the resounding victory over
John Grant of *Fiji Samachar* editor Vishnu Deo. A faction within the
Arya Samaj extended its *sangathan* ("consolidation") effort then, led by
Thakur Kundan Singh Kush and others seeking to organize the rural
Fiji Indians. This *sangathan* movement was never itself endorsed or con-
solidated by Fiji's Arya Samaj as a whole. The Arya Samaj organizations
in many parts of Fiji opposed it. But it received very favorable treatment
overall in *Fiji Samachar*.

By 1930 the aggressive activities of local Hindu Sangathan Sabhas
("Hindu consolidation organizations"), especially in the Suva-Rewa
area, led to many controversies. Some of the *sabhas* sought not only to
organize the Hindu community but also to enforce a social discipline. In
a few localities, Muslims were pressured to undergo *shuddhi* and become

Hindu; if they would not, Hindus were pressured to boycott them, at threat of being themselves out-casted. Pleas for protection were sent to the government, especially from Rewa and Vatuwaqa in early 1930, just months after the election and the beginning of the Legislative Council boycott.

This *sangathan* movement did not reorder the Fiji countryside. The government chose to avoid direct confrontations over boycotts on local levels, seeking to maintain classic colonial impartiality. But the Hindu Sangathan Sabhas were thwarted, ironically for their self-confident claim to represent religious Hinduism, by resistance from local Hindu communities themselves, at the same time that wide publicity was given to debates between Arya Samaj leaders and new Sanatan Dharm *pandits*. To understand this history we will have to connect the rural, local confrontations with colonywide debates, both religious and political, between Indian religious organizations and between Indians and the government. We have outlined the mission of the Arya Samaj—from principle to project in India, and then to its project in Fiji—to show that it was not simply a response to colonially constituted conditions in Fiji. We will discuss its fate, its failure, in chapter 8. Let us now consider other aspects of the Fiji situation, political and administrative, to establish the rest of the context for interpreting the key Fiji debates.

The New "Indian Problem"

On 15 May 1929 rituals of celebration and protest commemorated the fiftieth anniversary of Indian settlement in Fiji. A week before the anniversary date, Governor Eyre Hutson decided on advice of his Executive Council that the day would not be a public holiday; the government gazette published his decision. Three days before the anniversary date at a meeting in Lautoka, Indian leaders including Vishnu Deo, S. B. Patel, and A. D. Patel founded the Fiji Indian National Congress and called for a *hartal*, a day of fasting, prayer, and work stoppage, on the fifteenth. On 14 May the Governor reversed his gazetted decision and declared the day a public holiday. On 15 May, while the *hartal* was observed, a parade in Suva celebrated the "jubilee year." Elsewhere in Suva the Arya Samaj Modern Youth Society led by Vishnu Deo burned the indenture system in effigy (Sharma 1966: 188).

Why did the Governor make the day a holiday? It is possible that news of the impending *hartal* influenced him. His minute explaining the decision cites unspecified "private information from the other side of the island." He was also influenced by Maynard Hedstrom, European merchant and politician, one of the two European elected members of the Legislative Council appointed to the elite Executive Council.[1] Hedstrom arrived from abroad just in time to offer his support for the

1. In 1929 the Executive Council had eight members, including the two appointments of elected Europeans, and also six officials: the Secretary for Indian Affairs, the Secretary for Native Affairs, the Chief Medical Officer, the Colonial Treasurer, the Attorney General, and the Colonial Secretary.

holiday. But the main force within government for reversal was J. R. Pearson, the Secretary for Indian Affairs.

In the weeks before the event, the government realized that it had no laws through which it could control the celebrations. While new broader powers for the police were passed with haste (CSO 2691/29), the Governor was convinced not to grant the public holiday by members of the Executive Council who feared Indian celebrations without the police powers available. However, Pearson ("the S.I.A.") and his clerk Buksh had been working with an Indian Jubilee Celebration Committee that earnestly desired the holiday. Wrote the Governor in his explanation to members of the Executive Council (CSO 1561/29):

> The S.I.A. stated that the Committee had succeeded, not without difficulty, in combining the more moderate elements of the various sections of the Indian community and in preparing the program which would be acceptable to all. The Committee considered that a Public Holiday was an essential feature of their programme, and that the inability of the Governor to declare a Public Holiday would be regarded as a rebuff to the Committee by the opposing elements. They pressed for reconsideration of the question even if a half-day's holiday only were declared.

The event as a whole gives us insight into the emerging configuration of agencies and relations as the election approached in 1929. The so-called moderate Indians typified by the Jubilee Committee no longer claimed to represent the Indian community as a whole. Rather, they asked for a favor (even a half day) on the ground that they were in a political struggle, a struggle in which the best they could hope to do was to rally and unite "the more moderate elements" of "the various sections of the Indian community." The Suva moderates, led by European I. Hamilton Beattie (publisher of *Vriddhi*, a journal for Indians), not only had their parade on the fifteenth but founded their own Fiji Indian National Congress in Suva on the fourteenth, trying to forestall the assumption of colonywide Indian leadership by the Fiji Indian National Congress founded in Lautoka days before. Working with the moderates and advocating trust and authority for them was the Secretary for Indian Affairs, Pearson. He in turn met with resistance within the government, succeeding here in part because of Hedstrom's blessings. And meanwhile, the so-called radical sections of the Indian community observed the anniversary with their own separate rites—fasting, prayer, and, in Suva, dramatic public protests from the Arya Samaj.

"The Indian Problem" in Election Rhetoric

The election of Indians to Fiji's Legislative Council had been delayed for almost a decade, in part because of urgings by the government of India for a common roll voting system. India's official influence over Fiji, always mediated by the Colonial Office, waned in proportion to the likelihood of further sponsored labor emigration. By the late 1920s it was clear even to Fiji that further emigration proposals were futile. The fate of common roll voting proposals was sealed, most likely, by the reduction of colonial India's influence overseas. Ironically, however, the popular agitation for it in Fiji and the formal and informal communication among popular political associations in Fiji, Kenya, and India had barely begun. Official India's influence over official Fiji, and the influence of popular political movements in India over Fiji Indian politics, moved in inverse proportions but with similar results: official Fiji felt both as pressures, attempts to challenge its authority and limit its sovereignty.

Even in the early 1920s the anticolonial Indian nationalists were already infamous in Fiji. By the late 1920s India was known among Fiji Europeans as a land of religious and communal violence and all manner of agitation and strife. If Indian political voices had been illegitimate since indenture days, they were now dangerous as well. After the Fiji Indians elected to the Legislative Council in 1929 quit their seats and boycotted the council over the common roll issue, Fiji's new Governor, Murchison Fletcher, wrote to the Colonial Office:

The articulate element, in a very small minority, has little real understanding of or interest in the shibboleths which it is instructed to voice. I regard the local politician as the uninformed tool of an extraneous organization which is dangerously seeking every opportunity to use the Colony for the purposes of its world-wide attack upon the British Raj (CSO 289/30).

The basis of this version of the politics of the Indian community was that Gandhi had sent two barristers to aid the Fiji Indians, S. B. Patel and A. D. Patel (though they arrived with no coordinated agenda) and that increasing numbers of missionaries, teachers, and even lawyers were arriving under the sponsorship of Indian organizations, especially the Arya Samaj and the Muslim League. However, the point is not simply that Fletcher misunderstood the social and political means and ends motivating these visitors, and their relations with their Fiji Indian hosts. It is rather that he articulated quite sharply, in an important communication, the new "Indian problem" perceived and discussed by Fiji Europeans in 1929. The Indian boycott of the Legislative Council came less than a month after Fletcher's arrival from Hong Kong to become Governor of Fiji; he very quickly adopted, reproduced, and helped amplify the local Indian-problem rhetoric.

In indenture days, the "Indian problem" had been one of pollution;

Indians were an irritant and a drag on the new civil society. Though there were alarmist exceptions, most portrayals of an Indian threat (if one was perceived at all) described it as something like the threat of a virus to a young and growing organism. By 1929 the Indian problem was widely reported as an actual threat to European mastery, perhaps even a conspiracy. It was a matter of politics, not hygiene. To some, like Fletcher, this made it also a matter of deception. The average Indian was surely not interested in acting politically. Even the articulate local Indian leadership—no doubt he had Vishnu Deo in mind—"has little real understanding of or interest in" the topics they raised in public. And if the political must be a matter of deceptions, the deceptions were not only malicious but dangerous. To Fletcher, this politics could only be a sort of warfare, part of a "world-wide attack upon the British Raj." Thus the Indian problem shifted in the European imagination from an irritating presence requiring maintenance work to a dialogical guerilla war. Indian speech, or some of it at least, shifted from something laughable to something to be scrutinized for subversive intentions.

To understand the extremity of the Fiji Europeans' reactions to Indian political speech we might recall, first, that in the colonial world the range of genres for political exchange between the colonizers and the colonized, the terrain of normal politics in the Gramscian sense, was remarkably small. As we have seen, in the Fiji of indenture days the acceptable form of political exchange was limited to requests by humble petitioners, preferably individual. By the 1920s the government encouraged secret correspondence by loyal and trustworthy Indians about Indian affairs and dangerous radicals—as we have seen, such letters could go all the way to the Governor for action—and Indian "men of character" could be appointed to posts on commissions and even to the Legislative Council, though not given policy influence in either venue. Finally, by the late 1920s the government was experimenting with granting the moderates special privileges such as holidays, especially when those moderates reflected and promoted government interests. That the Indians were electing candidates to the Legislative Council was enough of a crisis for these Europeans, as we shall see.

The Indian boycott of the Legislative Council was not the beginning of a European perception of a war with the Indians, though it brought more widespread acceptance of the image. The earliest portrayals of a war with the Indians were more abstract. As early as the 1910s the Social Darwinist imagery of a racial competition for survival between indigenous Fijians and Indians in Fiji had been extended to describe a competition between the Indians and the Europeans, especially by polemicists in Australia for a whites-only policy there. When Rev. Henry

Worrall wrote "A Racial Riddle: The Clash of Alien Races in the Pacific" for Australia's *Life* magazine in 1912, he lamented "the passing of the Fijian" and declared "the immense importance of the Indian problem in Fiji." The pernicious influence of the Indians on indigenous Fijian Christians could only be solved by a major missionizing effort directed at the Indians, he thought, but the larger problem was the Asian tide itself:

> Through the partially opened floodgates of India, an ever-growing stream of coloured humanity flows toward Fiji, transforming, as it flows, the natural and domestic conditions of the group. . . . The Indian invader is not only destined to become numerically and commercially the strong man of Fiji, but the ultimate possessor of many other Island groups in the Pacific. . . . He has come to stay, and to work out a destiny for himself, and, it may be, for many other races who, watching him, may themselves launch out on enterprises that may re-mould Australian ideas on the Asiatic question.

Warfare imagery, a common Christian missionary trope, organizes Worrall's explanation of mission work—sections of his article are titled "The Real Struggle Now Begins" and "The Battle to Be Re-Fought." The war image connects in one theme his concern for indigenous Fijians seen as a dying race, his concern for Christian conversions and defense of converts, and his concern for the racial future of Australia and the world. In the 1930s even C. F. Andrews (1937) described the Pacific as a zone wherein the Indians as a race naturally competed well, while whites were enervated as a race by the climate. For Andrews the point was that the Indian presence in Fiji was natural and good, but even he accepted and employed the eugenical figure of a racial war for survival.

In the late 1920s this depiction of the Indian problem gained new referents with dramatic events in realms of real and direct competition. It was not the Fiji Indians' fault that a major international capitalist depression began in 1929, nor that the depression hit Fiji Europeans harder than Fiji Indians. Fiji Indian sugar cane growers were insulated from falling international sugar prices by CSR pricing policy.[2] But the

2. The international sugar market of the early twentieth century was quite volatile: in London the price of raw sugar per hundred weight was 11s. in 1910, 58s. in 1920, 6s. 7d. in 1930, and 4s. 8d. in 1935. (Tinker 1976: 408). Government of Fiji trade reports estimated the value of Fiji sugar exports per ton at £29 in 1920, £15 in 1928, and £9 in 1930 (Moynagh 1981: 122). But the company paid the same price for sugar cane from the mid-twenties through the 1930s: 13s. 6d. a ton with additions or deductions for sugar content. The company had settled the strike of 1921 with a promise of a fixed price, and it regarded a fixed price as the cornerstone of its management of Indian tenant farmers; in any case CSR still made a profit when the world market price was at its lowest (Moynagh 1981: 124, 132; Knapman 1987: 128). By 1925 Fiji's European settler/planters had been driven out of

collapse of the copra market severely hurt Fiji Europeans, mer-
chant/wholesalers as well as planters, and the Fiji European merchants
were already bitter about their "Asian" competition. If the Fiji Europeans were feeling the new pressure of economic competition with
Indians, they also had an excruciatingly concrete, if seemingly trivial,
political grievance against the new opening of Fiji Indian politics. The
new Letters Patent that granted the Indians their three elected seats on
the Legislative Council reduced the number of elected European representatives from seven to six. None of the sitting Europeans wished to
resign, and in a bitter election campaign three incumbents were forced
to contest with each other for two seats. In political speeches they played
a game of one-upmanship, addressing the same target with increasingly
strident rhetoric—Fiji Indian political aspirations.

Some of the fodder for their attacks was provided by Vishnu Deo in
his English-language Town Hall election speech on 1 September. To
quote from a pamphlet reproduction of the speech (available in CSO
6141/29), Vishnu Deo argued for a common roll voting system as a matter of equal citizenship, fairness, and justice. He denied allegations that
Indians sought to dominate Fiji or make it an Indian colony, noting that
the majority of official members over elected members on the Legislative
Council precluded Indian dominance regardless of how many Indian
voters could meet the standards of the electoral roll. He argued that
what Indians wanted was freedom (*swaraj*) for India and in Fiji, "a fair
field and no favour." He promised "co-operation" in Fiji but demanded
"the full and unrestricted rights of British Citizenship".

Two days later Sir Henry Scott, K. C., gave the first European candidate speech. Neither he nor the other European candidates were
reported to have made any explicit references to Vishnu Deo or his
speech, but all three devoted considerable time to "the Indian question."
Scott argued for agricultural and technical education over scholastic education for Indians, for the Christian missions to be given the funding
earmarked for an expansion of the Indian schools, and for an end to
biases he saw in the operation of school and hospital policies. "It was his
indelible impression that the Government was too prone to put the

---

sugar cane growing by a combination of Indian preference for their own leaseholds over
employment under Europeans and CSR's unwillingness to support European planters'
lifestyles when the cane could be bought more cheaply from Indians (see Knapman 1987:
58–64). The remaining European planters produced copra and other agricultural products; nothing protected them, or their European merchant/wholesalers, from falling
world prices. The depression was also said to have driven five hundred Indian traders out of
business (Knapman 1987: 94).

native Fijian in second place to the Indian. (loud applause). . . . He thought the Fijian the most loyal citizen anywhere. (loud applause)" (*Fiji Times And Herald,* 4 Sept.). His most extended comments concerned Indian political aspirations directly:

He thought the Indians of this Colony were entitled to some representation. The large body of Indians were all right, but it was the few leaders that caused all the trouble and wanted equal rights. Well, they had them now. (Hear, hear). There was one law for all, but if the Indians meant that the body of Indians should be treated with social equality, then he was on the other side. He had no desire to start strife, but when this question was raised by Indian agitators he could not remain silent. Was the future to have in store for them what he read in a local paper . . . where a meeting was called to prevent the Government moving Mr. Chowla to Savu Savu (laughter). If the employees of any local company did such a thing they could imagine what would happen. (Applause). He never heard of such audacity.

The reference to Chowla here is notable, because Chowla was a leader of the Indian Reform League. The meeting pushing the government not to dispatch him to a backwater advanced moderate, not radical, Indian interests. But Scott made no distinction, disliking all Indian leaders, blaming the moderates in particular for "audacity." His rhetoric reflected more of the earlier than the later Indian problem—his main concerns were the audacity of Indians as employees and the prospect of spending public money on Indians, even letting Indians share in Fiji's social institutions. In the questioning, when asked if Indians should be allowed to use Suva's public baths, he again replied that "he himself would not stand for social equality with the Indians. 'That's my opinion in a nutshell,' declared the candidate, among long and continued applause."

Scott thus demonstrated that anti-Indian remarks were popular with the voters. On 5 September Mr. Henry Marks, C.B.E., spoke, and Town Hall was filled again. Like Scott, Marks addressed questions of public spending on Indians, but more stridently, arguing that "the Indians wanted everything for nothing" (*Fiji Times and Herald,* 6 Sept.), that they should be offered fewer services and be made to pay more taxes. He was against including the Indians under such laws as the Workman's Compensation Act: "An Indian would go a long way towards killing himself for the sake of 5 pounds a week. (Applause)." Such remarks were afterthoughts, however, to the first half of his speech, addressed directly to Indian aspirations and the new Letters Patent:

He had no hesitation in saying that the King had been wrongly advised in giving them the amended constitution. (Applause).

This Colony had been sacrificed to pacify India (loud applause). In providing the machinery to elect three Indian members they had been manufacturing a whip to flog themselves with. He could see they would have much trouble, and in the end the Indians would take their proper places and be nominated. (Applause).

We have the Indians here and we must make the best of it and teach them "we" are the Colony and not the Indians. . . .

He traced the gradual rise of the Indians in status. They did not want car drivers, clerks and interpreters. They wanted agriculturalists and not to have their gaols filled with educated criminals. He thought the Indians should be taught to read and write and then put on the land, but we did not want them as lawyers and solicitors (laughter).

The policy of the Government of giving them secondary instead of technical education was wrong and should be stopped. They should be taught to be loyal to the Empire and to work in harmony with all their fellow citizens. The Indians were being altogether wrongly directed. Ninety five per cent of them would be content to work on the land, but for agitators. (Applause). . . .

The Government was not playing the game with the Fijian. (Applause). The Fijian was being side-tracked to make room for the Indians.

Marks picked up key themes from Scott—deriding Indian aspirations, contrasting agitating Indians to loyal Fijians, worrying about expenditure on Indians, and so forth. But he described a broad racial conflict, one in which "there would be much trouble" because "the Colony had been sacrificed to pacify India." The problem was already serious, the current state already dangerous. The Indians had to be pushed back. Marks abandoned the carefully nonracist rhetorical style exemplified by the 1910s *Fiji Times* discussion of justice and "a certain gentry." He argued explicitly that the whites must "teach them 'we' are the Colony and not the Indians." The Indians were aspiring to social, political, and occupational statuses they must not be allowed to sustain, not because they were polluting things for the whites but because they were a threat. The jails would soon be full of educated criminals, and the Indians needed to be taught loyalty to empire.

The third candidate, Alport Barker, editor of the *Fiji Times and Herald*, spoke on 6 September. He also argued that Indians were getting too many services for nothing and not paying their fair share of taxes, quoting income tax figures to show that Europeans payed the vast majority of taxes. Late in his speech, he turned to "the Indian question," which, he remarked, the other candidates "had threshed out" already. On the Indian elected members, unlike Marks he thought they should be given "a fair trial," but he proposed to applause that if they were "not a success" then the Secretary of State could be asked to amend the Letters Patent in three years. (There was, in fact, a major attempt in the mid-1930s to return the Indian representation to a nomination basis, an effort that failed when the Colonial Office refused to accept it.) He also connected Indian political aspirations with indigenous Fijian political rights:

He thought the interests of the Indians however had overriden the Fijians. The Fijians had not been given a fair deal. (Applause). He told several Governors his opinion. The Fijians were the owners of the land. When we took over the country we promised to protect their interests and he did not think they were doing so. (Applause).

In the course of these three speeches, then, a new European settler-politician rhetoric developed. The Fiji European electorate, which included Fijian-European "half-castes" as well as people claiming a strictly European ancestry, was very receptive to anti-Indian politics. In these speeches a link was articulated that became the organizing theme of anti-Indian political discourse, discourse at the core of Fiji's political order this century. From indenture days Fiji Europeans had propounded Social Darwinist analyses of race conflict between the indigenous Fijians and the Indians, and even before indenture days many of them made a paternalist and romantic commitment to the cause of protecting and advancing indigenous Fijian interests. In these speeches in 1929, Fiji Indian demands for political rights were read for their implications for this supposed racial struggle, and Fiji's Europeans concluded that Indian political aspirations were a threat to indigenous Fijian rights. From roughly this point onward in Fiji's political history, every Indian political request or achievement was discussed as both a threat to the future of indigenous Fijians and a betrayal of their cession of Fiji and their loyalty to empire. The real anxiety within the new Indian problem was that the Indians were seen as a political threat to the European rulers of empire. But further suppression of their political status could be justified when they were described as a threat to the future of the indigenous Fijians.[3]

3. A similar argument was used against the Indians in Kenya in 1923 and in the Colonial Office against common roll in Fiji in 1925. Tinker (1976: 9) summarizes it as the "Guardians of a Trust" and "sons of the soil" argument, used against overseas Indians throughout the empire. This argument spreads unevenly through different domains of discourse and social analysis. For example, confidential official deliberations on whether and how to restrict free Indian immigration to Fiji concerned questions of the sex disproportion in the Indian community, since most of the free immigrants came as single males, and, in the early, depressed years of the 1930s, questions about unemployment and the usefulness of the immigrants, who were primarily Gujarati and Punjabi. Not until June 1933 was there any mention of indigenous Fijian interests in relation to Indian immigration, and not until 1936 was the argument made that Indian immigration was a threat to the future of indigenous Fijians. By September 1937, however, the "grave danger" to in-

This rhetoric was to carry great authority in later political debates. After World War II it led to reaffirmation of indigenous Fijian paramountcy in political and social matters; in the late 1960s it motivated and justified disproportionate representation, special privileges, and protections for indigenous Fijians in independent Fiji's Constitution; in the 1980s it was offered as justification for indigenous-Fijian-led coups. In 1929 and the 1930s, however, official authority still had considerable license over policy and could override popular opinion when it chose to. Not only the Indian political leaders, led by Vishnu Deo, but also J. R. Pearson reacted with anger to the content and tenor of the European candidates' speeches.

Pearson thought that the speeches aided the Arya Samaj candidates in their own election successes, that they "induced a number of wobblers to vote for the more aggressive candidate as more likely to 'keep his end up' than the moderate" (CSO 6141/29). Vishnu Deo's margin of victory was so wide that this explanation is not entirely likely. If the speeches did have an effect on the Indian politics in fact, it was probably to cement the resolve of the Indian leaders to be aggressive in the council. At a meeting in the Arya Samaj Hall after the election to congratulate Vishnu Deo, the European candidates' speeches were reported to be the principal topic of concern to both Vishnu Deo and the other speakers. Vishnu Deo himself discussed the situation in terms of the European speeches on the one hand and a message from Gandhi on the other:

In view of the message of Mahatma Gandhi that India was unable to help us until the attainments of Swaraj, Indians in Fiji should endeavor to stand on their own legs. In view of this message he, with others, had accepted the communal franchise under protest, in order that we may try and improve our condition. He was aggrieved that we were accused of asking for social equality with the Europeans. Indians did not wish, nor ask for that, but what they asked for was equal opportunity and such political rights, as had been promised them. If, he said, our cooks and dhobis are so full of evil odour with the Europeans here, why are such retained in the employ of Europeans and not told to go on the land? . . . Would things really be better for them if they left such service? He referred, also, to the remarks which were made by Dr. Sapru at the Imperial Conference, that the Indians, as subjects of the British Empire, asked for a place within the house of His Majesty the King, and that they would not be satisfied with a place in his stable.

---

digenous Fijians was the second of three reasons given the Secretary of State by the Governor to justify radical limits on free Indian immigration, the other two being that immigration by single men perpetuated the sex disproportion in the Indian community, and that the free immigrants included "an undesirable element which would be liable to ferment discontent in any period of economic stringency."

The rhetoric that stung the Indian leaders was clearly that of Marks on the proper place of Indians and the real citizenry of the colony. The Indians did not decide upon boycott as a protest of their "communal franchise" situation until a month after the election at a Round Table conference led by S. B. Patel in October (Gillion 1977: 134).[4] But Vishnu Deo was already oriented toward the issues raised in the European speeches and the need for an aggressive reply, within days of the elections themselves.

Press reporting then raised the stakes further. The quote above is from one of two accounts of the postelection Arya Samaj meeting published in Alport Barker's *Fiji Times and Herald* of 17 September 1929. This account was marked "(contributed)" and probably written by an Indian; it was as nonjudgmental of the candidate and other speakers as were the press accounts of the European candidate speeches, ending as follows: "After partaking of refreshments and singing of the Arti, the happy gathering came to a close." The other account described the meeting quite differently and ended with a vague call for action against the Indian leaders:

MEETING OF INDIANS.
At Samabula.
Cooks' Strike Proposed.

The proceedings in the Arya Samaj Hall at Samabula on Thursday night were marked by a considerable amount of violent language and angry threats.

The ostensible reason for the gathering was to congratulate Mr. Vishnu Deo on his election to the Legislative Council.

But reference to some speeches recently in the Town Hall acted as fuel to a fire and all sorts of threats of retaliation were made.

These, it is alleged by reliable witnesses, included a suggestion that the cooks come out on strike as a protest against some remarks made during the previous week.

One old Indian resident, who rose to counsel moderation, was howled down and was not allowed to speak.

It is regrettable that the extremists should run riot with words. It stirs up bitter strife and will get the Indians and their cause nowhere. Moderation in speech and action might invite sympathy, but the ranting of agitators carries no weight in Fiji.

4. This Round Table also marked the end of Beattie's Fiji Indian National Congress. The delegates of Beattie's Congress formally accepted proposals passed unanimously at the Round Table in the name of a single, united Fiji Indian National Congress. The synthesis of the two congresses was ratified at a meeting on 7 November in Suva, two days after the walkout, that also elected new officers from the ranks of both original congresses and endorsed the boycott by acclamation (CSO 289/30).

We suggest that all public matters be treated in a calm and commonsense manner, and that any fanatical declamation be squashed in its infancy.

Such press coverage was itself a subject of protest by the Indians on the Legislative Council before their walkout.

If the Indian leaders felt beseiged, J. R. Pearson felt that a crucial opportunity was slipping away. At roughly the same time that the Indian Round Table was uniting the congresses and approving the boycott strategy, Pearson was writing and circulating a long memorandum, which he entitled "A Note Prompted by Certain Ebullitions of Anti-Indian Feeling In the Hope of Suggesting an Alternative to a Policy of 'Keep Under' or 'Clear Out' " (CSO 6141/29). He sent copies first to the victorious Scott and Barker and the losing Marks, and then allowed parts of it to be published when they did not reply or even acknowledge receipt of it. In the memo Pearson asked whether the view that the Indians should be kept as menial labor "can be reconciled with the basic standards of our civilisation." In any case, he went on to argue, "the Indians are here."

4. This being so, is not the Colony now on the horns of a dilemma? Either it must foster and control the urge for advancement or it must face the consequences of the community seeking satisfaction with outside aid and with the feeling that it is being thwarted by those who might help it.

5. On a very small scale we are faced with the same problem with which British administrators in India are faced, and I feel that to a certain extent pessimism about India is at bottom of a good deal of the pessimism and what appears to me lack of courage and confidence over the Indian problem here.

Pearson cited his "30 years service" in India and quoted the "profound truth in the saying of the present Viceroy" that "come what may the English people as well as the many peoples of India had each and all an essential part to play in India's destinies. In other words the English element in India is now so necessary to the whole growth that it cannot survive without it." He proposed, with his unsound theory of the future of India, to apply the lessons of the India expert to Fiji's problems. "It must be recognized," he went on, that the Fiji Indians had "progressed in a surprising way." The Indians were rising with education. Many Indians would stay in agriculture, creating "a thriving class of yeoman farmers as the mainstay of the population," but it was also "inevitable" that the "higher grade of economic organisation" "will not in future be so completely staffed by Europeans as at present." He wrote, "We must adapt ourselves to conditions as they are." Further, the indigenous Fijians must be encouraged because they also would inevitably advance. "It is not therefore a question of a possible clash between races, but one of working together for the best interests of three." Pearson sought to replace metaphors of war with metaphors of growth, fostering, and development. The Indians could not be kept to "one dead level":

13. Now my main contention is this—that everything points to the advantages of fostering and controlling the Indian advance. . . . There is a vast amount to be done to help on the Indian community materially and over communal organisation and education in the broadest sense of the word. . . .

19. And again in the wide field of communal organisation and the development of a spirit of responsible citizenship we cannot stay where we are. Leaders must arise, and leaders who can sway the multitude with no corresponding constitutional responsibility must be a source of danger. At the present moment we have no Indians with any authority to deal with the most petty disputes among their own people, no Council of Elders recognised and therefore responsible for seeing that they find reasonable expression. Our Indian officials in the districts have considerable responsibility the exercise of which is not at all easy to control owing to the deficiency of means of direct communication between rulers and ruled. We cannot keep the population down to one dead level. Graduation must come and it is for us to see that with it comes a sense of obligation to the authority that has conferred it.

Pearson proposed a two-part model of social development. On the one hand, the Indian society was a natural organism. As Pearson argued in his conclusion to the paper, "It is much easier to handle simple relations between master and contract laborer with the feelings and instincts of a small child. We have got beyond that stage now. The child is growing up and we have got to guide his steps." On the other hand, "we have got to guide his steps"—the natural process took different directions depending on the attitude of superior agencies toward it. This is a variation on the characteristic attitude of British political culture (see chapter 3); rather than "justice extended to the coolie," order descending pure and simple, here growth from below could be managed from the top down. When the inevitably developing society was raised like a growing child, then the leadership of the colonized society was obliged to the superior authority, the authority conferring new powers and privileges. This, Pearson believed, was the state of social fact in India and a state of affairs Fiji should seek. Because social advancement in the Indian community was inevitable, British authority should confer it in order to control it.

Pearson proposed a radically different course for Fiji's policy toward Indian political voices. However, in late 1929, after writing this memo, he departed Fiji on an eight-month leave of absence. He turned over the office of Secretary for Indian Affairs to Dr. Victor McGusty, a Fiji-trained colonial officer, on the very day that the new Legislative Council first met. Pearson left copies of his memorandum with McGusty, "in case it is considered of any value." But from the minutes in its file, the Governor was less interested in its contents than in the fact that Pearson had allowed parts of it to be published (anonymously, in Beattie's journal *Vriddhi*). The Governor queried the Colonial Secretary, who replied that he had not given Pearson permission, and on Pearson's return he was directed to the regulations restricting such publishing without permission. The Governor noted that he "in no way criticized the attitude taken up by Mr. Pearson," but neither did he endorse it. He simply required that the regulations controlling official discourse be "strictly observed," "a salutory safeguard against the possibility of unopportune or unwise statements on policy being published." The public discourse even of *European* electoral politics was not to be engaged directly, even anonymously, by policymakers without approval from the highest level. The distance between voices with power and those without it was to be maintained, the privilege of official communications preserved.

When Pearson went on leave, he had little inkling of the impending boycott and high hopes for the impact of Indian representation to the Legislative Council on policy. Late 1929 was also a time of official debates on reform of Indian marriage law (detailed in chapter 7); at the conclusion of a defense of Indian "personal law" in marriage against an attack by Fiji's Attorney General, written just before he went on leave, Pearson wrote that the reform "is preeminently one which should be referred to a committee of the Legislative Council on which the elected Indian members can sit" (CSO 3296/29). The walkout mooted his hopes, and for the crucial months of the opening of the boycott, Pearson was not a factor in government deliberations. His temporary replacement, Dr. McGusty, very much reflected Fiji's previous official line.

Boycott and Reaction

In November 1929 Vishnu Deo and the other Indian representatives asked a long series of questions in the Legislative Council concerning Indian rights, privileges, and standing in Fiji. The questions were designed to address Indian grievances by revealing inequities in colonial society at a moral plane. The same moral grounding for Indian political speech had organized his Town Hall election speech on 1 September (pamphlet version in CSO 6141/29), days before all the European speeches and a month before the boycott strategy was adopted by the Fiji Indian National Congress. Equality, he argued, was a matter of justice and right. Even in accepting an "inequitous" communal franchise system in order to run for Legislative Council he felt that he was committing a "sin."[5] He concluded:

Having so committed the sin, I feel that it is now incumbent upon me to suffer penance by offering myself as a candidate for the continuance of our constitutional fight to secure fulfillment of pledges of equality given us from time to time and to achieve our goal, namely EQUAL CITIZENSHIP THROUGHOUT THE BRITISH EMPIRE AND FREEDOM IN INDIA. [emphasis in original]

What the Fiji Europeans heard in September in Town Hall and in November in Legislative Council was not moralizing over injustices and "humiliation," and certainly not the self-doubt behind the self-righteousness as *swaraj* (self-rule) advocates tried to imagine how to achieve a nonhumiliating, respectable form of citizenship. They did not accept the declarations made by Vishnu Deo and others that the Fiji Indians had no desire to dominate in Fiji. The Indians would not accept as a premise that racial equality and empire were incompatible, and that empire came first; what the Fiji Europeans therefore heard, in all the Indian political speech, was an international war on empire. In the days before the beginning of the boycott, S. B. Patel visited several European politicians and officials, explaining the principle that the Indians wanted formal equality in an electoral common roll even without any effective political power, that they would not protest if franchise restrictions severely limited the number of Indian voters or candidates so long as the restrictions applied generally and voting was not separated by race. The answer Patel received, as he reported it to his London correspondent H. S. L. Polak, was that it was a matter of empire and imperial precedents. Hedstrom was most explicit: "Sir Maynard Hedstrom told me frankly that the Kenya Europeans have fought and were fighting their battle for them to keep the Indians off the common roll, and the Fiji Europeans would have to keep themselves in line with the Kenya Europeans and fight tooth and nail" (quoted in Gillion 1977: 136).

Thus the Indians arranged their boycott, seeking dignity and trying to make a moral statement, against Europeans explicitly preparing to "fight tooth and nail." In Legislative Council on 5 November Vishnu Deo moved "that Indians in Fiji should be given Common Franchise

5. The moral pressure on Vishnu Deo was not only in his imagination. As Gillion (1977: 133) describes, a prominent Fiji Indian named Chattur Singh visited London in 1928 and brought back to Fiji a stern warning from H. S. L. Polak, the Secretary of the Indians Overseas Association, that Fiji Indians could not accept a communal franchise without compromising themselves and other overseas Indians.

along with other British subjects resident in the Colony." He said (CSO 289/30):

I wish to make it quite clear that we have no desire to dominate, we do not wish to impose our civilisation, and we have no desire to deprive the Fijian native of his rights and of his liberties. We want to remain in Fiji and we want to see British justice meted out to all her citizens.

European responses to the motion did not address the issue of justice but took issue with two Indian claims—first, that Indians had been for fifty years "sacrificing their all in making Fiji what it is to-day," and second, that indigenous Fijian interests would not be harmed. To the first, Maynard Hedstrom retorted that most of the Fiji Indians "came from the Calcutta streets," in "utter poverty," taking advantage of Fiji to "better their lot":

When you think of those people coming off those steamers, with not five rupees per head among them, and then think of one of the same race in the Colony saying they "sacrificed their all" in making Fiji what it is to-day, it gives cause for laughter.

To the second, Hedstrom repeated the principle, fast becoming a cornerstone of Fiji politics, that Indian aims and intentions toward indigenous Fijians did not matter, that it was a betrayal of cession for Indians to gain any political power in Fiji; "the Fijians would inevitably, naturally, and bitterly resent any transfer of authority from the British race to the Indian race." Finally, newly reelected Sir Henry Scott contributed another theme to the official response to the Indian motion:

We should not come to this Council and theorise on abstract principles for the glorification of the personal wish of a few—and I advisedly use that word "few"—people who have come here and wish to make a name for themselves politically. I personally do not believe that this movement was started in Fiji. I refuse to believe that this movement has the support of the majority of the Indians in Fiji. But I do believe that it is a movement that has been studiously considered and brought over from India by certain emissaries. These emissaries are now living here, not for the betterment of the Indian community, but for their own aggrandisement, political and otherwise. I oppose the motion. (Applause).

The motion was then opposed by all members of council apart from the Indians, and the Indians walked out.

Fiji had to report upon the incident to the Colonial Office and determine its own course of action in reply. We have already quoted, at the outset of the section, the Governor's estimation of the Indian motives—following Scott, a picture of a worldwide attack on the British Raj—

which was included in his despatch of 1 February 1930 reporting on the situation. McGusty, in Pearson's place, had the job of more fine-tuned observing and advising, and he wrote a series of summary memoranda on the subject. In the first, in an echo of government investigations of indenture days, he began by disparaging the characters of the three Indian representatives:

2. The personal particulars of the candidates are not without interest. Mr. Vishnu Deo is an ex-civil servant who was dismissed on account of his having embezzled public funds. He is therefore a vigorous opponent of the Government. Mr. Ramchander Maharaj, prior to 1916, served two sentences, each of six months imprisonment. . . . He is the most moderate of the three ex-members, though his lack of character has caused him to form a close association with the other two. The third ex-member, Mr. Parmanand Singh, was employed as bookkeeper by an Indian merchant who mysteriously lost a large sum of money.

Then he went on to propound the Fiji government's consensus explanation: "At an early stage in my relations with them it became clear to me that the Indian elected members were activated by influences from outside the Colony." They did not really represent the Fiji Indians:

At the present time, the Indian nationalist party have succeeded in establishing a temporary influence over the so-called educated Indians in Fiji, by pretending to interpret the communal franchise as a racial indignity. Unfortunately it is almost impossible to voice the opinions of the great majority of Indians, and particularly of the tenant farmers, who are a contented people without political knowledge or ambition.

In the report of the eager McGusty, the European urge to suppress Indian "political knowledge or ambition" produced multiple layers of denial: the educated Indians were not the real Indians, but their education was only "so-called." The nationalists were not interpreting communal franchise as a racial indignity, they were "pretending to interpret" it so. Behind their moral declarations lay strategic connivance befitting such "lack of character."

McGusty's estimations came in the midst of dialogues local and international in the weeks and months following the beginning of the boycott, contesting its meaning and especially its relation to the "mass" of Fiji Indians. Scott had "refused to believe" that the majority of Fiji Indians supported boycott; Fletcher's letter to the Colonial Office called the "articulate element" a "very small minority" and declared that "the local Indian in the mass is ignorant and unintelligent, but he is prosperous and so contented, and he cares little for abstract political theories." McGusty worked to find and promote spokesmen within the Indian community to combat the influence of the untrustworthy nationalists. For a December 1929 conference at Government House, the Indians he invited either did not show or sided with the boycotters (the latter group including John Grant of the Reform League and Sahodar Singh, an editor from Beattie's press). In his memo on the conference (CSO 289/30), McGusty regretted that "the true voice of the Indian community was silent":

> If I had succeeded in my efforts to produce a farmer or other Indian with independent views, it is certain that Mr. Patel and his associates would have attacked him in force beforehand, and so bewildered him with their arguments about race and rights, that he would have come to the conference utterly voiceless as far as his true opinions were concerned.

In later memos he noted with hope a growing split between the Arya Samaj and the Christian and Muslim Indians. In January Christians and Muslims resigned from the Suva branch of the National Congress, the Christians at least led by John Grant. Muslims at a meeting in Nausori petitioned the governor to grant them a separate Muslim representative to the Legislative Council.[6] McGusty counseled Christian leaders in their efforts to oppose the Samajis politically and advised the government to consider giving the Muslims separate representation and other special privileges. In response, in March 1930 a meeting of the Fiji Indian National Congress passed and publicized an "emphatic protest" over the government's rumored intention to nominate an Indian to the Legislative Council and called "upon every Indian to refuse to accept nominative seats in the said council." No appointment was attempted. The congress also resolved, "Whereas efforts are being made by few self interested individuals to misrepresent Indian public opinion and thereby to force the unanimously rejected racial franchise on the Indian Community, this Public Meeting reiterates its unanimous opinion that no settlement other than the recognition of Indians' right to common franchise is acceptable to the Indian citizens of the British Empire . . ." (CSO 289/30).[7] To this the government published the Colonial Secretary's official reply, that "the Government is not aware of the alleged misrepresentation of Indian public opinion" and that the congress itself misrepresented the unanimity of Indian citizens of the empire, that "in certain parts of the Empire certain sections of the Indian community strongly resist a common franchise and demand a communal roll."

6. For more on these events see chapter 8.

7. At the same meeting, a third resolution was also passed, criticizing a rumored government intention to exclude English from Indian primary schools. The resolution "urgingly requests the Government to be so good as to include English as one of the compulsory subjects in all Primary and assisted Schools established and to be established throughout the colony." See the second section of chapter 7.

The dispute was raised in the Legislative Assembly in India. An Indian member referred to the December conference as a "Round Table" and asked if the Indian government was aware of "the fact that the Indian community in Fiji have unanimously asked for a common roll?" The Government replied that "so far as Government are aware, the demand for common electoral roll has the support of the bulk of the Indian community in Fiji." Asked what steps it had taken and would take to support the quest for common roll, the reply was that "Government are giving most careful consideration to this matter, and are not losing sight of it." Copies of the exchange were sent to Fiji and are also in CSO 289/30, with a memo attached from Pearson noting that "actually the bulk of the population are very little concerned about the matter." In 1930 and 1931 communal roll was still under protest in Kenya as well as Fiji. A June 1930 Colonial Office white paper named common roll voting as an objective for future Kenyan government, but a 1931 London parliamentary joint committee inquiry decided against it; in between, Kenyan elections in May 1931 had the same results as Fiji's of 1929, election of so-called noncooperators who boycotted their seats. India, both official and public, was still "concerned" about both cases but was concerned much more immediately by its own confrontations, as Gandhi's salt march opened new possibilities for contestation at home.

Official India was more willing to believe in Fiji Indian political aspirations than was official Fiji. But without admitting widespread dissatisfaction among its Indians, official Fiji became uncomfortably aware of the limits of its own knowledge of Fiji Indian affairs. McGusty boasted in a December 1929 memo, "I have personal experience and knowledge of the Indians in every part of the Colony," but by February 1930 he also urged the development of better intelligence gathering on the Indian "extremists." Because "Ghandi" [sic] advocated noncooperation, he wrote (CSO 289/30), the government should expect "that the agents of Indian nationalism will make renewed efforts to promote discord in Fiji." Therefore it was "extremely important that the Government should have first-hand information concerning the movements of the local extremist leaders." His concern led to the organization of an Intelligence Committee, whose first meeting took place in September 1930.

Pearson returned mid-1930, and it was he, not McGusty, who sat as SIA on the new Intelligence Committee. Reviewing McGusty's memoranda on the political situation, Pearson was skeptical. In his third memo McGusty confidently declared that the goals of the boycott amounted to "political domination of the colony by Indians."[8] Pearson

8. This quotation, and quotations from Pearson below, are from CSO 289/30.

wrote, "I doubt whether the designs of the party which engineered the boycott are quite so sinister as Dr. McGusty makes out, and 'Indian nationalism' for India itself can now hardly be stigmatised as extremism." Pearson was more concerned about the fact that Fiji was beginning to see Indian religious and factional controversies of the sort much feared in 1920s India. By then the serious efforts at Hindu *sangathan* ("consolidation") organization had begun, in Rewa near Nausori, the locus of the Muslim break from the congress.

Hindu-Muslim conflicts particularly worried Pearson, and he wrote another lengthy memorandum, this one concerning sectional conflict in general. In it he argued that it was "a grave mistake to ascribe the trouble solely to" particular Indian leaders and societies. "The societies are symptoms, not causes," symptoms of "progress." For Pearson it was always a matter of a social evolution, an evolution to be managed properly or improperly. He therefore argued for quick and active intervention in Indian sectional affairs by European authorities, especially judicious mediation of disputes as they arose. He saw no government interest in promoting sectional schisms. Rather, "early checking of mischievous tendencies is what is needed," as the potential for harm was great, while with proper guidance, all the societies could be beneficial, even the Arya Samaj. Despite the fact that "it seems to rely for its appeal on its militant attitude towards other religions and its advocacy of an ardent and uncompromising Hindu nationalism," Pearson had great hopes for its influence:

Climate and conditions in Fiji appear to exercise a sedative effect on these missionaries. Several who have come out full of missionary zeal have now settled down as quiet and peaceable workers in the educational field, following the example of the best disciples of the sect, who have done much for the educational cause in Northern India.

Pearson's estimation of the Arya Samaj was answered by McGusty, indirectly but effectively, in early 1931. A confidential report reached Suva from the Lautoka District Commissioner in December 1930, when the boycott of the Legislative Council was still ongoing, that two mysterious Europeans were "operating in this District," spending time with both Indians and Fijians, spreading propaganda. Official Fiji was baffled and alarmed. "It is possible that these people belong to some International Society and are paving the way to spread communism among the people and it may be worth while to make enquiry concerning them." They were Jehovah's Witnesses missionaries.

Further confidential inquiries were ordered, and Dr. McGusty was dispatched from Suva to Lautoka, as Governor's Commissioner, to investigate. In January he turned in a confidential sixteen-page report, which began by revealing the threat Fiji faced:

2. *Communist Activities.* In a confidential letter to me which was dated the 19th December, Mr. G. H. Allen, Manager at Ba of the Colonial Sugar Refining Company, stated that he had reason to believe that communistic agencies, supported by proselytising and disloyal influences of the Arya Samaj, were becoming active in the northern districts, and were intended to discredit the Government in the eyes of Fijians and Indians. Mr. Allen stated that his principal source for information, so far as it concerned the Fijians, was the Reverend A. D. Lelean of the Methodist Mission at Ba, whose opinion on such matters he considered authoritative. At about the same time a letter was received from the District Commissioner at Lautoka reporting the activities, suspected to be communistic, of two Europeans named MacGregor and Auchterloni. . . . I was afforded an opportunity of being present at an interview. . . . With fanaticism that was, I think, wholly assumed, he [MacGregor] voluntarily spoke of the aims of his Association, which he said were in no way connected with bolshevism or communism, but were essentially religious and intended to interpret and to disseminate the many prophecies of the Bible, and prepare the world for the establishment of a promised Perfect Kingdom on Earth. . . . I am satisfied that the overthrow of the old order, which is essential to the establishment of the Perfect Kingdom, cannot be effected without bloodshed, and that, however inspired the teachings of the International Bible Students Association may be, its proclaimed objects are intended to arouse distrust and hatred of the existing order, and therefore of existing forms of government, in immature minds, and in this Colony in those of the Fijians and Indians. . . . I have reason to believe that after some investigation the Arya Samaj have accepted the representatives of the International Bible Students Association and have decided that their gospel is likely to further their own ends. . . . It is hardly necessary to prove that the International Bible Students Association is using religion to cloak its communistic activities, since its teachings in their admitted form are intentionally disruptive, and I am therefore prepared to support the opinion of the District Commissioners and of all other thoughtful persons with whom I have consulted that MacGregor and Auchterloni should be deported as soon as possible, and quite definitely before their activities can achieve what is assumed to be their immediate purpose, namely, to cause industrial disturbances at the time when the Sugar Mills are expected to commence the season's operations.

Thus were two representatives of the Watchtower Bible and Tract Society depicted as they tried to pamphleteer in Fiji. In fact they never were deported; they eventually gave up and left after failing to interest either the Indians or the indigenous Fijians in their apocalyptic Christian message. But their effect on the Indian community was in another sense much more lasting: in response to their appearance, the organization of government information-gathering on Indian affairs was completely transformed.

McGusty's report, while beginning with their "communist activities," then turned to:

3. *Arya Samaj activities.* The activities of this body in Fiji are undoubtedly far more political than religious. Its object is not merely to work in sympathy with Indian nationalism, but to prepare the way to convert Fiji into an Indian colony with a wholly Indian administration. The influence of the Arya Samaj is naturally strong in the northern districts, where a large Indian population is closely knitted together by good transport facilities. I have been told that the future Indian administrators of the Colony have already been chosen in secret; that Raghvanand, a clerk and interpreter, is Indian Governor elect, and that theatrical meetings of our future administrators are secretly held. Foremost among the active adherents of the Arya Samaj are some of the Government clerks, and in this connection the names of Raghvanand, the Secretary of the body, Gujadir Singh and Chowla were particularly mentioned. It should be noted that Raghvanand was recently granted leave for the ostensible purpose of winding up the estate of his father, the late Badri Mahraj, and that his time is said to be devoted to Arya Samaj matters rather than to his own affairs. . . . A confidential report from the Colonial Sugar Refining Company might throw some light on this matter. The obvious value to the Arya Samaj of a close association with clerks and interpreters should now be met by an open recognition of the political aims of the Arya Samaj, and the discountenancing of any active participation in it by Government officials. . . .

With regard to their influence on the Fijians . . . efforts are being made to promote association . . . by spreading insidious suggestions of over taxation of Fijians . . . [and] by using every available opportunity to discredit the system of native administration. Efforts to proselytise are still in their infancy. The danger of this constant stream of propaganda, more remote than immediate, is its effect on the untutored mind of the Fijian . . . and the certainty that any disruptive internal movement in the Fijians will be encouraged and used by the Arya Samaj to the best advantage.

The Arya Samaj influences, while they must always be regarded as an unknown quantity, and therefore as a power to be reckoned with, are probably less momentous than they were a year ago. The efforts of the Patels [not, in fact, connected with the Arya Samaj] and other leaders to promote Indian unity have been unsuccessful, and to the Muslim opposition has now been added that of the orthodox Hindoo, who regards their activities with undisguised suspicion. Furthermore the tranquilising influence of prosperity, for Indians have not yet participated in the general depression, and particularly the contentment of a very large body of cane farms present problems which will largely continue, under existing conditions, to perplex the agitator. 'Divide et impera.'

McGusty's report constituted the Arya Samaj as, pure and simple, an enemy to the European government, an organization to be thwarted. Efforts to unite the Indian community, especially those led by the Patel barristers, were presumed to be connected to a secret Arya Samaj plot to replace the colonial government with an Indian hegemony. They were to be frustrated and defeated by a "divide and conquer" strategy, keeping the Indian community disordered—exactly the opposite of Pearson's hope of increasing organization through government tutelage.

McGusty's report, after going on to discuss the latest rumors concerning Apolosi Nawai, a Fijian "agitator," turned to recommendations for future action. McGusty had visited the District Commissioners' conference, and found them lamentably uninformed about the conspiracies under their noses. He therefore recommended that steps be taken to free them for more community work and community observation. He recommended, next, that a more formal and efficient intelligence service be instituted, principally through the constabulary. Raghvanand should be forced to resign from the Arya Samaj, and Indian clerks generally should be forbidden to participate in politics. Further, the clerks should be instructed to furnish monthly reports on "the Indian situation" to their "Superior officers," reports which "are unlikely to provide information of any intrinsic value but which may be useful as a guide in estimating the fidelity of the clerks." All packages entering the colony sent to people "whose integrity is not obvious or established" should be searched to prevent the introduction of seditious literature, "which is undoubtedly entering the Colony." Finally, McGusty recommended that suspicious immigrants be scrutinized more carefully and not be allowed to land in Fiji "until they have established the fact that they are not associated with any subversive movements."

Within a month, virtually every bit of conspiracy data unearthed by McGusty was found to be groundless gossip by the very authorities whose powers he sought to strengthen. Such figures as the missionary Lelean and the CSR official Allen (who had transported McGusty around the west during his investigation) were regarded by the police as "alarmists," Allen in particular known to be "obsessed" with fears of Indian revolutionaries in Fiji. Constabulary investigations found all the allegations to be hearsay. The Watchtower missionaries were what they claimed to be, missionaries. There was no further evidence of an Indian secret government. Indians, Pearson determined, were uninterested in the Watchtower materials, which they regarded as still more Christian propaganda. But while the report was found to lack substance, the very uncertainties it had raised fomented an intelligence crisis in the Fiji government. Every one of its recommendations, except the deportations and perhaps the extra screening of arrivals, was accepted and implemented within a few months of its writing.

In early 1931 all Indian clerks were forced to resign from all "sectional associations." The Reform League alone was excepted, because Pearson saw it "as of the nature of a social club." Pearson was not happy to be ordering the resignations. He wrote of one clerk, "I know myself that he has been instrumental at times in getting these Societies to adopt a moderate and reasonable attitude." But the higher authorities of the Fiji government wanted the clerks' loyalty undoubtable. The Governor, in particular, was alarmed to find that only one of his District Commissioners could speak Hindi, "with the result that the D. C. is largely in the hands of his Indian clerks—a position which must be remedied. . . . I understand that Indian clerks stay for long periods in one post, and it would appear to be high time to have a general change round." Their moderate influence and their role as political mediators was to be tightly constrained, in the siege mentality of the new Indian problem. In the course of the year, a clerk intervened and pleaded for calm during a particularly stormy debate in Suva between Arya Samaj and Sanatan Dharm leaders. He was observed doing so by the police, and he was reprimanded and told not to involve himself in sectional affairs again.

The clerk who had to bear the most suspicion was Raghvanand, the son of Badri Maharaj. Both the Governor and the Colonial Secretary were anxious to force his resignation from the Arya Samaj, and he did indeed resign, despite Pearson's observation that he had been "instrumental in stopping the headquarters organisation of the Arya Samaj from embarking on the 'sangathan' movement, which has been giving us so much trouble in Rewa." The Colonial Secretary minuted that Raghvanand, "though openly friendly with the European is, I am convinced, secretly and violently anti-European. I have for a long time thought that his activities should be curbed by transfer to a remote province but immediately upon his transfer to Savu Savu [clearly, the intended graveyard of troublesome Indian clerks] being ordered he found the pretext of his father's estate to remain on Vitilevu where he is the central figure in the Arya Samaj movement." After McGusty's report, in which he figured so prominently, Raghvanand's leave was terminated, his resignation from sectional societies forced, and his activities closely monitored for years. He was even rejected in his application for approval as an Indian Marriage Officer, to conduct marriages "according to Vedic Dharm." Despite his Brahman status, his fathers' having been licensed, and Pearson's intercession on his behalf, he was denied the license on order of the Colonial Secretary.

Apart from the new treatment of clerks, the most important result of the McGusty report was the new intelligence apparatus. Perceived Indian threats dominated the business of the new Intelligence Committee, and its information-gathering was elaborated and routinized. It coordinated a series of intelligence-gathering procedures, including the Indian clerk reports and reports of constables, the efforts of the Postmaster to intercept seditious materials, and the monitoring of the Indian vernacular press by the Inspector of Indian Schools, the Rev. A. W. McMillan. The interception of seditious materials never worked particularly well, because the postal staff was incompetent to read the materials arriving in multiple Indian languages. Further, as time went on, in cases of both imported and local Indian vernacular press accounts the Fiji authorities had great difficulty in deciding what was seditious. The Exports and Imports Control Ordinance of 1920 gave the Governor broad powers to prohibit importation of goods, and in 1922, after the Indian strikes, the Governor gazetted a proclamation of his intention to prohibit goods with any words, marks, or designs of a seditious nature, or of a nature calculated, in the opinion of the Governor, to disturb the peace and good order of the Colony," an intention to interdict symbols of Indian nationalism at the border (CSO 2868/22). But censoring news was a more complex matter; sedition laws required that materials be false to be considered seditious, but much of what the Intelligence Committee wished to interdict and censor was, unfortunately, true— news accounts of nationalist successes in India. In 1931 a new sedition ordinance was drafted and passed, making the definition of seditious materials depend only upon the "intention" of the writer, covering both "seditious libel" and other "seditious acts."[9]

When asked if he could provide press summaries, Rev. McMillan had queried whether his reports should deal with interreligious matters principally, or with general matters. In response he was given a broad charter to report on "inter-communal and inter-religious relationships, alleged grievances of Indians, criticisms of Government, the nature of comments made in the vernacular papers on the political situation in India, Round Table conferences, etc., and in fact anything which appears in the local Indian press likely to give D.C.C. [the District Commissioners' Council] information as to what Indians in the Colony are thinking, and doing." Over time McMillan became an influential member of Fiji's official community of Indian experts. As we shall see, his press reports played a critical role in Vishnu Deo's downfall.

In sum, a new discourse on "the Indian problem" emerged in 1929 in Fiji's electoral politics and found its way into official dialogues also. In the first arena, a rhetoric welding Indian political aspirations to betrayal

9. The Ordinance defined "seditious intention" very broadly to include everything from calls to arms against empire to efforts "to raise discontent or disaffection among His Majesty's subjects," or even "to promote feelings of ill-will and hostility between different classes or races of such subjects." The largest-scale use of this ordinance was not to come until World War II, when many Indian newspapers were shut down, most notably *Fiji Samachar* after it reported on the Fiji Indian Round Table that decided upon Indian noncooperation in the war effort.

of indigenous Fijian interests was developed to protect European interests and mask an underlying fear of an Indian political threat to the Europeans. In the realm of the confidential, the latter fear was played out in a dramatic overreaction to the arrival of Watchtower missionaries. Yet the overreaction did not falsify the fear, but rather reinforced it, for it proved to the Governor and other high officials that nothing, really, was known about Indian political affairs. "It is obvious that we require a much better system of intelligence than we have at present," the Governor minuted in January 1931, and in response Indian clerks were remade into reporters, Indian public discourse was monitored. In the process, Pearson's efforts to encourage Indian moderation by building bridges between government and Indian moderates were overriden by official imperatives and perception of conspiracy and war. The experts on Indian affairs, and even those reporting on them, were to be insulated from direct involvement and contamination; Indian authorities, rather than being built up to government specification, were to be held down. It was a clear choice of McGusty's "divide et imperia" over Pearson's managed evolution, as Fiji European discourse moved from dislike of Indians and fear of Indian contamination, to antagonism toward Indian political demands, to fear of Indian politics altogether. This fear of the Indians, and this distancing strategy for dealing with them, emerged within and informed areas of law and policy well beyond intelligence-gathering, as we will now see.

Policy Debates: *Panchayats,* Education,
and Marriage Reconsidered

Unfortunately for the European authorities, increased information-gathering could not solve the problem underlying their administrative ignorance of Indian affairs. As was detailed in chapter 4, the Indians had withdrawn from the administrative institutions of European colonial society. In February of 1930, ten months before the Watchtower panic, three months after the Legislative Council boycott, just when the *sangathan* ("consolidation") controversies were beginning to arise in Rewa, while Pearson was on leave and Dr. McGusty was acting SIA, McGusty noted the problem in a major administrative memorandum (CSO 553/30):

> It is a remarkable fact that with the increase of the Indian population and its dispersal throughout the Colony principally in groups or settlements, no co-ordinating system has evolved or been introduced with the object of bringing Indians into direct contact with the administration.
>
> 2. The European population is literate and accustomed, through the press and other agencies, to keep in touch with administrative matters that are relevant to its interests. The still communally living Fijian has a very direct line of communication which passes successively through his village headman, Buli, and Roko or Provincial Commissioner to the Native Department. But practically the only agency of contact between the Indian community and the administration is the Constabulary.

The Indian withdrawal, a fact of the 1920s, was a problem needing a solution in 1930. This chapter will first trace out the reconsiderations about Indian administration launched by this memorandum, then consider new debates on education and marriage laws.

Panchayats

In indenture, the agents of contact between government and Indians had been the Inspectors of Immigrants. But after indenture, McGusty's memo argued, there was a "break in their contact with the administration," which now had to be "repaired."

McGusty described, in a bit of political anthropology, the development of the rural Indian communities as he understood them. "Naturally," following "the gregarious instinct," the Indians scattered on their plots of land formed communities "as the topography of their settlement permits, and in each community a local esprit de corps develops." He then noted the existence of what the Indians called *bara admi*, "big men": "There are, I believe, in some of these Indian communities headmen who generally attain that position by virtue of some personal influence, which is generally a religious one." These individuals were often made use of to suit the "convenience" of local administrators, but it was time, McGusty thought, for official recognition and "centralising organisation" through "a system of village or community headmen."

Fiji Indian leaders often imagined a rural organization based on *panchayats* empowered to arbitrate disputes. Badri Maharaj, in perhaps the last effort of his political career, wrote to the government in July 1930 suggesting that the time had come for official *panchayats*, now that Fiji had a Secretary for Indian Affairs with experience in India to oversee the institutions (CSO 1895/30). However, it was McGusty's call for headmen, not Maharaj's request for *panchayats*, that began a long deliberative process which resulted in 1932 in the chartering of what is still the only institution of rural government for Indians in Fiji: District Advisory Committees.

McGusty imagined a headman who would mainly be an information conduit. He would instill community spirit, communicate all essential administrative matters, and bring matters of community welfare to the attention of government authorities. He would report crimes but would have no police powers. In the plan of this Fiji-trained officer, these Indian headmen would perform functions markedly similar to those of the government-appointed headmen of indigenous Fijian villages, the *turaga ni koro*. McGusty's memorandum was well received by the Colonial Secretary and the Governor. The Colonial Secretary noted that Pearson had been attempting to devise some sort of organizational scheme for the rural Indians but had gotten "little encouragement." McGusty, however, "has now placed his finger on the real needs of the Indian community."[1]

1. These quotations, and all others until the end of this section, come from CSO 553/30.

McGusty's memorandum was circulated to the District Commissioners, most of whom were skeptical. Money was a primary concern of the Rewa District Commissioner, who saw the offices as either inherently corrupt, if supported by Indian contributions, or as a drain on government funds. Further, he doubted that headmen could be found in Rewa, scene of building *sangathan* ("consolidation") controversy, who would be acceptable to all communal factions. The DC Navua claimed that Inspectors of Immigrants used to try to appoint and use headmen, but "the experiment was unsuccessful owing to the difficulty in obtaining reliable men." He could see the value they would have, but "I do not think the necessary material is available at the present time." The DC Nadi agreed that "the right material" did not exist and noted that scattered, unclustered settlement would made boundaries difficult. Payment by community would make the office a focus of favoritism and further strife, and payment by government "would probably lead to an unwarranted assumption of authority by the recipient," a delegation which he, along with the other DCs, was loath to make. The DC of Lautoka, home of Allen and much of the CSR officialdom, suggested that CSR overseers themselves played much of the role suggested; "I have found a number of these overseers helpful to the administration of certain matters especially in distribution of information to the people." The DC Ra, who had also minuted against Maharaj's *panchayat* plan as he passed the request on to the central government, thought simply that the headman scheme "will surely lead to failure" because of the "isolated tiny settlements . . . different castes and religions, coupled with lack of education and lack of sportsmanship."

By the time opinions were gathered, Pearson was back, and the matter was turned over to him in mid-1930 for comments and suggestions. Pearson agreed with McGusty that action was advisable, quoting the paragraph of his memo against Scott and Marks on the inevitability of the rise of Indian leaders. "We risk the springing up of irresponsible leaders among the Indian community. . . . Citizenship must come in the circumstances of the Colony in the local field before it comes in the political field." Pearson solicited McMillan's opinion, raising the possibility of *panchayats* instead of headmen, and McMillan endorsed the *panchayat* option. McMillan stressed the value of plural councils to check the authority of individuals and suggested that special efforts be made to include Christian Indians and Indian schoolteachers on the *panchayats* selected. Anticipating his role as vernacular press monitor, he included in his note a quotation from *Fiji Samachar* praising the tolerance of the Indian Christian community (while criticizing the political agitation of the Muslims). Finally McMillan suggested that, especially while the

Indians were boycotting the Legislative Council, overarching district Advisory Councils could be constructed from the *panchayats* to represent the Indian community generally. McMillan was vague concerning the functions to be undertaken by *panchayats* and Advisory Councils, as was Pearson. But Pearson chose a clear direction, toward delegation of "petty functions of a statutory nature," even "actually empowering individual panchayats to settle petty disputes." "We cannot continue to keep an adolescent community indefinitely in leading strings," Pearson concluded, "and we must sooner or later attempt to inculcate a definite sense of responsibility."

After further discussions, in August of 1930 Pearson drafted a more definite scheme. Noting that "even in Fiji there is an almost instinctive tendency towards reference of disputes to a panchayat of arbitrators," he favored a *panchayat* system. He agreed with the proposal to appoint Christians and schoolteachers whenever possible and with the concept that the principal function of the *panchayat* was information conduit. He also suggested further powers: for the members to be qualified to sign burial certificates, attest notices of marriage, register births and names of fathers in cases of illegitimate children and unregistered customary marriages, and possibly, register births and deaths in general. Further, he hoped to give the *panchayats* authority where practicable over "petty criminal complaints and civil disputes." "Powers to the local Magistrate to send cases to the Panchayat for decision might be given," Pearson argued. "I strongly recommend investigation of this possibility."

By January 1931 Pearson had toured Fiji and discussed the proposed *panchayats* with District Commissioners and sugar company officials. "Not many I am bound to say are particularly enthusiastic about the proposal," he minuted to the Colonial Secretary, "but I think they recognise that something of the nature has got to come." He proposed to start slowly, building *panchayats* first in carefully selected areas, and put up papers explaining how the program would begin. In the course of explaining the *panchayat* functions, he included an aside about "sectional societies" in general:

Religious societies do exist and must be recognised. It is in fact very important that local officers should keep in touch with local branches, and not treat them merely as alien and semi hostile bodies at bottom of most of the friction that exists. The Indian community is composed of followers of different faiths, and sects. With the general progress increased attention to tenets must develop and with it to some extent increased divergence in customs. We have got to assist the community to adjust relations to these developments and restrain the more ardent, but we cannot treat any particular sect which is sincerely devoted to its tenets as purely hostile and outside the pale. There is good and bad in every sect and it is our duty to help on the good.

These papers and this opinion were sent by the Colonial Secretary to McGusty for his views the day after McGusty filed his confidential memorandum on the Watchtower, Communist activities, and the Arya Samaj. McGusty minuted firmly against *panchayats,* arguing again for appointment of headmen, strictly for communicative purposes. The matter of headmen versus *panchayats* was discussed at the meeting of the District Commissioners—the same meeting at which McGusty revealed the secret conspiracies lurking under their noses—and, the Colonial Secretary reported to the Governor, there was more support for *panchayats* than headmen, but more fundamentally, "neither proposal met with much support." Further, "it may be said quite definitely that none of the D.C.C. [District Commissioners] envisaged the creation of a number of local *panchayats* with the functions suggested by the S.I.A. [Pearson]."

The Governor tentatively approved the headman scheme and set the matter on a February 1931 Executive Council agenda. Pearson asked for a delay, to reconsider the headman scheme himself, and was granted it. A week later he put up further papers, written by himself and others including McMillan, arguing for the superiority of the *panchayat* scheme. They emphasized the ability of *panchayats* to overcome sectional disputes by bringing sectional representatives together and the superiority of the *panchayats* as "training in the duties and responsibilities of citizenship" (McMillan). Pearson concluded:

[While] in my view the headman scheme implies another grade of petty Government official, not fully trusted as a "Government man", and probably as a self seeker, the panchayat scheme, however slowly introduced, works in the direction of combining diverse elements to work together in co-operation with the Government, with joint responsibilities towards it.

The Colonial Secretary, preparing the papers for the Governor and the Executive Council, then came out definitively on the side of McGusty and the headman scheme. In his analysis, "headmen would have no powers, statutory or otherwise, but would have certain duties to perform, panchayats would be invested with certain powers and would perform practically the same duties." The headman system had advantages:

3. The Government will not be committed to a scheme, the effects of which cannot easily be foreseen.
4. It will not raise hopes amongst the politically minded of the establishment of a form of Indian self-government.

Fiji's higher authorities argued from their fear of Indian culture, the same fear displayed earlier (and we shall soon see, contemporaneously) in debates on Indian marriage laws. They disliked schemes articulate with Indian forms, "the effects of which cannot easily be foreseen." And in the post-Watchtower atmosphere, the "politically minded" Indian was simply to be thwarted.

The Executive Council met, considered the question, and appointed a committee of McGusty, McMillan, and Pearson to meet together and plan a system for the creation of experimental advisory boards. In July 1931 the group proposed a scheme to create boards to be called "district *panchayats*" but to have strictly advisory functions on a district-size scale. Pearson still hoped for the development of local *panchayats* with more concrete functions, to be subsidiary to these district advisory groups, and noted, "I am anxious that this development should be kept in view."

The plan was then discussed at a meeting of the District commissioners, chaired by the Governor. The District Commissioners approved the plan, but only after several insisted with the support of McGusty that the *panchayats* not be allowed to hear disputes and that their authority be constituted as strictly advisory. The Governor concurred, but only after lowering the term of appointment from two years to twelve months and changing the name of the bodies from *panchayats* to "Indian Advisory Committees." These Indian Advisory Committees became the basis of rural Fiji Indian government. Pearson's hope that they could become coordinated with local *panchayats* never materialized. However, their membership did eventually become elected, and informal ties were established between the committees and local religious and labor organizations when their leaders were elected to the committees. It was not so easy in 1932. In early 1932 the first Indian Advisory Committee was constituted, in Rewa, consisting of men of property from the various subdivisions of the Indian community. No one connected with the Rewa *sangathan* movements and no one identified as an Arya Samaj member was appointed. The Muslim representative was one of the signed complainants against the *sangathan* organizers.

Education

In education policy, again, official efforts to sponsor responsible Indian social improvement conflicted with efforts to constrain the Indian community and thwart its agitating leaders, but here the results were different.[2]

2. These events in Fiji are similar in some respects to debates in India after the events of 1857. Then also, colonial policymakers had second thoughts about the advisability of ad-

We have already seen that in their campaign rhetoric the elected Europeans were implacable foes of government spending on Indian education. Further, even if the world depression did not seriously affect the vast majority of the Fiji Indians until well into the 1930s, the Legislative Council was already concerned about finances by late 1929. After the Indian walkout it bitterly resisted efforts to spend government funds on Indian schools. When an acting Governor, A. W. Seymour, announced a program of new expenditures on Indian education, the elected Europeans not only tried to block the measures but even asked London to remove him from Fiji. Indians protested with public meetings in support of the acting Governor, and in London the new Labour Secretary of State used the occasion to snub the elected members, insist upon the expenditures, and back Seymour (who in November 1930 became Colonial Secretary to the new Governor, Fletcher). For London, Seymour's authority was itself a vital issue. Gillion quotes a Colonial Office minute: "Fiji is on its way to becoming a little Kenya—the unofficials are not yet too stout to be dealt with—we must make sure that they don't become so—on no account must Mr. Seymour be thrown to the wolves."[3] From that point onward for years, the Colonial Office countervailed against the "unofficial" wolves and pressured Fletcher and Fiji to allocate higher levels of funding for Indian education.

The language of instruction for Indian education was another area of education controversy decided in 1930–1931. It was policy, following a 1926 Education Commission recommendation, to regard English as the lingua franca of the colony and encourage instruction in English as the basis for Indian curriculum. However, the elected Europeans and the CSR officials were strongly against this, and the new Governor, Murchison Fletcher, was convinced by the arguments for Indian vernacular education. "The indiscriminate teaching of English will lead people away from their present contentment," Fletcher wrote to London in February 1930, the fourth month of Legislative Council boycott. He reproduced the image of the Indians as an agriculturalist race and announced his intention to avoid the "very costly and very tragic mistakes" of other colonies; "the mainspring of his demand for education is his determination to get away from the land" (quoted in Gillion 1977: 126). In February 1930 the Executive Council ordered the Department

---

vanced education for Indians, on the grounds that such education led Indians away from their proper place. For an interesting discussion of education policy in India see Viswanathan 1989, especially 142ff. Fabian 1986 traces a more complex colonial contest of this sort, with different results, in the Belgian Congo. See also chapter 5, note 2.

3. This quotation and the details of this debate are taken from Gillion 1977: 123–24.

of Education to prepare a curriculum in which Indian primary and secondary education was entirely conducted in the vernacular. McGusty, then acting Secretary for Indian Affairs, wrote the minute instructing the Board of Education with explicit scorn for "the insistent clamour of the political agitator for an English education."[4]

Hearing of the decision, the Indian politicians did protest. At the same March meeting in which they protested government representations of Indian opinion on the boycott, the Suva Congress Committee of the Fiji Indian National Congress passed a resolution calling for English-language Indian education. On stationery topped with an image of a spinning wheel, an image of the Indian nation as a goddess, and other key symbols of Indian nationalism, a letter to the Board of Education reported the resolution; it was signed by Vishnu Deo as President of the Suva Committee. The letter was merely acknowledged, and its resolution was not important in the continuing policy discussions.

In January 1931 (but before McGusty's Watchtower report) the Governor wrote to defend his decision to the Secretary of State:

It is no doubt true . . . that all effective education unsettles the mind at the start, but an ineffective English education tends to unsettle the recipient permanently. The Government of Fiji cannot attempt to impart a sound knowledge of English to all Fijian and Indian children, and the smattering of that language which is acquired in inefficient schools is sufficient to entice the child away from the land, while it is quite inadequate for purposes of enabling him to earn a living other than an agricultural occupation.

Fletcher was trying to effect a major policy shift. Before Fletcher, as in the report of the Education Commission in 1909, official Fiji had opposed the arguments against Indian education. But like the 1929 Fiji European politicians, and like the CSR and settler witnesses before the 1909 Education Commission, this Governor now sought to justify a policy against Indian education based on an eternal racial stratification of Fiji. Fletcher's argument inverted the relation of education to realization of human potential; denying the possibility of true education, he suggested that the efforts to educate would only "unsettle" the colonized and "entice" them away from their most satisfactory real possibility, agricultural labor. The project articulated by the commission in 1909, the hope to use education to make Indians into citizens "useful" and "trustworthy," was temporarily abandoned.

Pearson did not find out about this controversy, which went on largely in his absence, until late 1931, near the end of his time in Fiji. He then

4. This quotation and those following, until otherwise noted, are from CSO 5738/29.

wrote a long minute protesting the vernacular emphasis and suggesting on many grounds the practical and social necessity for Fiji Indians to learn English. In this instance, again, the resolution of dispute was through the fiat of the Colonial Office. The Colonial Office, Gillion reports, "stressed the advantages in spreading a knowledge of English as a second language: a higher standard of education, the bringing together of the races, and the avoidance of a situation where the Fiji Indians looked to India for all their ideas and policy. . . . If all were taught English, there would be no gap between a small English educated class and the rest of the Indian population" (1977: 127). In the interpretations of the Indian boycott official Fiji had been insisting that the bulk of the Indian population was distant from the westernized elite, and London now used that claim against them. English and the aspiration to fully educate the Indians returned to Fiji's curriculum. In this matter Pearson won out despite his minimal involvement, as a later minute from the Board of Education noted: "Mr. Pearson's views are the basis of our present Policy on Indian Education" (CSO 5738/29).

The letter from Vishnu Deo and the congress had not made a serious impact on the education policy debate. However, at last insofar as the simulation of decision-making was concerned, the petition of another Indian spokesman did. In 1928 a newly formed Suva Sanatan Dharm Sabha wrote to prominent Hindu leaders in India and requested that a "Pandit-Teacher (Vaishnav)" be sent to Fiji to "uphold the principles of Sanatan Dharm" and "to work for the Sanatan course." In late 1930 two Sanatan Dharm missionaries arrived in Fiji and became the principal opponents of Vishnu Deo and other Arya Samaj leaders in the religious debates. One of these missionaries, Ram Chandra Sharma, was cited by the Fiji Governor, in his dispatch defending his education policy, as an advocate of Indian vernacular education. According to the Governor, Ram Chandra requested that Hindi only be taught in primary and elementary schools, "up to the fourth standard," and "that English, where taught, should be taught thoroughly in separate schools."

Thus in education, as in many other matters, the Sanatan Dharm and the Arya Samaj leaders began to work at political as well as religious cross-purposes. On the *sangathan* ("consolidation") question, and specifically the anti-Muslim boycotts, Ram Chandra also took exception to Arya Samaj rhetoric and opened all his meetings to Christians and Muslims, encouraging them to attend and participate. For these and other reasons, the Fiji Arya Samaj branded the Sanatani missionaries as "traitors." We turn next to the social matter in which their disagreement was most extensively debated: marriage law.

Marriage

Debates over marriage law were the most extended and possibly the most acrimonious of all the conflicts that developed between Pearson and the rest of official Fiji. They were also the point of sharpest public cleavage between the Arya Samaj and the Sanatan Dharm. In this debate the Arya Samajis sided with the Indian Reform League and favored promoting westernizing reforms of Indian marriage law. The political emergence of the Sanatanis was connected more closely with the marriage questions than with any other public issue of the day. It would be too simple to say that the Arya Samaj and the Indian Reform League sided with Pearson, attempting to defeat the Fiji establishment on the one side and the Sanatan Dharm on the other. On marriage law the Indian reform societies sometimes allied against Pearson with the official establishment, though for reasons incongruent with each other and with official plans, leaving Pearson without any allies in his efforts to establish a moderate paternalism. The official debates were more concerned with the principles of order for colonial law than with the social relations among the Indians; the Indians' interest in gaining equality with the Europeans and authority over their own affairs needed to be articulated with their interest in resolving particular problems in the legal and "customary" forms for their social relations. We complete in this section our map of the official discursive terrain that the Indian organizers sought to penetrate.

In chapter 4 we reviewed the situation when the Neill Committee considered reforms of Indian marriage laws in 1927. Neill, the last Agent-General of Immigration, had patronized the Indian Reform League and regarded it as the voice of Indian opinion. On his arrival in 1927 Pearson inherited the problem of resolving the final details of the new ordinance the committee had decided upon, an ordinance to require that all Indian marriages be registered. He held a meeting with Indian leaders to discuss the details of the amendments, and its very constitution suggests the shift in attitude toward the Indian community. Neill had appointed two members of the Reform League as the Indian members of his commission; Pearson invited eight Indian spokesmen to his meeting, only one of whom represented the Reform League. The others were two Sanatan Dharm *pandits*, Vishnu Deo to represent the Arya Samaj, two Muslim League members, a representative of the Madras Maha Sangam (a South Indian communal society), and a representative of "the Sikh church." With their advice he set a one-year grace period for customary marriages to be registered and also made other adjustments to the proposed reforms.

More generally, Pearson made his estimation of the situation clear in his early notes on the situation (CSO 4563/27):

I would at the present juncture risk a certain amount of confusion and irregularity and even fraud in isolated cases in order to get the procedure worked and old marriages legalised. . . . The marriage scandal has continued so long and has affected the social life of the Fiji Indians so adversely that it seems urgently necessary to make every endeavor to put matters on a better footing.

He advised tabling all other reform concerns in order to push through the ordinance requiring Indian marriages to be officiated by licensed marriage officers and to be registered. The Governor noted his approval of Pearson's plans, but suggested holding the papers for the arrival of the new Attorney General, P. A. McElwaine. McElwaine arrived in early 1928. Soon after began his extended combat with Pearson.

In his first minute on the subject, McElwaine argued broadly that "it is, I think, most advisable that there should be only one law of marriage in the Colony." He was most concerned that the current law potentially allowed incestuous and polygamous marriages, and his target for repeal was the second change in Fiji's marriage law insisted upon by India in the late 1910s: the provisions respecting the "personal law" of the Indians. "I do not know how in practice the personal law can be proved in this colony as a question of fact" (CSO 4563/27). Pearson replied by suggesting that Fiji adopt a practice common in India—reliance upon Indian experts. "If a question of this nature was ever brought to the court, would it not be possible for this to be dealt with with the aid of assessors as expert advisors of the court?" (CSO 4563/27). It was a question official Fiji was not prepared to consider; it received no answer in the papers.

Pearson succeeded in dividing the reforms requiring marriage registration from the personal law issue, and the ordinances were revised in 1928. Indians had until April 1930 to register their customary marriages. In June 1928 McElwaine raised the personal law issue again, as he considered the revisions of the Letters Patent giving Indians communal electoral representation. If the Indians were to be given "a distinct share in the affairs of the Colony" then they should be "in the same position as other persons" in such matters as marriage law (CSO 2602/28). While their voting roll was to be separate, their legal forms should be the same; if they were to enter the civil society of the colony at all, it should be with adherence to European legal terms.

McElwaine pressed his position further in July 1928 in connection with a particularly scandalous case that Pearson, as Secretary for Indian Affairs, was called upon to arbitrate (CSO 3113/28). The parents of a fourteen-year-old Fiji Indian girl had a Fiji European lawyer draw up a contract between themselves and a Fiji Indian Christian man who was already married and registered as married to someone else. By the terms of the contract, they would send their daughter to "henceforth" live with the man and to marry him "according to Hindustani Custom" when she reached the legal age of fifteen, in exchange for gifts and general financial support from him for themselves. If he failed to continue to support them, they could call the girl home and the contract was void. Another European lawyer had approached Pearson on behalf of the girl and the Indian man with whom she currently resided. They claimed that her parents had agreed to have her live with him before the "higher bidder" had turned up. They wished for Pearson to override the custody laws and give permission for her to marry the man with whom she lived.

Pearson gave the petitioning couple official permission to marry and declared the later contract "both immoral and illegal." He was outraged by the practices of Fiji lawyers. Though "willing to admit that English Lawyers must find it difficult" to advise Indian clients given the "decidedly chaotic state" of parts of the Indian population, he felt "very strongly" that the English lawyers should "realise" their duty "both as professional men and as members of the race which controls the Govt. of Fiji" to help improve Indian social relations "and to avoid pandering to immoral practices." Otherwise, "the difficulties in the way of reform will be greatly increased."

In fact, what needed reform was precisely the system of manipulations that such lawyers' contracts had created, strategic manipulations employing contract forms and English authority to undermine both legal and customary marriages by playing them against each other. The lawyers' offices were not simply confronted by immoral practices, but were actually a cause of them, the instrument of many manipulations and the condition of possibility for them all. In the Fiji of the 1920s the European lawyers sold a new type of authority, used in various ways for intimidation and leverage in the Indian community especially in marriage matters. This indeed is what registration of all marriages stopped.

Upon seeing the papers and Pearson's comments the Governor wished to prosecute the European lawyer involved in the case, one "Capt. Leleu." McElwaine resisted the suggestion, however:

Capt. Leleu in preparing [the contract] possibly thought that it was a marriage agreement "in accord with the personal law of the parties." I am not disposed to think that Capt. Leleu deliberately or knowingly drew an illegal agreement. So long as sec. 43 of the Marriage Ord. stands I should be surprised at nothing which relates to Indian "Marriages." . . .

Pearson agreed with the decision not to prosecute Leleu, because he had already discussed the matter with Leleu to his own satisfaction, but replied more generally to McElwaine's argument:

The Indian law is not quite in the chaotic state the Attourney General seems to imagine. There are quite a number of English judges and barristers in India concerned with its administration. I am willing to admit it is not easy to ascertain personal law in this country.

The next confrontation came over McElwaine's final drafting of the 1928 amendments to the marriage ordinance (CSO 3167/28). Despite Pearson's and the Governor's wish for speed in the matter, McElwaine raised new questions. He was not happy with the provisions for the registration of existing marriages and complained about the "quasi-marriages" and "loose marriages" of the Indians. He also disliked a clause that allowed for the woman to be represented by a parent or guardian when marriages were registered directly before the District Commissioner. It did not protect the women, McElwaine argued, citing the case just discussed. In a naive, formalistic way he wanted the women to be heard, to enable them to express their intentions. But his real intention was not to empower women's voices so much as to control Fiji's legal forms. His horror was that the law

may put ideas of Purdah in these people's heads. So far the Purdah system with its resultant unsatisfactory Court procedure laws is not recognized in Fiji and I have no doubt the system was not introduced by the Indian Immigrant class.

"Purdah," like "suttee," was a British symbol of the bizarre and immoral in South Asian culture and a focus of reform campaigns. It also provided the colonial British with one of their favorite metaphors for their relation to Indian culture, "penetrating the veil." McElwaine wanted to keep all such veils out of law in Fiji. Pearson disagreed, denying in general that Indian customs were unmanageable and denying in this case that an Indian custom was even at issue, citing a "universal instinct common even among European peoples of bashfulness at the beginning of married life."[5] More broadly, he attacked McElwaine's underlying attitude

---

5. Pearson relied most often on universalistic forms of social theory, as here and in his organizing metaphor of the Fiji Indians as adolescents in a process of social development. However, it should be noted that he also at times stereotyped the Indians as racially different, as when in March 1931, requesting that police prosecute in a violent *sangathan*-related incident, he noted, "We have got to recognise Indian mentality, the ease with which the strong and persistent can domineer over the weak and the tendency to group excitement and violence when it is aroused" (CSO 2600/30).

and laid down his own analysis of Indian marriage relations and general program for marriage reform:

I do feel constrained to say in view of his [McElwaine's] other comments that this problem will never be approached in my opinion from the right angle, if it is assumed that the present state of affairs here is due mainly to the defects inherent in the marriage system these people brought with them from India. It must be clearly understood that the Hindu marriage system is based on caste and regulated by caste controlling authority. There may be defects in the recognition of infant marriage, and the prevention of widow remarriage but as a general marriage system considering the millions of people governed by it, it is wonderfully successful and operates with extraordinarily little friction and litigation.

4. I am afraid we have got to recognise that the present defects here are largely due to the very artificial conditions imposed by the immigration system which resulted in grave sex disparity for many years. Indian women were at a premium and girls on reaching maturity became chattel because there were so few of them, and the standard of morality and of marriage relations fell far below that of the people of their own country. It would be futile now to discuss how far the people themselves were to blame, and how far the fault lay with the system. So far as I remember, it was certain outspoken statements about sexual relations which had become inevitable, which contributed more than anything else to the abolition of indenture system.

5. But it is no use now aiming at the introduction of the full Indian system. Caste has almost disappeared here, and there is at present little or no social cohesion. Nor can we impose on them an entirely alien system of English Christian origin. The problem is more complex and we have got to help them evolve a system of their own. There is the greater obligation on us to help, because I do not think it can now be denied that we have some responsibility for the present state of affairs. From this point of view I cannot understand the opposition to an attempt to legalise large numbers of customary marriages.

. . . One has only to talk to the people themselves to realise how ordinary decent village folk carrying on in their traditional way are being suddenly confronted by complications over registration which are seriously affecting their family life. I am not speaking here of the cases where the customary marriage has been deliberately resorted to, in order to avoid risk of too binding a union.

7. I consider the present bill the first step towards putting family relations in this country on a better footing. . . .

I think it clear that the Fiji Government is bound to recognise that marriage customs are intimately connected with religion and we must give Indians some measure of freedom to follow their own customs and rites even though we have to help them to modify them to suit conditions.

More than any other official in Fiji, Pearson was aware of the role of contradictions in sexual relations in the demise of indenture and of official "responsibility for the present state of affairs." Further, he proposed a solution that, while not a return to "the full Indian system," was to establish and legalise an Indian marriage system involving Indian forms of "customs and rites."

The governor, in approving a final draft of the amendment, sided with McElwaine in requiring women to appear when their marriage was registered before a District Commissioner. On the more general question of McElwaine's proposal to cover Indians also under one general marriage ordinance, the Governor argued on Pearson's side, but with less than a ringing endorsement, that the Indian immigrants still required "protection" and that "I do not consider that the time is yet ripe to remove such legislation" (CSO 3963/28).

The controversies continued when, late in 1928, Fiji received an inquiry from the League of Nations, part of the worldwide inquiry into "white slavery," prostitution, and "traffic in women and children" (CSO 4691/28). Simultaneously, several individual Indian marriage cases were under discussion by Pearson and others in the administration (CSO 4904/28, 4914/28). Pearson was asked whether the problem in the Indian marriage system fell under the purview of the League of Nations definition of "traffic in women and children." He argued that it did not, because it was not "exploitation for immoral purposes" but simply "exploitation in an immoral way."[6] Fiji eventually answered the league by noting that "under the cloak of custom and religion some bartering of children does exist among the Indians. Every effort is made to discourage it by suasion. No such practices exist among the other races." In the course of deliberations and discussion of cases, the broad disagreement between Pearson and McElwaine again erupted.

In his original opinion on the league inquiry, Pearson cited Garnham's pamphlet *Moral Conditions among the Fiji Indians* (1918) and added that the same conditions persisted, that occasionally, parents or guardians of young girls

use her to attract a man to the farm to whom she is united by a temporary union that may be disolved [*sic*] at any time. They get another helper on the farm, retain the services of the daughter and can get rid of the temporary husband and take on another at any time they like. . . . It seems largely to be the result of artificial conditions here. . . . It is to be hoped that the Attorney General will be able at

6. All the Europeans, even Pearson, tended to imagine sexual motivations behind Indian marriages involving underage girls. However, as we shall discuss in more detail in chapter 9, it is unlikely that lust was the motive of the men seeking girl wives. They could find sex other ways, but child brides were a means to wives, households, and families in the long run. Female informants in Fiji who had married at young ages in arranged marriages reported sleeping separately in the boy's parents' house for years after their marriages.

some time to go into the matter. I have been trying for some time to get his opinion on questions related to the traffic without success.

The Attorney General, however, was generally unwilling to discuss the matter except in connection with his objections to personal law. In the case discussed in CSO 4904/28, the return of betrothal gifts was at issue in a court case over a betrothal that did not become a marriage. By Fiji law, Indian betrothal gifts, usually jewelry, had to be returned if the woman's side did not carry through with the marriage. McElwaine resisted regarding Indian betrothals as special in law, however, and argued that gifts connected with "these so called betrothals" should simply be treated the way gifts between parties in anticipation of marriage were treated in English common law. More directly, in 4914/28, the Attorney General resisted prosecuting in an egregious case of "trafficking," on the grounds of the personal law clause.

In this latter case, three successive men were allowed to live with a girl by her guardians. Pearson minuted:

> The case is a bad one. . . . Some sort of ceremony is gone through with each successive lover, and the man lives in the house and does some work until it suits the couple to turn him out or he gets tired of the arrangement. . . . I need hardly say that caste law in India would not tolerate proceedings like this. The demoralisation is due to the people having lost the moral sanctions imposed by caste, and having gained nothing to replace them. . . . We cannot expect the community to settle down under stable conditions here so long as they are tolerated.

Pearson was particularly concerned because, he reported, the girl's guardians had recently gained guardianship of two other young girls, essentially by purchase. He wanted guidance as to the grounds on which he could declare parents unfit and assume guardianship. The Attorney General declined to prosecute, however, and offered no advice on legal steps to prevent further trafficking except repeal of the personal law clause:

> This case is another illustration of the complexities which arise owing to the peculiar status of Indian women arising from marriage "in accord with the personal law of the parties." . . . What the personal law of the parties is, I do not know and have no means of ascertaining.

While the authorities were stalemated, Indians began to call for reform. The Indian Reform League sent its resolutions for reform to the Colonial Secretary in December 1928, principally a call to raise the marriage ages to eighteen for males and fifteen, seventeen without parental consent, for females. They argued on "both Medical and Social grounds" (CSO 934/29). Vishnu Deo was more immediately involved in a particular case in 1929, a marriage planned for a twelve-year-old girl, which Pearson described as follows (CSO 4691/28):

The father is determined on the marriage and is supported by an orthodox Hindu Pandit who holds the view that no girl is safe once she is verging on puberty until married, and that the orthodox Hindu religion enjoins this. The father's brother protests and he happens to be Pt. Vishnu Deo of Samabula School notoriety. [The Arya Samaj had recently attempted to take control of the school through its school board; the government removed Thakur Kundan Singh Kush from the post of headmaster and replaced him with a Christian Indian teacher.] He and his society are I think quite genuine in their attempt to rid Hinduism of early marriage and he of all people is imploring me to declare his brother by reason of his determination incapable of taking charge of his daughter, and hand her over to the Seventh Day Adventists!! Christianity may be an anathema in a Head Master, but apparently is a safe haven of refuge for a niece in peril of early marriage.

By 1929, then, Vishnu Deo was already extraordinarily committed to combating the "orthodox" on questions of marriage. A similar case would become controversial in 1931.

In 1929, however, the main parties in contention continued to be Pearson and McElwaine. In another file in March, McElwaine cited the opinion of S. B. Patel that Indians would accept one marriage law with Europeans (CSO 835/29). At the time Patel was seeking to establish the legal bases for asserting the common status of Indians and Europeans in Empire, and therein the basis for common roll in voting; for those very reasons the Governor had decided he opposed a common marriage law. Pearson replied two days later that since the European law set twelve, not even thirteen, as the age of marriage, the change would be a disaster. In a case in May, McElwaine was asked whether the woman married by a government worker "according to Indian custom only," and their children, were entitled as beneficiaries to his government pension. McElwaine replied, "As it is doubtful whether marriages by Indian custom are monogamous it is doubtful whether the widow of such a marriage is a beneficiary at all" (CSO 2488/29). In this matter Pearson was never consulted, but the case was resolved in favor of the widow. Finally, in June Pearson and McElwaine's most extended and important conflict of the year began, over a murder case (CSO 2488/29, 3296/29).

In June 1929 a man was tried, convicted, and hanged for the murder of his "mother-in-law." To follow the court report on the case (CSO 2992/29), he married a girl aged ten or eleven "according to Indian custom" in June 1928. After the marriage he lived with her family; later he wanted to leave and take his wife with him. The parents objected that the girl was too young. A local, unofficial "panchiad" (*panchayat*) was held in December without result. On February first, the man shot and killed his mother-in-law. "The motive for the crime appears to be revenge for being deprived of his wife after the purchase had been completed," wrote the Chief Justice at the conclusion of his report.

The father of the girl reported that the arrangement had been for the man to live and work at the girl's parents' farm for one year, at which point a second marriage was to be held (so the court recorded—possibly this was to be the marriage following an original betrothal, possibly a second ceremony, this one to be registered officially). Then the man could leave with his wife. After the man lived with them for several weeks, building a new house for them, he and the girl's father had a major quarrel and the man wanted to leave. The girl's father denied that the man had given him large sums of money and, in cross-examination, denied that the man had asked for his money back. He did admit, however, that the *panchayat* had asked him to let the girl go, and that he had refused. The accused made no statements in his own defense until after he was convicted. Then he said, "All the money I earned and previous money I handed to them. I borrowed five pounds from Loku and gave that money to them also. All my clothing and cooking utensils are in [their] house. For this reason all this has happened. That is all."

Pearson was incensed when he read a minute concerning the case written by the Attorney General. McElwaine wrote the following, and his views were elaborated by another government officer:

> I have expatiated at large and at length on the marriage law so far as it affects Indians. I think it rotten but my views are not shared by the Secretary for Indian Affairs or the Government of India. This paper does not concern me.
> P. A. McElwaine

> The Attorney General has spoken to me. He considers that the reason for this murder was that the accused had paid money for his bride and was not allowed to take her.
> If Indian marriages were on the same footing as other marriages under which the husband and bride live together at once after marriage the provocation for crimes of this sort would not arise.
> A. A. Wright

Pearson replied in a long, angry letter to the Acting Colonial Secretary (CSO 3296/29). By this point, mid-July 1929, the elections were growing close. The Governor who had partially supported Pearson, Eyre Hutson, had departed the colony. The new Governor who would mistrust him, Murchison Fletcher, was yet to arrive. Pearson's own leave also approached. He wrote that he regretted to hear McElwaine's conclusion that reform was held up "by the support given to this 'rotten' system by the Government of India and me." While he "would be only too pleased to cooperate" in reform,

I cannot agree that the Att-Gen. is right in his diagnosis of the cause of the trouble in the cases on which he has noted. . . . I think it is a mistake to make too much of a bogey of this personal law. So far as I can make out it has had nothing to do with the cause of the trouble in these cases, or in any other case that I have come across in which parties have cohabited. . . .

The personal law of the parties had nothing to do with the refusal to hand over the bride who had already lived with her husband. On the contrary . . . the pernicious custom of insistence on retaining the bride is a local one due to unnatural sex conditions, and directly opposed to the personal law of Hindus. The delay in [amending marriage law to require registrations] was the cause of the trouble. Neither I nor the Government of India are responsible for the delay, and I am forced to add in view of the tendency to attribute all the evils in social conditions to Indian custom that the Fiji Government received fair warning of what was likely to happen owing to the persistence of importing disproportionate numbers of male labourers, from one of its own officers so far back as the annual report on Indian immigration of 1902.

7. The last portion of [Wright's] note apparently conveys the Att-Gen's opinion. How the fact that he is married in a tail coat and in a church under the personal law of Christian English people instead of by progressing round a fire hand in hand with his bride in accordance with Hindu personal law puts a bridegroom in a better position "to get delivery of the goods" into his sole and separate custody I cannot conceive.

Pearson went on to deny that polyandry and bigamy were real problems; although the former might be known "in some out of the way parts in the Himalayas," neither was part of the personal law "of any Indians in Fiji." Child marriage was already forbidden by the minimum legal age requirements. The main personal law issue was "that the actual ceremony is in accordance with the religious rites of the parties." It might even be possible to amend the personal law clause to refer only to personal law in the "celebration" of the marriage:

It would be at any rate worthwhile exploring the feasibility of amending in this way, subject always to the consideration that personal law among Indians practically implies religious law and that with Hindus marriage implies a religious status not a more or less civil contract.

Despite his anger Pearson was willing to see the personal law clause substantially reduced in scope, if it would make the Fiji government take responsibility for supporting proper social relations in the Indian community. What the Attorney General and other Fiji authorities desired, however, was to avoid the terms of Indian culture altogether, to imagine the Indian marriages as a form of civil contract. They refused to see cultural content in such legal forms as banns. McElwaine replied to Pearson tersely. "I have already offered a solution," he minuted. He was willing to allow "any religious rites which the parties desire," "but the qualifications and disqualifications of intending spouses should be the same in all cases and what constitutes a marriage should be the same in all cases." His primary concern was still securing Indian adherence to European legal forms. Pearson left on leave without reply, but by mistake the paper was returned again to McElwaine. In Pearson's absence he provided a stronger last word: "I do *not* wish to see this paper again. If or when I am permitted to raise the Marriage Ordinance this paper will even then be unnecessary to me."

Pearson's letter in this file had concluded with his vision, appropriately moderate, of the next step to be taken in marriage law reform: the matter was "preeminently" one for a Legislative Council subcommittee including the elected Indian members. Pearson wrote, "I shall hope to see such a committee appointed at an early date." The walkout made this hope irrelevant and left the matter in official circles of debate. In March 1930 the new Labour Secretary of State who had insisted upon funding for Indian education replied to a dispatch that had forwarded the Indian Reform League's proposal for raising the marriage age. In the same progressive spirit, he wrote, "I should be very glad to approve any legislation to check child marriages which approves itself to the best Indian opinion and is likely to be effective" (CSO 934/29). Before this, in January, the new Governor asked for the papers on marriage in response to a McElwaine minute describing the Indian marriage laws as "the worst piece of legislation we possess" (CSO 6158/29). These events opened many doors for McElwaine and McGusty, for the Indian Reform League, and for the Arya Samaj.[7]

In January McElwaine wrote the new Governor a long memorandum on the need to reform the Indian marriage laws. He reviewed how the personal law clause had been "added by the steam roller" in 1919, and how the Attorney General then, along with the elected members of the Legislative Council, had been sharply opposed. The Colonial Secretary, in passing the papers to the Governor, noted that India's influence had coincided with the labor migration and that "the S. of S. will today permit this administration more independence of action, and we need not be as fearful of Indian opinion." Further, he noted, "various Indian bodies" had requested a raising of the marriage age for females. The

---

7. References to detail, and all quotations, to the end of this section are drawn except where noted from CSO 6158/29.

Governor, reading the papers, instructed the Attorney General and the acting SIA to "consult representative Indian opinion." The Attorney General then got the file and sent it to Dr. McGusty, the acting SIA, asking him to consult with "respectable" Indian opinion on a wide range of amendments.

In early April 1930 McGusty and McElwaine met with four selected Indian representatives to discuss amendments to the marriage laws: John Grant to represent the Christian Indians; Abdul Sahu Khan, a government clerk, to represent the "Mohammedan"; Vishnu Deo to represent the Arya Samaj, and Umadatt Maharaj to represent the "Orthodox Hindoo." McElwaine wrote the memo concerning this consultation. The Indian representatives objected to the requirement that Indian women had to appear before the District Commissioners to register their marriages (and, as McGusty noted elsewhere in the file, only 186 more Indian marriages had been registered, two months before the end of the period for legal registration of previously constituted customary marriages). McElwaine wrote, "I explained that there never has been Purda in Fiji and that the Government did not propose to introduce it. This, the Indians recognised; indeed they did not appear to have any desire for the introduction of Purda." He then concluded against amending the requirement.

The discussion turned to the age of marriage:

> The majority of the Indians [i.e., the Christian, the Muslim clerk, and Vishnu Deo] agreed that the marriage age of females should be raised.
>
> Mr. Umadatt [the only "Orthodox Hindoo" consulted] was the only person who did not welcome the proposal, but on being assured that the marriage age has recently been raised both in England and in India he said in a resigned way that he would leave it to the Government.
>
> His point of view is interesting. He thinks that if the girl does not marry at 13 her parents have difficulty in preserving her virtue. I pointed out that the Criminal Law Amendment Ordinance 1889 could be invoked in aid.
>
> It was agreed that the marriage age should not be raised for another year or two to allow the process of enlightenment on the evils of child marriage to spread.

And finally,

> The Indian members were unanimous that the reference to the personal law of the parties in this subsection should be repealed.
>
> I most heartily endorse this view.

McElwaine also found the Indians to be in agreement with him on the repeal of several other clauses, including the one requiring return of betrothal gifts if marriage were refused. He concluded, "The proposals go a long way towards unifying the law of marriage in the Colony—a consummation devoutly to be wished."

By 12 May McElwaine had his bill drafted and approved by the Executive Council for submission to the Legislative Council. Its "Objects and Reasons" section described it as "the result of a Conference with representatives of the Indian Christian, Hindoo, Arya Samaj and Muslim communities who unanimously agreed to the amendments. . . . Its object is to bring Indian marriages in Fiji more into accord with the marriages of Europeans." The bill explicitly forbade registration of polygamous marriages, established a table of proscribed relations coordinate with those for others in Fiji, and removed several clauses, such as the betrothal clause, that made special reference to Indian relations and circumstances. The amending ordinance also deleted all references to personal law, a change that "removes an ambiguity," explained the "Objects and Reasons" section succinctly. The bill was passed by the Legislative Council on 16 May 1930, a few weeks before Pearson's return. However, the law had another obstacle course to run: review in London and in India.

When the Secretary of State had notified Fiji in April 1929 that the King would not disallow the amending ordinance requiring Indians to register their marriages, he made specific reference to a paragraph in a McElwaine memorandum that had been enclosed in support. In that memorandum McElwaine had suggested that the "personal law" clause be repealed (CSO 2573/29). The Secretary of State had instructed Fiji, in light of McElwaine's view, that the government of India would also be consulted in the event of any further proposed amendments to marriage law for Indians in Fiji. Thus the review process for the new ordinance was complex and long. It took almost a year for the reply to be formulated, but when it arrived, in April 1931, the Colonial Office passed on a government of India query about McElwaine's favorite amendments. McElwaine's obsession with maintaining European form in law was mistaken by the government of India as a matter of immediate practical effect. Not realizing that the obsession had led McElwaine *not* to interfere in all manner of Indian practices, they supposed that he wished to forbid practices the Indians sought to continue:

I am accordingly to request that the Government of Fiji be asked whether in actual practice Indians have applied to be married under their personal law in India, and, if so, with what result. It will also be an advantage if some idea could be obtained as to the number of such applications. The Government of India hope that when the result of this inquiry is known, they will be given a further opportunity of offering their opinion on this provision of the new Ordinance before it is actually brought into force.

Further, the London India Office took umbrage at the suggestion that it had "steam rollered" the personal law clause, and it doubted the advisability of repealing it.

In mid-July 1931 the matter was back in Pearson's hands. He wrote a detailed memo on the history of the marriage reform questions, noting that the latest amending ordinance was drawn up and passed while he was on leave and despite his earlier expressed doubts on the matter. He then attacked McElwaine's memo on his "conference" with Indian representatives and made his own general argument:

> 6. According to the note on this consultation . . . the Indian representatives agreed to the removal of the references to the personal law in both sections. I have spoken to some of them about this, and personally I have considerable doubts whether they really understood what they were agreeing to. . . .
>
> 7. In any case my personal opinion is that there is very great force in the objections raised by the India office note and the Government of India letter. I am afraid I have all along differed from Mr. McElwaine over a fundamental point. He considers . . . a uniform marriage law for all classes and races in the Colony "a consummation devoutly to be wished for." . . . I remarked on the inadvisability of imposing on Indian Hindus and Muslims "an entirely alien system of English Christian origin."

Pearson declared McElwaine's 1930 ordinance a "retrograde step," and it was never made law. He again proposed a panel of arbitrators to decide whatever questions of personal law might arise in practice to be "presided over by the Secretary for Indian Affairs," but this panel, too, was never realized in fact. Late in 1931 the Governor endorsed, in a meeting with Muslim leaders, the principle that "marriage relations of the community should be governed by the laws and customs peculiar to their religion" (CSO 267/30), and shortly thereafter he approved Pearson's idea, developed from earlier negotiations with McElwaine, of new and separate legislation on Hindu and Muslim marriage law. McGusty minuted in favor of a uniform marriage code, suggesting that custom primarily covered the ceremonies solemnizing marriage, but Pearson, going much further than he had in 1929, defended the notion of differences:

It seems to me doubtful if Dr. McGusty realises how intimate is the connection between religion and marriage in the case of Hindus and Muslims. The Muslim point of view [objects to the difficulty of divorce in Christian-influenced law]. With Hindus it has been said that marriage is a sacrament and necessary to spiritual salvation. . . . It is not merely a question of the ceremony which is in issue, but also that of the conditions precedent to and the implications of the marriage.

It might seem that Pearson won his battles over the question of marriage law. But in many ways the matter was stalemated. No new law had taken effect, and the Fiji authorities recognized no clear standards for the forms to be taken by Indian marriage and divorce. They simply registered the marriages conducted by their official marriage priests and then judged matters of inheritance by what was registered; divorces were rarely brought to their attention. The matter of actually writing new Hindu and Muslim marriage laws was no simple business, as Pearson was aware. The matter of drafting separate laws was, inevitably, to be a matter of close consultation with the experts of the Indian communities concerned, exactly what official Fiji had been avoiding up to and through the tenure of Pearson's service, which was to end in 1932. By this time—in fact, since November 1929, the month of the boycott, and shortly after the amendment requiring marriage registration came into force—Muslim leaders petitioned for their own separate laws of marriage, divorce, and succession. They argued that English law, based on "the teachings of the Bible," was "imposing certain hardships" on Muslims, especially in regard to divorce (CSO 267/30), and official Fiji was increasingly sensitive to the utility of emphasizing Muslim difference, just as it had been suspicious of S. B. Patel's effort to establish sameness. Official Fiji put itself into a position rejecting Indian sameness and difference, soliciting Indian leadership when it was useful but withdrawing itself as far as possible from any regular administration of Indian marriage customs. Marriage laws would be debated officially for more than a decade before more permanent compromises were reached, compromises facilitated by the demographic balancing of the Indian community. By then Pearson and his agenda for Fiji Indians in Fiji's law were long gone.

Pearson's Departure

J. R. Pearson's tenure in Fiji ended in 1932, shortly after Vishnu Deo's obscenity conviction. In September 1931 confidential discussion began concerning what should be done about the post of Secretary for Indian Affairs when Pearson's contract expired in May 1932. Pearson offered to stay on another year. But Governor Murchison Fletcher suggested that the time had come, for financial and other reasons, for Fiji to appoint its Secretary for Indian Affairs from its own ranks. He asked the Colonial Secretary and Pearson to submit their views in writing. A. W. Seymour, the Colonial Secretary, noted that Pearson was better qualified than anyone local, and that in any case an officer from India would be necessary. He raised the spectre of India insisting upon an Indian civil servant of Indian race, an event that would be "a great embarrassment to this Government."

Pearson, asked to comment on the question apart from personalities, expressed himself at length and in no uncertain terms. He argued again that the Indian community was in the throes of an "awkward adolescence" and required an experienced officer to avoid "absurd" misunderstandings. The situation was exacerbated by two facts, "firstly the admitted weakness in the knowledge of the Indian vernacular and understanding and touch with Indian matters among European officers, and secondly, not always passive resistance among an element in the European community to even minor concessions to Indian aspirations." In Fiji, he said, the linguistic skills of the few in government service with any knowledge of Indian languages were greatly exaggerated, "the smatterer being considered a real pundit." He also returned to the central theme of his years of infighting. "Any collection of human beings" would generate leadership. The question was

whether such leadership is to be that of grievance mongers and irresponsible prophets of the millenium or that of responsible leaders, recognised, fostered and controlled by the administration. Those who persist in trying to keep the community down to one dead level are merely laying up for themselves trouble for the future and the risk of being forced to concede far more than they might give with good grace. The desire to preserve European interests in the Colony is probably based on sound Imperial instincts and European characteristics will probably conduce powerfully to this result. Local prejudices tinged with pessimism about India's connection with Empire cannot be allowed to interfere with the plain necessity of guiding and controlling Indian aspirations to a legitimate place in the population of the Colony.

He argued again for the importance of a *panchayat* scheme and for other reforms. He even criticized the treatment of Indian clerks:

The favourites tend to go up like a rocket and down like a stick. I had to protest against the practise of marooning capable clerks in small places owing to the difficulty of controlling their activities in bigger ones. It seems to me of very great importance to the future of the Colony that it should foster the growth of an intelligent and conscientious body of Indian officials with adequate scope for promotion and the exercise of talent. There are avenues for employment of Indians still to be explored. They cannot be left indefinitely in wholly subordinate positions. Trust will engender a sense of responsibility and the Indian analogy proves that the Indian Service can be invaluable both as a means of satisfying legitimate aspirations and as powerfully conducing to the stability of the whole community.

He complained that the government was inattentive in general to Indian affairs. No cadets had ever been assigned to train with him on Indian questions, despite his repeated requests. He concluded, "I am afraid I cannot say that I consider that there is at the present moment, any officer of the Fiji service, in every way competent to hold charge of the department."

A few days later, with only the Colonial Secretary dissenting, the Executive Council decided to appoint "an officer of the Fiji service" to the post of Secretary for Indian Affairs at the end of Pearson's contract. The Colonial Secretary then wrote a vigorous protest, noting that Indian opinion had not been consulted, that given their great distrust of the Fiji government the Indians would surely favor an outside officer, and that because the local officials were linguistically incompetent, "if a local officer were appointed immediately the Government would get completely out of touch with Indian opinion." He cited a concrete example, the claim of McGusty in early 1930 that "the majority of Indians in Fiji were in favour" of the marriage ordinance amendments of that year, which had simply not been the case. The Colonial Secretary, licensed by the Letters Patent, required that his dissent be brought to the attention of the Secretary of State.

The Governor himself then wrote a ten-page confidential letter to the Secretary of State, justifying his decision to replace Pearson with a local officer. He argued that it had become necessary for officers concerned with Indian affairs in Fiji to be "possessed of special experience of conditions in Fiji." He denied that local Indians cared whether anyone from India was appointed to look after their interests: "The demand, such as it is, comes from a discontented class of soi-disant leaders and teachers, who take their cue from disloyal elements outside the Colony." Pearson was never assigned cadets because of "distrust of his ability to impart the requisite instruction." "Old beyond his years," he did "not possess the energy, initiative, and drive" necessary for his office. It was true, the Governor allowed, that Fiji government officials were weak on Indian languages, but they were improving. McMillan was more fluent than Pearson, and McGusty "has been studying Hindi for some time past" and was as reliable a translator, he found, as Pearson was.

He then argued that local race prejudice was grounds for a local appointment. "The Europeans—and here I include myself—resent the underlying suggestion that the local Indian requires some sort of special protection which the Fiji Government is not competent or cannot be trusted to give." A local officer would win more cooperation. He suggested therefore that McGusty be appointed. In closing, he addressed the points of Seymour's dissent, noting that he disagreed about McGusty's ability to interpret local opinion and remarking, "I consider that, if necessary, the Indians should be made to understand that the Government will not tolerate any dictation from them. I do not in any way share Mr. Seymour's fears."

In 1930 a Labour Secretary of State had supported Seymour to keep the elected Fiji Europeans from dictating education policy. In 1932 a Conservative-dominated government in London helped Murchison

Fletcher suppress Fiji Indian "dictation." The Secretary of State approved the replacement of Pearson with McGusty as Fiji's Secretary for Indian Affairs in a one-sentence telegram. For McGusty the appointment was not even full-time; he continued also as Fiji's Inspecting Medical Officer. Under his oversight, the District Advisory Committee system spread through Fiji, but all official talk of *panchayats* ceased. While the bureaucracy of "Native Affairs," later "Fijian Affairs," continued to grow, under McGusty's leadership the office of the Secretary for Indian Affairs became simply a kind of ombudsman's office for the problems of individuals (see Gillion 1977: 143). Its staff was not wholly specialized in Indian affairs but, like McGusty, was trained first in "Fijian affairs" and transferred into and out of Indian affairs according to other needs. Even in its heyday the office of the Secretary for Indian Affairs was not a high priority, as is revealed in part of Pearson's 1929 defense of himself (CSO 4579/29) for allowing clerks to see confidential papers:

> The conditions of work especially in my Government Buildings office are bad. I have only one small room in which my clerk or clerks have to sit with me. The room is at the center of the Buildings and the verandah outside is constantly thronged by people coming to see me, or visit other departments. I have only a half time stenographer and she may be heavily engaged elsewhere or on leave. I have on occasion to type papers myself, ask for help from the C.S.O. or take papers away from my office to the Native Department or Colonial Secretary's Office [for typing].

At McGusty's retirement in 1945, the post was abolished entirely.

Pearson had thought that European tutelage was inevitable and desirable for the evolving Indians. In India the Indian leadership evolved the British authorities themselves out of power. Recognized authorities such as the barrister Gandhi turned one by one against the colonial hierarchy itself and used their powers to mobilize an anticolonial party on Indian cultural themes and at the same time to manipulate colonial forms against their old masters. In Fiji colonial authorities built a much firmer barrier, leaving the forms and agencies of Indian culture in a permanently separate status. Following Pearson's lead, Fiji's social field might have been reintegrated, at the cost to the Europeans of allowing Indian cultural forms, and Indian authorities to interpret them, into the courts and other offices of power. But official Fiji refused. Vastly different was its relationship with the loyal indigenous Fijians, whose traditional authority structure was integrated into colonial law (and of course, remade in the process). Provincial Councils, a Great Council of Chiefs, and native stipendiary magistrates were officially empowered and supported in their judgments about traditional matters. Indigenous Fijian dissenters resisted on occasion (see Macnaught 1982; Kaplan 1989, 1990) but Fijian custom was routinized and reified. For the Fiji Indians, the gap between colonial law and Indian marriage practice created the opposite situation, as Pearson was aware. Not only did the Muslims not have "Islamic law," but "Indian 'Hindu personal law' clearly cannot be applied and under present conditions it would I fancy be impossible to say that any Fiji 'Hindu personal law' had been established by customary observance" (CSO 6158/29). It was left to the Indians on their own to articulate their standards of decency and virtue, law, and custom, not only what they should be, but what they were.

"The Need is for Pure and Holy
Patriots": The Religious Debates and
the Fall of Vishnu Deo

From the late 1920s until key defeats in 1931 and 1932, the Fiji Arya
Samaj attempted to reorganize the Fiji Indian community politically,
socially, and religiously, in Arya Samaj terms and under Arya Samaj
leadership. Its rival in Hindu self-representation, an organization calling
itself Sanatan Dharm ("eternal *dharma*" or "eternal religion") began to
organize later and was far less coordinated in its efforts in Fiji. Why then
did the Fiji Hindus not become Arya Samajis? How did the Arya Samaj
project fail?

To this point we have reviewed a complex history of discourse and
dialogues leading up to and intersecting with the Indian sectional debates of 1930–1932. No one arena of dialogue or genre of discourse
established the context for these debates. Our inquiry has ranged from
anti-indenture agitation and religious debates in India, to the exchanges
between official India and official Fiji, to the dialogue in Fiji triangulat-
ing among Fiji Indians, Fiji Europeans, and official Fiji, to the conflicts
within official Fiji. This chapter begins with a final bit of background,
political controversy in India itself in the 1920s, and then narrates the
events of the Indian religious debates in Fiji. My hope is that the reader
will now find these events understandable, without losing sight of how
extraordinary they were.

The Collapse of Fiji Indian Political Unity

By 1929 interest in Indian nationalism was widespread and intense in
the Fiji Indian community. However, after the failed strike of 1921 led

by Gandhi-promoting Bashishth Muni, no further attempts were made to articulate and apply Indian nationalist principles in Fiji on a major scale until 1929, when the Fiji Indian National Congress was founded and a Fiji Indian Round Table decided to boycott the Legislative Council. Much had happened between 1921 and 1929 in India, including notably the rise of conflicts between sectarian-political organizations.

Gandhi called off a major noncooperation *satyagraha* ("insistence on the truth") campaign in 1922 after an outbreak of Hindu-Muslim violence and called for social unity and communal uplift as a prerequisite for further direct anticolonial political action. While opinions at the time differed over the advisability of suspending political action, there is no doubt historically that the call for community-building instead generated the opposite result: a focus on schisms and differences between factions of the Indian population. As different groups promoted their own visions of communal reform and new national order, the political community that had followed the Indian National Congress began to split apart in a national schismogenesis.[1] By the mid-1920s the political focus in India was on intercommunal, principally Hindu-Muslim, riots and violence, focused in many places on Hindu *shuddhi* ("conversion") and *sangathan* ("organizing") projects (see, e.g., Pandey 1978: 115ff.). India's Muslim League's politics also shifted dramatically, away from support for the anticolonial *swaraj* ("self-rule") movement and toward concern for the Muslim community as a threatened minority. This move, it became clear, played into the hands of the colonial authorities seeking to justify their own presence, leading to further debate and acrimony between Muslim and other political voices.

As some Fiji officials alleged, Fiji Indian politics was in some measure a delayed function of political events in India. The principles of noncooperation, applied successfully in South Africa in the late 1900s and early 1910s, and in India in the 1910s and early 1920s, were articulated in Fiji by Bashishth Muni in 1921. And it was not until the late 1920s that Fiji's sectional associations—a Muslim League, a South Indian–oriented Sangam, various Sanatan Dharm societies—were founded and began to make public self-representations, not until 1930 that they

---

1. "Schismogenesis," a useful analytic concept coined by Gregory Bateson and first discussed in *Naven* (1958), refers to a pattern of conflict development in which opposition provokes further opposition, and conflicts lead to clarification of group boundaries, articulation of new points of difference, and new conflicts; conflict in one area of life generates conflict in others as the principle of opposition ramifies through previously unaffected discourse and practice. Bateson used the concept to explain social organization in New Guinea where it was not in equilibrium; it also describes very precisely the fracturing history of nationalism in India in the 1920s and among the Fiji Indians in the late 1920s and early 1930s.

began to clash with each other seriously. Further, as in India, the Arya Samaj was organized in Fiji, actively seeking to uplift the community, long before the societies that grew to oppose it. However, the idea of a delayed function is imperfect. Fiji Indians were directly and intimately involved in the anti-indenture campaign, one of the major early *satyagraha* movements in India. And on the other hand, Fiji's Indian National Congress was attempted when the sectional associations were already constituted and recognized, and it was very short-lived.

In any case, the Round Table in Fiji, its boycott decision, and S. B. Patel's enthusiasm (quoted at the beginning of chapter 1), all suggest that in 1929 Fiji Indians united politically, their agenda inspired by Indian nationalism and oriented to local circumstances.[2] They sought communal uplift, equality with Europeans in Fiji, and "swaraj", self-rule, in India. They sought to establish their Congress as a political institution. And if the pollution of indenture, the denigrating rhetoric of Christian missionaries and other colonial voices, and indigenous Fijian contempt for Fiji Indians (Neill once minuted that the mutual disdain of indigenous Fijians and Fiji Indians was "highly amusing to observe") all provoked a Fiji Indian search for dignity and their own form of virtue, that search needed to find its voice. The *swaraj* projects in India itself articulated not an established sense of "honor," racial or otherwise, but a search for self-respect, self-control, and "uplift" individual and communal. The Fiji Indian community in 1929 hoped to achieve something for itself in its Legislative Council boycott. But in the short run, all that was achieved was political stalemate. Its only real hope for reform was that official Fiji, or more realistically London, would sooner or later respond to their protest, together with protests from India and Indians elsewhere. But the stalemate was its own space, in which efforts to articulate the project of the Congress and its boycott led Fiji into its own schismogenesis.

In the atmosphere of that stalemate, the activities of the Arya Samaj and other sectional associations began to carry a new political weight, as matters to be evaluated in light of the need for Indian unity. Antagonism between the Muslim League and the Arya Samaj was already established. At its second annual general meeting, in Suva in December 1928, the Fiji Muslim League passed several resolutions, including an appeal to the government to "take rigid measures" to prevent importation of "contentious literature" into the colony. Their Honorary

2. Even Indian Reform League leaders were participants in the Round Table and later National Congress discussions endorsing boycott. However, John Grant later told Fiji officials that his signature on a call for a common roll was coerced.

Secretary, X. K. Nasirud Dean, sent their resolutions to the Colonial Secretary, writing in his cover letter that this resolution was an outcome of "the nefarious activities" of the Arya Samaj and complaining in particular about a Samaji pamphlet called *Shuddhi Samachar,* which he translated as "news of purifications." The cover of the pamphlet showed a crowd of *maulvis* ("Muslim Priests") having their beards and hair shaved, performing a *havan* rite, "i.e. conversion to Hindooism." "A worse picture than this can hardly be imagined." "These trouble makers should not be allowed to disturb the peace and tranquility which the Indians in Fiji are enjoying," concluded the Secretary. Already, before the elections, these religious issues were connected to political ones. The general meeting also resolved that it "feels alarmed at the anti-Islamic propaganda which is being assiduously fostered up all over the Colony by a certain section of the Indian Community and respectfully appeals to the Government to take every precaution in safeguarding the interests of the Muslim Minority Community when political privileges are extended to the Indians of Fiji." But in 1929 Muslims participated in the Fiji Indian National Congress and in the Round Table decision to boycott. Shortly thereafter, Rewa became a focus of increasing concern.

In 1929 Arya Samajis had publicized their conversion (*shuddhi*) of a few Muslims in Rewa. Rewa was a site of local Hindu-Muslim tensions, dating from failed efforts to prevent a local Muslim from opening a butchery in 1926; Arya Samajis participated in that conflict, but the protest against the butchery was led at least equally by people later in the moderate camp, notably Dr. Beattie himself.[3] In December 1929 storms

3. In 1926 Muslims and Sikhs in Nasinu, an area midway between Suva and Nausori in Rewa, apparently exchanged complaints about public cow and beef slaughter. A Muslim applied for a Board of Health license for a butchery, and a European who was contemplating building on a nearby lot tried to block the license. The Board of Health asked the constabulary to send a European constable to investigate the site, but the constabulary sent a Sikh officer, who, the Colonial Secretary later alleged, was "well known to be a very strict believer" and was no doubt "the cause of all the trouble." Fiji's few Sikhs, favorites for employment in the constabulary in Fiji as well as India, had a low profile in the debates of 1929–1932. But in 1926 the constable's visit was followed by protests against the license in (1) a petition to the Colonial Secretary from eighty-five Rewa-resident "loyal Hindu subjects of your benign government," most of whom marked, rather than signed, their names, (2) a letter to the Board of Health from "the Senior Indian Sergeant of Constabulary," another Sikh, who wrote in his capacity as President of the Sikh Gurdwara Committee, (3) a memo to the Colonial Secretary from the District Commissioner of Rewa, (4) a letter to the Colonial Secretary from Badri Maharaj, (5) a letter to the Colonial Secretary, citing a *Fiji Times* news report, from the Suva Arya Samaj, and (5) a petition to the Governor from about four hundred "humble petitioners" who were "residents of the Colony," apparently mainly from Suva, most of whom could write; the scripts of the signatures were, in order of frequency, devanagari, roman, gujarati, tamil, and arabic; the

led to flooding on the Rewa river. Vishnu Deo's Suva branch of the Fiji Indian National Congress collected and distributed relief funds and supplies, in explicit competition with the government relief efforts. In the same month, at the Governor's Conference on Indian franchise (see the second section of chapter 6) no Indian voice against the council boycott emerged. But shortly thereafter, Vishnu Deo was accused of distributing the relief charity unequally in Rewa, overfavoring Samajis. In the first ten days of January 1930 he refused to allow Christian and Muslim leaders to call a meeting of the Suva branch of the Congress, and they resigned. On 5 January the mass meeting of Fiji Muslims in Nausori generated the memorial to the Governor requesting a separate Muslim representative in the Legislative Council; rumors followed that a Muslim would accept appointment to the Legislative Council and break the boycott, something that never happened. The chairman of the Provisional Committee for the Attainment of Muslim Political Rights created at the meeting was a *maulvi* named Abdul Karim; the Secretary was X. K. Nasirud Dean.[4] In their memorial to the Governor, also signed by four others, they complained particularly about

Hindoos, fired by the state of affairs in India . . . oppressing the Muslims by organising, wherever possible, a commercial, industrial and social boycott campaign against the Muslims. In short, the Hindoo aim seems to be to convert Muslims to Hindooism by bringing economic pressure to bear upon the Muslims and thereby to diminish the strength of our Community. As a matter of fact their efforts are proving successful in certain districts where Muslims are sparsely settled amongst the Hindoos.

They also complained that "the agitation for a Common Electoral Roll is conducted by the Arya Samajists and other Hindoos of their ilk. . . . The 'Fiji-Indian National Congress' has become a mere tool in the hands of a few agitators."

---

petition was submitted by Durga Prasad, described by the police as "a disciple of Rev. McMillan" (CSO 4940/26, 5506/26, 5517/26, 5325/26, 5550/26). The government filed these letters and petitions in multiple separate papers, with little comment. A meeting in Rewa followed, run by Raghvanand, Chattur Singh, Dr. Beattie, and others, and confidential papers were opened, recounting the visit to the Governor of a delegation led by Beattie. The Colonial Secretary characterized Beattie's remarks in the Indian meeting as "impertinent, impudent, and characteristic of an unbalanced mind of an extremist and religious fanatic"; the Governor replied to the delegation that he could not revoke the license, by then granted to the Muslim butcher, and that "I advise the Hindoos and Sikhs and Mahommedans to maintain their present attitude of loyalty and to aim at exercising tolerance towards the religious beliefs and liberties of their compatriots which they are privileged to enjoy under His Majesty The King's Government."

4. This memorial and related papers are in CSO 289/30.

In the midst of these frustrations, within the larger stalemate, the *sangathan* efforts of Arya Samajis in Rewa were abruptly invested with colonywide political significance. In response they apparently accelerated their effort to strengthen the Hindu community; at least, they did not desist. Efforts to convert Muslims and boycott those who refused to convert continued. Boycotts of Hindus refusing to boycott the Muslims emerged, as did isolated cases of violence. According to the Rewa constabulary, the Arya Samajis "conducted a house to house visitation among isolated Mohamedans and countered refusals [to convert] with threats." The constabulary labeled Samaji teachers, including Kundan Singh Kush, as "troublemakers" but also noted that some Muslims, in turn, taunted and threatened the new Hindu converts and "killed cattle & carried meat about" (CSO 1577/30).

On 10 February 1930 a group of Hindus wrote to the Colonial Secretary, complaining that a group of Arya Samajis including Kundan Singh Kush had pressured them to contribute to a fund the Samajis were collecting. The fund was to aid in the prosecution of a group of Muslims alleged to have murdered an Arya Samaj member; it was alleged that the Fiji Muslim League had already underwritten the defense. When the Hindus refused to contribute, "the abovementioned collectors threatened us with boycott and assault and said that in future we would be treated as out-castes from the Hindoo Society." Complaint was also made that "the Hindoo Sangathan Sabha" had orchestrated an assault on a Muslim whose father-in-law purchased cows and sold them to butchers, an assault they alleged took place the day after a Samaji offered two hundred pounds to underwrite it. Further, a *sangathan* leader "advised the Hindoos under threat of boycott to refrain from purchasing goods from the stores of Muslims or to help them in their cultivation or in any other way."

In the same minute paper, 531/30, was filed a letter with extensive complaints from leaders of the Rewa Muslims:

The Hindoos of this district have organised a general boycott campaign against the Muslims. In every locality they have formed cliques under the name of "Hindoo Sangathan Sabha" the main object of which is to unite the Hindoos and convert the Muslims to Hindooism by bringing economic pressure to bear upon the Muslims. As a matter of fact their efforts are proving successful in places where Muslims are sparsely settled amongst the Hindoos. The Hindoos have decided to boycott all the Muslim barbers and this has resulted in many barbers changing their faith to Hindooism. The majority of the Muslims or others who are dependent on the Hindoos converted to Hindooism so far are barbers by occupation. The Hindoo feelings were driven to a high pitch during the last Elections and it resulted in pro-Hindoo and Arya Samaj candidates entering the Legislative Council to obstruct the activities of the Council. We are opposed to this attitude by the Indian members of the Council and this has aggravated the position. There is not the least doubt in it that the Hindoos whose number of voters in the very short time will vastly outnumber that of all the Muslims, Christians, Europeans and possibly Fijians put together are seeking dominance in this Colony. The Muslims have withdrawn from the Fiji National Congress.

In certain places the Muslims are coerced to conform to Hindoo rites and ceremonies. . . . The mid-wifery profession amongst the Indians has been confined to the Chamars who are Hindoos. These Hindoo women now refuse to attend Muslim confinements and consequently our women of the poorer class are greatly distressed when they confine. Some of these mid-wives stipulate that they should be paid at the rate of 2 pounds per hour when attending Muslim women as there is every danger of their being ex-communicated from the Hindoo society. Every Hindoo who has anything to do with Muslims is either boycotted or punished in some form or another. On one occasion a Hindoo was boycotted because he greeted a Muslim and on another occasion a Hindoo was fined four pounds by the Sangathan Sabha because he gargled his mouth with water given by a Muslim after the former had a tooth pulled out. . . . Even Mr. Basvanand of your office was refused admission to a Hindoo Bhandara at Vuci to which he was invited because he was accompanied by a Muslim, Mr. G. N. Buksh, of the same office. . . .

In conclusion I would like to say that the Muslim forbearance is about exhausted and the Government should take immediate steps to avert any catastrophe which may be brought about by Hindoo aggression. The instances of Hindoo oppression given herein are just a few out of numerous. A whole book could be written about the anti-Islamic attitude of the Hindoos.

The Muslim complainants, demanding government intervention, related local boycotts against Muslims to Muslim withdrawal from the boycott against the Legislative Council and reflected on intemperate Hindoo ambitions in contrast to their own "forebearance."

This Muslim letter had been solicited by the Rewa District Commissioner after he received the letter from the Hindus and a letter defending the Hindu Sangathan Sabha movement written by its leaders. In their letter of 27 February 1930 the leaders of these Rewa Sangathan Sabhas described a rise of beef-eating among the Rewa Muslims, disrupting the days when "the Hindus dealt with their Muhammedan brethren as if they were sons of the same mother." (In July 1930 Pearson, back from leave, noted in this file that beef-eating "was at the bottom of the present friction.") Muslim *maulvis* forced Hindus to boycott Muslim social functions by insisting on the admission of beef-eaters and later, in 1928, refused to let Hindus put soil on the grave at a Muslim funeral. Muslims stopped accepting the ritually prepared sweet foods from Hindu rituals, pronouncing them to be "unholy," while the Hindus were still willing to accept ritual sweets from the Muslims. Further, the Muslims began to refuse to eat meat killed by non-Muslim butchers.

All these events led to the formation of a society called "Hindu Sangathan." . . . The only rule which it has, that has anything to do with the Mohammedans is that it prevents the Hindus from eating and drinking with the Mohammedans. The root of that rule is, that just as a Mohammedan is bound by his religion to exclude Hindus from some things so is a Hindu bound by *his* religion not to eat or drink with anyone who kills or eats the animal sacred to the Hindu Religion.

No doubt many petitions must have reached the government from the Mohammedan Community complaining many thing against the Hindus and their society but the society has no other laws that effect the Mohammedan than the one mentioned above. It has nothing in the way of an anti-Mohammedan movement. So far no petition has been sent to the government by the Hindus because the affairs with which they deal are religious and not political. The Hindu Sangathan is not a political "Sabha" or society. It is simply a religious society trying to keep the Hindus from ignorance.

The original anti-*sangathan* movement letter from "Hindoos" in Rewa was written in English and typed, typed on the same machine that later produced the letter from the Muslim leaders (judging from unmistakable details of the typeface), probably by the same person (judging from the formatting and manner of introducing corrections to the text). The twelve "Hindoo" signers of the original letter were listed neatly by name, father's name, and address, and all signed by means of a thumbprint. The five signers of the Muslims' letter signed by hand, three in roman script, one in devanagari script, and one in arabic script. The first two signers of the Muslim letter were Abdul Karim and Gulam Nabi, the first and fourth signers of the memorial of the Provisional Committee for the Attainment of Muslim Political Rights of the month before—a document also prepared, probably by the same typist, on the same typewriter. The letter defending the Hindu Sangathan Sabha was also in English, but handwritten; it declared itself to be from "the Hindu Community of Rewa," and its thirty-two signers all wrote their own names, twenty-one in roman script and eleven in devanagari. Thakur Kundan Singh Kush was not among them.

As well as revealing the extremely close connection between local "religious" and colonywide "political" boycott controversies—Pearson later put it succinctly in July 1930: "The Arya Samajists are bitter over what they term the betrayal of the Indian National party by the section of the Indian Mohammedans which were formerly associated with them" (CSO 1837/30)–these details of the letters suggest some of the ambiguities of representation that can surround Indian letters to the government. By 1930 these letters reflect wider mastering of English prose and colonial letter-writing genres. The two letters from the typewriter both finish "We beg to remain, Sir, Your most obedient servants," the later one spreading this across three lines, while the *sangathan* defenders' letter concludes, spread over two lines, "We are The Government's most loyal subjects:—". But precisely because English literacy was still so thinly spread, and because the first letter prearranged for its signatories to sign by thumbprint, we might wonder who was speaking, mediated by what letter-writing agencies, especially when the "Hindoos" of the first letter wrote of the murder case that "we knew that the Muslim League's name was implicated merely as a bait" and that "it was unnecessary for the Hindoo Community to retain the services of a lawyer."

The *sangathan* movement represented itself as religious and not political (in contrast to the Muslim claims connecting local and colonywide boycotts), as dedicated to keeping the Hindus from ignorance, as responding to Muslim boycotts, as seeking to protect what was sacred in the Hindu community, as the organized voice of the Hindu community. But as we can see, the Rewa Muslim leaders read the project as political and responded politically. This active, though very local, effort to organize and discipline the social ranks of Hindus brought into question colonywide the matter of Arya Samaj hopes to lead and represent all Fiji's Hindus.

By mid-1930 many non–Arya Samajis had withdrawn from the Hindu Maha Sabha as well as the Fiji Indian National Congress, severely damaging the claims of the organizations to represent, respectively, the Hindu community and the Indians as a whole. On 29 June 1930 the Hindu Maha Sabha held its general meeting in Nausori, Rewa, elected Thakur Kundan Singh Kush its president, and passed more than a dozen resolutions, including, reported the *Fiji Times,* one "requesting Hindus to organize themselves and to adhere to the teachings of the Hindu Dharma as regards diet and to disregard all those who willfully vex Hindus by their activities," and another "supporting all resolutions passed by Sangathan Sabhas and Ba Young Men's Sabha appealing to Indians to boycott Dr. Beattie and his Pacific Press and Vriddhi." (On this boycott, see below.) The chairman of the meeting, a Kabir Panthi *mahant* named Pingal Das, in his opening speech declared it as a goal of the Maha Sabha "to promote greater solidarity among all sections of the Hindu community and to unite them more closely as parts of one organic whole, to protect and promote Hindu interests and Hindu rights whenever and wherever necessary." Pearson (in CSO

1837/30) passed judgment: "This Maha Sabha has really fallen largely into the hands of a sectional organization but seems anxious to pose as the general association representing the Hindus of the colony and to advertise itself as such."

In July 1930 there was another cow-slaughtering controversy, in Vatuwaqa, an area outside Suva. But more importantly, controversy took a new turn as spokesmen for the "Sanatan Dharm" began to make explicit challenges to the Arya Samajis, sometimes using Beattie's publications against Vishnu Deo's *Fiji Samachar*. McMillan noted about the cow-slaughtering, on 28 July 1930, that "the Arya Samajists are so preoccupied with their controversy with the Sanatan Dharmis, that there may be a temporary lull in the Moslem question" (CSO 1774/30). In the same file on 29 July, the Chief of Constabulary also noted the "considerable amt. of feeling round Suva and Rewa between the Arya Samajists and the Sanatan Dharm. The Arya Samajists have issued a challenge backed by fifty pounds for a religious argument. The pundit selected by the Santanists who took up the challenge was assaulted by an Indian taxi-man."

Thus began the debates between the Arya Samaj and the Sanatan Dharm, at a time when Indians boycotted the Legislative Council, Muslims petitioned for separate representation, McGusty and Pearson debated *panchayats,* and McElwaine awaited word on the revision of the marriage laws he had passed in Pearson's absence. Perhaps most important, it was also a time of *swaraj* revitalization in India, following Gandhi's salt march of 12 March to 6 April. To Fiji's Indian language press, the accelerating events in India, and the nationalist modes of evaluating them, were the basis for understanding and evaluating all that was happening in Fiji as well; with this understood we can approach the controversies between Beattie's publications and Vishnu Deo's *Fiji Samachar,* which were also accelerating at the time.[5]

Everything that became controversial for the Indians in 1930 provoked a new deployment of Indian nationalist rhetoric. The Fiji Indian National Congress was in 1929 the moral champion of Indian nationalism, consensus vessel of its wisdom and its project. As Fiji Indian unity unraveled in 1930, a competition emerged to capture the authority and virtue of the Indian nationalist voice. We can see this happening if we consider some excerpts from Fiji Indian vernacular newspapers gathered by the newly watchful Fiji government.[6]

5. See note 5 in chapter 5 for a survey of the Indian-language press in Fiji at this time.
6. I do not have the original articles, but only the translations, as they appear in the confidential government files monitoring potentially "seditious" literature.

Vaidik Sandesh, a Fiji Arya Samaj newspaper, used some of the tropes of the nationalist rhetoric when describing the situation in India in April 1930:

> Readers are aware of the continuance of terror in India. At this time the Government, being incensed, is using strong measures of repression. Just as when a lamp is blown out it gives one final flame, so the Government realising its last hour has come is showing its last flare, and is by repressive measures seeking to stamp out the non-co-operation movement. Lovers of this country have vowed that rather than remain slaves it is many times better to be martyred for the good of one's country. This fight will be recorded in letters of gold in the world's history. The success of this struggle depends upon India's people. We admit that at this time they do not possess machine guns with which to oppose this brute force, but they have an effective weapon before which brute force cannot linger, viz., the infallible weapon satyagrah, such as has been tried in Africa and other places.

One might have expected revolutionary rhetoric of this type to be opposed by the *Pacific Press,* Beattie's trilingual newspaper, generally supportive of and supported by the Indian Reform League. Fiji's government, at least, hoped it would be more "moderate" and was sharply disappointed to find the following in its 31 May 1930 issue:

> In connection with the satyagrah (soul-force) movement, instigated by Mahatma Gandhi last March to bring independence and salvation to India, all brave and good sons of India are taking part with mind, body, and wealth. A number of leaders of this non-violent satyagrah have already been punished with imprisonment. But Mother India's inoffensive, resolute and worthy sons have made up their minds to take breath only when India has been made independent.

While "immoderate," however, the *Pacific Press* was not declaring allegiance with the Arya Samaj newspapers and cause. In fact, Samajis and their newspapers had recently begun to call for a boycott of the *Pacific Press,* because *Pacific Press* had published criticisms of K. B. Singh, an Arya Samaji schoolteacher involved in the *sangathan* controversies, attributing to him slanders against Mohammed.[7] The *Pacific Press* article quoted above continued:

> At this time we overseas Indians ought with one heart and one voice to pray to Almighty God the Father to grant the desire of these brave and worthy sons of

---

7. In CSO 1837/30 Pearson connects the newspaper boycott also to the "differences of opinion over the Indian Congress organisation, the Jubilee Celebration and Council politics apart from differences over religious matters, and natural resentment against Arya Samaj attacks on Christianity." K. B. Singh eventually went on to replace Vishnu Deo on the Legislative Council, as discussed below.

Mother India and speedily make India free. But, sad to say, the very opposite of this is taking place. Today the fires of dissension and division are flaring up, especially in Suva and Nausori. Indeed it is this which keeps Indians ever in subjection. . . . (Here follow references to the announced boycott of Dr. Beattie and his papers.)

Tropes of Indian political unity and struggle—brave hearts and selfless, undivided loyalty, support for Gandhi's *satyagraha* campaigns, and appeal to God (though here "God the Father") for political salvation— were employed by the *Pacific Press* to criticize the campaigns of some of Fiji's leading Indian political organisers. The rhetoric of nationalist struggle became a means of scoring points in sectional disputation.

Fiji Samachar replied with its own version of the rhetoric of nationalism. In May 1930 *Fiji Samachar* published an article by Shri Krishna Sharma, written from India. Sharma intended to return to Fiji at the time but was shortly thereafter denied entry by the Fiji government. He wrote:

India will be free, there is no question about that: but when the history of Independent India is written, then a stain and a black mark will be placed against the names of those communities and individuals who today are not taking any part in this holy war. A few religious fanatics make the excuse of self-preservation and are crying out for communal representation.

This is a time when every son of India, whether here or overseas, should make this [the?] one objective of his very religion, that he will either sacrifice all and win independence, or else lay his body upon India's altar and receive immortality. No, no, but it should be the desire of every young man to repeatedly lay down his life upon the country's altar and be re-born until India wins complete independence.

There is no need for leaders in the service of the country who, making secure their own positions, make an outward display of Hindu-Muslim unity by beseeching Muslims and cursing Arya Samajis: but the need is for pure and holy patriots who will care nothing for pleasing or offending anyone. That is the spirit in which matters are progressing in India today, and Youth Leagues being formed.

The Arya Samajis appealed on nationalist grounds for support for the Arya Samaj and opposition to other sectional groups. They argued by means of the standard Indian nationalist trope of devout disinterested self, corrupt self-interested opponents.[8] The "pure and holy patriots"

8. For the development of this trope see especially the history of nationalist interpretation of the Bhagavad Gita: Vivekananda, Tilak, and then Gandhi each found in the text a charter for distinguishing the selfless and good from the selfish and evil. Further, each in his own way found in the text a call for all good people to serve their nation, a special Indian nationalist political or economic duty. I discuss this further in Kelly 1988a, 1988b, n.d.b.

had to oppose especially the Muslims and others who, in India and in Fiji following the boycott of the Legislative Council, called for separate and special protection of their separate communities. Nationalist interests were, to such Arya Samaj spokesmen, to be furthered by organizational efforts such as the *sangathan* movement, with a goal of creating one politically effective national community. Anti-Muslim (and anti–*Pacific Press*) boycotts were justified on the grounds that the boycotted group was obstructing nationalist organizing efforts.

By mid-1930 the Fiji Indian newspapers, the Indian Reform League, the Fiji Muslim League, and the Fiji Arya Samaj were tangled in self-righteous accusations and counteraccusations. Because the colonial government did not reply to the boycott with any offer of reform, there was nothing left in colonial politics for the Fiji Indian politicians to do. Most awaited word of events elsewhere, especially Kenya (where the Kenyan Indians finally abandoned their noncooperation campaign in 1933), and hoped for help from India and London. In the meantime attention focused for two years on the sectional and religious controversies. As the clerk to the Suva Police Magistrate, A. G. Sahu Khan, put it in his confidential report on Indian affairs in March 1931:

> My report is principally on religious manoeuvres for there is no other activity amongst the community which I may report. "Religion" is the talk of the moment amongst the Indians.

The Arya Samaj and the Sanatan Dharm

The targets for the powerful anticolonial rhetoric were shifting, from the British to perceived enemies within the Indian community, enemies with religious identities. But if the anticolonial tropes were newly mobilized in communal religious disputes, we should also recall, first, that many of them were already religious in origin and substance, and second, that the religious disputes already had a long and intemperate history. In a sense, serious public controversies over religious matters among Fiji Indians began with the preaching of such missionaries from India as Shri Krishna Sharma in 1927. By then a tremendous body of propagandistic religious literature was available in India for use in Fiji, and despite the Muslim League call for its interdiction, it is important by all sides. And we might touch, for a final time, on an important, earlier beginning to this religious discourse and counterdiscourse.

The Christian mission to the Indians in Fiji stressed the uniqueness of Jesus with a particular theme: that of all great religious figures, Christ was the *only* one who never sinned. This claim was probably part of the rhetoric of Burton and other missionaries in indenture days. It was certainly present circa 1930 (as confidential clerk reports of a Christian/Muslim debate in Lautoka in 1933 suggest) and was still part of Christian mission rhetoric in 1985, as I had occasion to observe when the Sai Baba organization invited a Catholic nun to address them on Easter about the significance of the holiday. As was discussed in chapter 4, this rhetoric also had a concrete reverse aspect—the disparagement of other religions.

Not only did the Christian missionaries, in India and in Fiji, express disdain in general for the non-Christian practices of the Indians, generating a need for others to defend the morality of their own religion. The Christians also developed explicit attacks on the morality, especially the sexual morality, of the gods and prophets of other systems. When Fiji constables were sent in 1927 to question Shri Krishna Sharma confidentially about his plans and habits, he complained to them about the way he and Hindus in Fiji generally were harassed by the Christian missions. In evidence he produced a pamphlet entitled *Shiva Pariksha,* "Shiva Tested," published in 1918 in Allahabad. Pearson soon after approached Rev. G. H. Findlay of the Methodist mission to the Indians and found that, indeed, the mission had several copies of the pamphlet and at one time had made use of it in its work in Fiji. The pamphlet was quite simply an attack on the morality of a Hindu god. To quote the government translation of key passages,

When Narayan (a god) disguised as a woman, then Shiva wanted to commit an offense and pursued Narayan. To save himself from the evil desire of Shiva he cut off Shiva's male organ.

Beloved [address to reader] for remission of their sins Hindus worship such shameful thing now a days. And those that go to Kashi for pilgrimage in the hope of salvation they go and see that part.

* * *

Hindus why do you look upon the drunken Shiva as your god. Why do you trust such a sinner for your salvation, which I cannot understand. Alas! Had Shiva been in this Hindustan today he would have consumed ganja, charas, opium, bang, todi liquor etc. same as his servants and would have become like animal.

Such rhetoric established a discursive space in which, in the 1920s in India and Fiji, Arya Samaj and Muslim polemicists joined combat both with the Christians and with each other. By 1930 their literature, some of it banned in India, was circulating in Fiji.

In 1930 and 1931 both the Arya Samajis and the Muslim League wrote to the government to protest the importation of literature offensive in its criticism of their religions (CSO 2226/30, 2600/30). The Muslim League primarily concerned itself with imported Arya Samaj literature. The Arya Samaj portrayed itself as hounded by Muslim, Christian, and even Sanatani sources—in 1931 accusing Sanatanis of importing a famous anti-Samaji pamphlet written by a Sanatan Dharm *pandit* in Karnal, Punjab, *Rangila Rishi*, "The Colorful Saint." According to McMillan's summary for the Fiji government (CSO 2600/30), *The Colorful Saint* extracted quotations from Dayananda's autobiography and a biography of him, then made comments casting doubts on everything from his parentage to his celibacy. It suggested that he became an ascetic to flee crimes he had committed and that the logic of his writings could be accounted for by his drug use. But this pamphlet, *Rangila Rishi*, was actually written in reply to an Arya Samaj pamphlet, *Rangila Rasul*, "The Colorful Prophet," which was a subject of Muslim protest in Fiji. The Samaj pamphlet had also attacked the sex life of the founder of the other's religion. *The Colorful Prophet*, first published in 1924 in Lahore, is described by Thursby (1975: 43–44) as follows:

The assumption upon which the pamphlet proceeded was that each founder of a religion or each great religious personage made some *distinctive* contribution to our understanding of the possibilities of human life through his teachings and actions. . . . For example, the author claimed that Swami Dayanand exemplified the type of the life-long celibate and was symbolized by the Vedas. . . . Muhammad, according to the author, embodied the type of a widely "experienced" person and would best be symbolized by his wives. . . . An accepted convention required that the essay, which had the surface appearance of being a lyrical and laudatory evocation of the meaning of Muhammed and his teachings . . . should begin with appreciative couplets. . . . They set the tone of the pamphlet: . . . "The bird serves the flowers in the garden; I'll serve my Rangila Rasul."

The Fiji Muslim League wrote to the government in late 1930 to protest such literature and to report a rumor that large quantities of it had been sent for by the Arya Samaj. In its protest it relied on a phrase from the nationalist rhetoric: "Serious trouble will occur when this literature arrives and is released. There will be a terrible clash between the Hindus and the Muslims, because the Muslims will sacrifice their all to vindicate the honour of their Prophet and the sanctity of their religion" (CSO 2226/30). In the same months, however, the Samaj accused the Muslim League of circulating defamatory pamphlets of their own, with titles such as *Swami Dayanand, a Critical Study of His Life and Teaching*, and *Beef Eating among Ancient Hindus*. In 1931 the Samaj complaints concerned *Rangila Rishi*, which was highly recommended in the pages of the *Pacific Press*. The Sanatan Dharm missionaries denied allegations that they imported the pamphlet to Fiji.

By December 1930 the field of religious debate was already highly charged, with attacks and counterattacks from both the Arya Samaj and the Muslim League on record with the government and in the press. Further, the competition between the Samaji *Fiji Samachar* and the Christian-sympathizing *Pacific Press* had become endemic. Through 1930 and 1931 Vishnu Deo carried on published debates with Methodist missionary G. H. Findlay and others concerned with whether God had bodily form—as we have seen, a favorite topic for Samaj ridicule of the logic of other theologies. The Christian-Samaj controversy was not always so highbrow. In the confidential files on the Indian press, Pearson noted, in mid-1930, that the *Pacific Press* published "in the course of an argument with the Arya Samaj over religious matters and orthodox Hinduism an astoundingly outspoken reference to the phallic side of worship which though perhaps tolerable in Hindi would certainly lead to a prosecution for gross indecency if published in English." From the days of *Shiva Tested* and Shri Krishna Sharma on, a specifically sexual side of the controversies was also building.

Then a key event in December 1930 changed the situation. In the month of official Fiji's obsession with the arrival of the two Jehovah's Witnesses, and possibly even on the same ship, arrived Ram Chandra Sharma.[9] Ram Chandra Sharma was an effective Sanatani *dharmopadeshak*, "preacher of *dharma*," the Sanatani *pandit* requested by a nascent Fiji Sanatan Dharm leadership years before. The Fiji Arya Samajis had never faced such articulate opposition when they contrasted themselves with the blind traditionalism of "orthodox Hinduism." Ram Chandra gave a new vitality and a specific content to a "Sanatan Dharm" that was explicitly anti–Arya Samaj.

We will begin to understand Ram Chandra's Sanatan Dharm mission with the preface to a book he later wrote, *Fiji Digdarshan,* "Fiji Survey" (1937). The book was written in Hindi but included a foreword in English written by J. R. Pearson, who described Ram Chandra's mission from his own point of view:

Pt. Ram Chandra Sharma arrived on a much more definitely religious mission [than the Arya Samaj]. Whatever his political opinions may be he kept them in the back ground, though he had in fact gained experience as a propagandist in India in support of moderation in politics and trust in British good faith. But he would be the first to admit quite frankly that he came primarily as a missionary of the Sanatan Dharm perturbed at the hold the Arya Samaj was gaining on the Hindu community in Fiji and eager to guide it to the ancient and traditional faith. . . . It was at once apparent that Pt. Ram Chandra's teaching made a great

9. Or at least, Gillion (1977: 110) cites December 1930 as the time of Ram Chandra's arrival. But the *Pacific Press* of 18 October 1930 prints a *bhajan* citing Ram Chandra Sharma as composer; he may have come earlier in 1930.

appeal to large numbers and that it was giving them what they had been long seeking for. His abilities as a popular preacher and as conductor of revivalist meetings are on a high order and his hymns and music were received with great enthusiasm. He was untiring in his work as a missionary throughout the Colony and in his efforts to give organization and cohesion to the great body of Sanatanist adherents and inspire them with his own sincere devotion (pp. 11–12).

The politics of Ram Chandra Sharma were anything but "in the background" for Fiji's Arya Samajis. Within two months of his arrival in Fiji, they were circulating a leaflet attacking him as a traitor to Hinduism in Fiji (translation only, in CSO 2600/30). The immediate cause of the attack was not colonial politics—by no reports did Ram Chandra advocate, with the Christians and Muslims, an end to the Legislative Council boycott—but *sangathan* ("consolidation") politics. The leaflet was written and circulated shortly after a meeting in Rewa. Ram Chandra was invited to a meeting at a school there but caused dissension among the school managers by requesting that the meeting be opened to Christians and Muslims. The meeting, when held, was controversial. It was boycotted by those committed to the *sangathan* movement; in protest of their boycott, it passed a resolution in criticism of *sangathan* movement leaders Thakur Kundan Singh Kush and K. B. Singh. Following this came the leaflet calling Ram Chandra a traitor, and a meeting of a Sanatan Dharm Mahamandal ("great mandali," "central society") of Nausori Rewa condemning "the Christians, Muslims and so-called Sanatanists" who had criticized the *sangathan* leaders. The leaflet argued:

By being a Sanatani Brahman, I consider it my duty to notify the whole Sanatanist of the world that at this time some self interested (people) are trying openly and secretly to uproot the Hindu religion. From reading History it is found out that Jaichand mixing up with non-Hindus ruined India. . . . Yes the same way trick is being made to break the Rewa sangatan. Rumor is going round to destroy the Sangatan anyway as possible. By taking out notices in the name of all Indians, Sangatan will be made to disappear. Behind the preaching of Sanatan Dharm, non-tolerance and differences will be spread to cause disunity. When these sort of attempts are being made with the consideration of bringing Hindus ruination, then I consider at the least my duty to warn my Sanatan Dharmis.

At issue, in short, was the hope of the *sangathan* movement, for its local societies to its Hindu Maha Sabha, to represent and organize Hindu society as a whole. They were losing control. The name "Sanatan Dharm," "eternal *dharma*" or "eternal religion," was a name the Arya Samaj could also apply to the religion it advocated. But it was slipping from their grasp. Despite this effort to use it against him, the name "Sanatan Dharm" was usurped by Ram Chandra, the representative of the anti–Arya Samaj movement going by that name in India, the movement the Samajis had hoped to discredit in Fiji with the debate challenges of mid-1930. Their efforts to challenge his authority led next to violence at Ram Chandra's home, when he refused to come out to debate and one of his supporters was attacked by a Samaj member. The event received great publicity, much to the detriment of the Arya Samaj.

To establish in more positive terms "the ancient and traditional faith," the *sanatan dharm*, taught and supported by Ram Chandra Sharma, we can consider his own argument in *Fiji Digdarshan*. Unnoticed by multiple outside observers and interpreters, at the time and since, the Sanatan Dharm mission of Ram Chandra and others was not simply dedicated to a defense of miscellaneous "orthodox" rituals and dogma, but instead had a concrete focus: the propagation and definition of community around a particular text. He wrote (Sharma 1937: 27–29, my translation):

> The great Tulsi Ramayan delivers the medicine of immortality to the foreign-dwelling men and women, teaching the true lesson of constancy; the fruitful result of this hopefilled effort is that the singing and telling of the Ramayan every day, and especially at festivals, in religious places, and even in the homes of these Hindus, continues to today. Each year, in the month of *ashvin*, beautiful performances of Ram Lila are to be seen in excellent brilliance, which make manifest the existence of *bhakti* (devotion), produced by the Ramayan. . . .
>
> The Ramayan is the fifth Veda in the colonies, teaching Hindi and doing good for people. . . .
>
> God, who protects the eternal religion (*sanatan dharm*) with ordinary and extraordinary powers, knew that descendents of simple devotees would spend lives in foreign countries in the indenture system. Protecting Vedic rules against this environment would be not only hard but impossible. Thus God transformed Tulsi Das from unworthy to worthy, and gave the great power to him to put the essence of the four Vedas, eighteen Puranas, and six Shastras into his Ramayan. Today it is a great blessing that the name and glory of Ram has spread from India across the seven seas. In India, even without this Ramayan there would be people who know the Sutras, and simple people would be saved because the Vedic truths would still be known. But the foreign-dwelling simple ones trapped in evil work have no other religious protection. In foreign countries the solution for the protection of Hinduism is the Ramayan.

Ram Chandra Sharma himself asserted firmly that the Tulsi Das Ramayan was already known and recited, Ram Lilas performed, and so on, before his arrival in Fiji. As we saw in chapter 2, Ram's exile and Ravan's deluded evil were already being used as political metaphors in Fiji in indenture days. Thus the place of the Tulsi Das Ramayan in Fiji Indian Hinduism should not be traced solely to this Sanatan Dharm mission. But it was the purpose of his mission to promote this text as the basis of Sanatan Dharm, to make it and its version of devotionalism the focus of "traditional" Fiji Indian Hinduism—and in this, the mission succeeded. A significant part of the story concerns the rest of the events of Ram Chandra Sharma's first full year in Fiji, 1931.

As the year went on, many sources attest, the Sanatan Dharm missionaries criticized Vishnu Deo, the other Suva-Rewa Arya Samaj leaders, and their *sangathan* project in successful and well-attended meetings. Ram Chandra, and also a more combatative Sanatani arrival named Murarilal Shastri, were particularly well received on the western side of Viti Levu; even the Arya Samaj groups there (following leaders such as Raghvanand) were already largely against the *sangathan* project. The Sanatani preachers were revealing that the Fiji Hindu public was skeptical of the aggressive Suva-Rewa Arya Samaj groups. In response, broad attacks on the politics and theology of the Sanatani preachers began to appear in *Fiji Samachar*. The 28 February issue[10] printed a satire of Ram Chandra's politics, in the form of a petition he was purportedly submitting to the government calling for prohibition of the sale of *ya-qona* (kava, a mildly intoxicating, popular social drink) and of beef, "as it offends the religious scruples of the Sanatan Dharmis":

3. that, as high and low caste Hindus cannot eat, drink, or sit together, therefore separate schools for separate castes be established by Government, and that only high-caste boys be allowed to study in Government high-schools;

4. that, as leather defiles Sanatan Dharmis, all leather washers in water-pipes be removed and rubber ones be substituted;

5. that, as leather is a forbidden article to Sanatan Dharmis, State aid be afforded to import canvas shoes and fibre trunks, and that an effort be made to stop the importation of leather goods by imposing a very heavy duty;

6. that, as the age for legal marriage in Fiji is contrary to Sanatan Dharm teachings, the Ordinance be amended to make marriage legal for girls of ten and boys of twelve years of age.

It is reported that there will be five signatures on this Petition, and that it will be presented to Government on behalf of sixty thousand Sanatan Dharmis.

The point of the satire was that the political and social convictions imputed to the Sanatan preachers were not only irrelevant and impractical for Fiji, but also, in matters such as caste and marriage age, actually immoral. The satire also sought to reverse a criticism frequently leveled at the Arya Samaj and the Hindu Maha Sabha, by suggesting that Ram Chandra (only a few months into his mission) was pretending to a leadership he did not have. A small Sanatan Dharm newspaper called

10. I quote again from the government press file, and from McMillan translations. At this point the file is not confidential; this quotation and those following are from CSO F51/6.

Sanatan Dharm appeared on occasion to reply, but the Sanatanis did most of their replying at public meetings. I have no accounts of Sanatan Dharm meetings in 1931 clear enough to determine what Ram Chandra and Murarilal advocated in fact about caste and marriage laws. Ram Chandra himself was known to keep to a strict vegetarian diet and to be particular about his cooks, but on the other hand, as both his open meetings policy and much of the rhetoric of *Fiji Digdarshan* suggest, he was an advocate of tolerance and praised the Hindu-Muslim tolerance and religious sharing of indenture days.

The real point for the Arya Samaj leaders, however, was the need to organize the Hindus and press forward on a political and social agenda. The central criticisms of the Sanatani *pandits* concerned their interference in this project. Thus, while an anonymous writer to *Fiji Samachar* on June sixth found fault with "Sanatan Dharm pandits who block the path to unity and concord," one of the Rewa schoolteachers active in the *sangathan* movement called for its support in explicitly political terms:

K. B. Singh of Tausa writes at length on the need for organized union among Hindus. The writer shows that just as great fishes swallow little fishes, or one experienced gambler impoverishes less skilled players, so powerful races swallow up weaker ones. As Bismarck unified the states of Germany so that, welded into a powerful whole they were able to defy the whole world and just as Japan has so organized that she is able to hold her head up in the world, so different sects of Hindus need to combine together and present a united front. Therefore organise Sangathan Sabhas in every settlement and a Hindu Sabha in every district so as to be well organised to oppose external forces.

In fact, by this time the *sangathan* movement was already collapsing, even in Rewa, where South Indian cultural organizations were emerging to criticize efforts to force a separation between South Indian Hindus and Muslims and convincing South Indians in the *sangathan* movement to leave it (CSO 2600/30). The challenge to *sangathan* posed by the Sanatan *pandits*, however, came at a more fundamental level. At issue was the overarching principle of the Arya Samaj that political struggle was the *dharma* and *satya*, duty and truth, of this age.

In late 1930 and through 1931, the Indian vernacular newspapers reported challenges to debate, from the petty ("An offer of five pounds by Shambu Das . . . to anyone who can prove certain things connected with the life and teachings of Kabir Sahib," 13 June 1931 *Fiji Samachar*) to the bold ("Poem, over the name of Surendra of Suva, boastfully calling upon Pdt. Ramchandra Sharma to accept a challenge to religious debate, failing which he is only fit to be called a jackal," 6

June 1931 *Fiji Samachar*). As early as March 1931, according to the confidential clerk's report for Suva of A. G. Sahu Khan,

the various sections of the Indian community have been much enthused by the prospect in the near future of a public (religious) debate between the Arya Samaaj leaders and the Sanatan Dharam Pundits. . . . The Christians and the Muslims are somewhat jubilant about the impending debate, for in it they see a frustration of the Arya Samaaj design to crush the non-Hindoos in this Colony by uniting, organising, and strengthening the various sections of the Hindoo community under their own (Arya Samaaj) banner. . . . In the afternoon of 22nd March, 1931, a public meeting was held at Samabula under the auspices of the Sanatan Dharam Sabha with the object that, as arranged by correspondence, the Pundits of the Sabha would question the leaders of the Arya Samaaj on theological matters and thereby prove to the general public the falsity of the Arya Samaaj beliefs. This was done in response to a notice published in the Fiji Samachar by the Secretary of the Arya Samaaj. The Arya Samaaj leaders attended this meeting somewhat belatedly and refused to have any discussion, on the ground that the time arranged was 7.30 P.M. and the place "Arya Mandir." Great talking ensued from both sides and I am told chaos prevailed. The Pundits declined to go to the "Arya Mandir" at night, preferring to have the discussion during the day time and in a place where all and sundry can attend. A similar meeting was again held at the Imperial Picture Theatre on 29th March, 1931. The Arya Samajists, shrewd as they are, will not fall an easy prey.

In May, according to Pearson, "the invasion of the Arya Samajists of the Sanatani meeting at Navua ended in uproar and challenges to 'step outside.' The Police had to interfere."[11] The confidential clerk's report for Navua reported this encounter as a victory for the Sanatanis:

Two Sanathan Dharam priests, late arrivals from India, came over to hold a religious meeting. A number of Arya Samajists followed them from Suva and were present at the meeting with a distinct purpose of causing a disturbance. They interrupted the meeting but the audience being Sanathans, the Arya Samajists' object failed and they had to leave in shame and fear, realising their position unsafe. The Sanathan Dharamists were jubilant over their achievement.

But the conflicts were far from over. By late May, negotiations for more proper debates were advancing. Pearson wrote on 21 May:

Controversy simmers on, mainly over the question whether an open debate should be held as to the points of doctrine at issue. The Sanatanis insist that the whole question of the Arya Samaj interpretation of the Vedas (the Hindu Scriptures) should be gone into if a debate is to be held and claim that they are only being forced into it by taunts from the Arya Samajists. The Arya Samaj

11. This quotation and other quotations and references to these debate controversies, unless otherwise noted are from CSO 2600/30.

paper the "Fiji Samachar" is publishing replies, piece-meal and rather trying to make out that their faction are not the challengers.

By mid-June, meetings devoted to debates between the organizations were a reality. The newspapers carried complex correspondence concerning them, both establishing the rules for future debates and criticizing the conduct of past ones. Quarrels over procedure were at times a part of the debates themselves. For example, in meetings (apparently designated for Sanatani reply to Arya Samaj questions) in Suva on 21 and 23 June, Murarilal spent several hours criticizing "unsavoury practices" of the Arya Samaj. At the second meeting, Vishnu Deo was given five minutes to reply. Wrote the Inspector-General of the Constabulary: "He endeavoured to continue. On an attempt being made to stop him, his adherents rushed to the platform and high words ensued. Odin Ramrakha intervened in the interests of peace, urging that it was only fair to give Vishnu Deo a few minutes more. The Police, who were present, also called for order, which was restored." Ramrakha, a government clerk, was chastized for taking part in the meeting, even as a peacemaker. Concerning the content of the debate, Pearson minuted that it was "all about some rather obscure Arya Samaj tenet relating to marriage"—almost certainly the form of liaison called *niyog*.

By July Indians were arrested in Nausori for "riotous conduct" in connection with a Nausori (Rewa) debate, in which references to obscene conduct by Hindu deities, according to the Inspector-General of the Constabulary in a confidential file, "were used by the Arya Samaj as arguments to show that the Sanatan doctrine is unsound or unworthy of adherence." In the July issues of *Fiji Samachar*, Vishnu Deo printed many of the "obscene" excerpts read and criticized in the Rewa meeting. Rev. McMillan made his newspaper report confidential and refused to translate the obscene passages. Instead he gave them for translation to Pearson's Indian clerks, then corrected their translations. (E.g., "'touching ——— and thighs' should be 'touching curly hair, thighs, waist-band and ———,'" "'took Radha and went away' should be 'took Radha to a lonely place and ———'" "at the end, after 'with both her hands,' add 'and cooled her feverish desires.'" Blanks were reportedly also present in the original texts.) When the Governor saw the translations, he wished to prosecute, finding that "the obscenities are of a nature which cannot be tolerated in a British Colony," but Pearson and others disagreed, Pearson minuting that "standards of decency differ." In any case, the Inspector General of the Constabulary had lost the file for months, and when the Governor saw the file in October, it was too late to prosecute.

There were no further debates after July. The Sanatanis chose to stop participating; on 25 July the Sanatan Dharm Sabha wrote to the government to protest:

My Sabha have the honour to submit the following facts for the information and consideration of the Government:

That a religious controversy was carried on by the Arya Samaj and the Sanatan Dharm Sabha both of Suva for the last few months, and finally it was agreed by the both parties to read once only questions and answers of the debate in their own respective meetings.

It was also agreed that the Samajists were to confine their answers to Vedas only (Ancient Holy Books). But they have quoted from Hindu Holy Books and also from Christian Bible contrary to the Agreement.

Further they have read the said "Questions and Answers" in their four meetings, thrice in Suva and once in Nausori Picture Hall with abusive criticisms contrary to the agreement which aroused much commotion and an assault took place in the meeting at Nausori, and only by timely arrival of the police saved what might have been much more serious consequence. The matter is still in the hands of Rewa police.

While determining his response to the Sanatani protest letter, Pearson minuted his view of the debates as a whole:

The controversy between the Arya Samaj reformers and the orthodox Sanatanis culminated in a debate of the nature described. The Sanatanis persisted in accepting the challenge in spite of my advice and now each side accuses the other of breach of faith and claims a victory. This was only to be expected. Controversy centered not on questions of theological doctrine but largely on questions of sexual morality. The Arya Samajists taunted the orthodox with believing in Gods whose amours are described in what to European ideas seem grotesque and obscene detail in the old religious books. The Sanatanis retorted by challenging certain doctrines relating to sexual relations preached by the founder of the Arya Samaj faith. It is not easy for the non-Hindu to appreciate distinctions in the many shades of interpretation of Hinduism between extreme literalism and extreme symbolism especially as some popular forms are tinged with the phallic cult. The whole controversy appears to our eyes on a deplorably low level.

In his confidential report for June, the only one to address the debates in detail, Sahu Khan noted more simply that meetings led by Vishnu Deo for the Arya Samaj, and Murarilal Shastri for the Sanatanis, "are held nearly every week. . . . Profane expressions of the worst possible nature are made from both sides." He also noted that when the "Hindoo Maha Sabha" met on 21 June 1931 only 150 people attended; the "orthodox Hindus boycotted," and Murarilal's meeting to criticize the Arya Samaj at the Imperial Picture Palace, on the same day, drew a crowd of three or four hundred. The political program of the Samaj was stalled. Sahu Khan concluded, "If, at the present juncture, a capable 'Orthodox' Hindoo (Sanatanist) offers for election, Mr. Vishnu Deo is likely to suffer a sure defeat; but, fortunately for Mr. Vishnu Deo, the orthodox Hindoos find no such person in their community."

In chapter 9 we will discuss in greater analytic detail the turn these debates took, the matters of sexual morality and "profane expressions." To conclude this chapter let us finish the historical narrative. After the Sanatanis refused to participate in further debates, the Arya Samaj tried to keep the matters alive through *Fiji Samachar* and to shore up their position by raising local reform issues. In October, while the government was still stalemated over the problems in the "trafficking" of young girls, *Fiji Samachar* sought to focus new debate on the question of the minimum legal age for marriage for Indian girls. In November it sought to become the champion simultaneously of Hindus and of a higher minimum marriage age by attacking Pearson for attempting to arrange the marriage of a thirteen-year-old Hindu girl to a Muslim man. The case (Supreme Court civil case 73 of 1931) became a multi-sided controversy. Pearson accused the girl's mother of exploiting her as a prostitute and virtually holding her prisoner. He asserted that the girl herself wanted to marry the Muslim man in question. The girl's mother first sought to force Pearson to return the girl to her, then to have her turned over to G. H. Findlay and the Indian Girls' Orphanage of the Methodist mission. In court documents Pearson argued that "the girl's best chance of settling down now is for her to be married as soon as possible into a respectable family," and he opposed the assignment to the orphanage in favor of the marriage to the Muslim. The mother swore in court, "I do not wish that my daughter, a Hindu, should marry a Mohammedan. Such a marriage would be contrary to Hindu belief and custom." The court assigned custody of the girl to the Methodist mission and enjoined against her marrying the Muslim for two years. This was in effect a victory for Vishnu Deo, who again preferred Christian mission custody to marriage at a young age for a Hindu girl, especially marriage to a Muslim.

Such controversies could not resolve the fundamental issues between the Sanatanis and the Arya Samajis, however, and the Samaj was still not willing to withdraw from controversy. Instead, through the final months of 1931 *Fiji Samachar* announced the intent of the Arya Samaj to publish an account of the debates with the Sanatan Dharm. As time went on, the publication was delayed, and seems to have been expanding in size. The 25 July 1931 protest letter of the Sanatan Dharm Sabha had primarily been concerned to request that the government prohibit such publication. Citing rioting and murder in India after the publication of

Rangila Rasul, "The Colorful Prophet," the Sanatanis asked the government "in the interest of peace and order" to prohibit the pamphlet, as it was "bound to bring commotion and hatred among the Indian people." However, the government refused to intervene, Pearson minuting that "government can hardly object to a reasonable account of the debate."

The Obscenity Prosecution

The Arya Samaj put its account of the debates on sale in January 1932. The Executive Council of the Fiji government, annoyed by the misadventure over prosecution in 1931, had already ordered that "in the discovery of future obscene publications the Intelligence Committee should act immediately and directly through the Attorney General, without delaying to refer such matters to the Inspector General of Constabulary." On 9 January Rev. A. W. McMillan went one better. Having purchased and read the debate book as soon as it was available, as part of his duties in monitoring the Indian vernacular press, he sent the book and his report on it directly to the second-ranking official of the entire government, the Colonial Secretary. Because I do not have a copy of the book, shortly thereafter banned,[12] I can only quote from McMillan's description to give a sense of it and its contents:

4. The cover of the book reads thus:

Om.

DEBATES WITH THE ARYA SAMAJ IN FIJI

—in which the Suva Sanatan Dharm Sabha
suffered heavy defeat.

Publisher:
Arya Samaj, Suva, Fiji.

. . . 6. The book contains 117 pages. I have been through it. The Introduction refers to the coming to Fiji of the two Sanatan Dharm propagandists Pandits Ramchandra Sharma and Murari Lal Shastri, their reception, the religious controversy that developed, the terms of the debate, and the way in which the Arya Samaj suffered abuse.

Pages 1–14 reproduce Pdt. Murari Lal's statement on behalf of the Suva Sanatan Dharm Sabha (May and June), also correspondence with the local secretary Ram Shankar.

The rest of the book (nearly 100 pages) is devoted to the reply of the Arya Samaj.

12. A few copies are known to exist but, for obvious reasons, are not generally made available by the Fiji Arya Samaj.

7. The Arya Samaj endeavours thus to defend the character of their founder Dayanand, whose celibacy is questioned by Pdt. Murari Lal. An attempt is then made to defend the Arya Samaj practice of 'Niyog' (a sort of companionate marriage or temporary alliance for the procreation of children by a woman when her husband is dead, impotent, or spending considerable amount of time in a far-distant place).

There is no debate on questions of doctrinal belief, on God, scriptural inspiration, karma, idolatry, transmigration, sin, ritual etc.

8. The main effort is to throw discredit on ancient Sanskrit literature, most if not all of which is accepted by the orthodox Hindus as sacred, by quoting passages in Sanskrit, and then giving a Hindi translation of the passage, showing up horrible obscenities. The thrust is then driven home. "And this is the filth the pandit delights in!" or, "That is the kind of stuff the orthodox Sanatanis would have us accept!"

9. Practically the whole of the book deals with sex matters. A percentage of the stories deal with the immoralities of gods and goddesses, but not a very large proportion. . . .

. . . Merely to discredit ancient writings did not require that practically a whole book should be devoted to nauseating stories of sexual excesses.

The court records and the confidential file on the obscenity case include a few translated passages from the book. Some are descriptions of sexual play of minor and major divine figures, and others seem to be statements from manuals on sexual activity. Shiva and Krishna, perhaps especially the latter, seem to have been principal targets for criticism; play of Krishna and his *gopis* (female devotees) that McMillan called "amorous excesses" were described in graphic detail. A matter not completely clear is whether the passages ridiculed were literally excerpted from Puranas and other sources. In later confidential correspondence with the government (his 1932 request for a pardon), Vishnu Deo names "the Bhagwat, a Puran" (*Bhagavata Purana*), a principal Krishna-*bhakti* text, as the source of many of his quotations. But one of the translated passages, at least, seems to have been a summary of material rather than a quotation from a Purana. The year before, McMillan noted the same about the "obscene" material published in *Fiji Samachar:* "Most of the stories are taken from Hindu religious writings, but they do not appear to be actual quotations, being given in abbreviated form."

The government acted quickly upon receiving McMillan's 9 January report. Pearson, who had apparently set McMillan to watch for the book, minuted that he had warned those responsible that the "previous publications were objectionable." The Governor was anxious to prosecute and to seize and destroy the book. The matter was sent to the Attorney General on 11 January; he minuted that the publication was clearly obscene, and also seditious if the intent was to incite hostility. A prosecution for sedition would have meant a political trial and Sanatan Dharm witnesses. Therefore, he favored a prosecution for the common-law misdemeanor of selling an obscene publication, for which the circumstances of a sale of the book were required. His original intention was to prosecute the managing director and the secretary of the responsible publishing company, neither of whom was Vishnu Deo. But when on the same day a purchase was staged to establish grounds for prosecution, the purchase was made in the *Fiji Samachar* office—from Vishnu Deo.

Whether it was designed or accidental to involve Vishnu Deo I do not know. In any case, on 12 January, the day after this purchase, the police raided the publishing house and seized all copies of the book still there. Vishnu Deo and another Arya Samaj leader, Babu Ram Singh, secretary of the publishing company, were brought to trial for selling an obscene publication. At their trial in March in an overflowing courtroom, they changed their pleas from not guilty to guilty and had their European barristers argue in defense of the Arya Samaj's social project. Singh's attorney argued (in the paraphrase of the *Fiji Times,* 9 March 1932):

Succinctly, it was a theological discussion which had inadvertently wandered into court. . . . We have here history repeating itself; it is the conflict between ancient and modern—a conflict that raged in Athens in Socrates' day, when the attack on the questionable words of the Olympian hierarchy commenced. . . . This prosecution constitutes a singular and signal vindication of the principles for which the accused are contending. In effect, the publication is an attack on these offending passages and intended as a condemnation of them. . . .

. . . With the Lordship's permission, may I be permitted to express the hope that the religious teachers may expurge from the religious literature these offending passages, or at least permit them to drop into obscurity. No one more readily recognises the splendid monotheism and spirituality of the great philosophers of India; but all these great heritages of mankind ultimately fall into the hands of clay of the commentators, who besmirch the face of Deity itself.

I also express my hope that, while the Hindu intellect may proceed untrammelled in its pursuit of truth, all controversy may be lifted to the plane of pure fact, where reason holds complete sway, undeflected by passions and emotions.

Vishnu Deo's lawyer argued, more particularly, that no real corruption had been intended or accomplished, if one took into account the state of the Sanatani Hindu mind:

To our mind, said counsel, the book was certainly disgusting, but he would ask his Honour to consider the fact that the object of the publication was not to corrupt, but to defend their teachers. If the book had been published in English, he would certainly not have attempted to excuse the offense in any way.

He submitted that the corruption, in the main, would be on the Indian community, and he would ask his Honour to consider the fact that the matter complained of was contained in the Puranas, which could be bought freely throughout the Colony.

His Honour: Yes, but that is not the point. If I took extracts from the Bible and published them apart from their context it would be obscene.

Counsel said he would ask his Honour to consider the limiting effect of the book, and the fact that the Indian mind was already well seized of the matter complained of.

As their lawyers admitted hopefully in their defense summaries, Vishnu Deo, Babu Ram Singh, and, in effect, the Fiji Arya Samaj were "in your Lordship's hands," entrusted "to one whose comprehensive knowledge of men and affairs will enable him to deal wisely and well with a difficult position." The judge then condemned their publication. While leveling only a token fine, he criticized both men and the tenor of the Indian public debates more generally. In particular, he argued, the accused must realize that "no community will permit an outrageous and obscene attack upon the religious beliefs of any section thereof." He then gave an instruction to the entire Indian community, and especially to the Arya Samaj:

Before I leave this case I would like, even if it be somewhat without my province, to offer a word of advice. Sitting on this bench as I do, independent alike of the executive and the community, my only duty being to administer the law, tempering justice with mercy, this impartial position urges me to ask the Indian community to leave religious disputes out of the purview of public debate or controversy.

In this colony of Fiji there are both Europeans and Indians whose religious ideas can never merge in a complete unity. Among the Europeans are members of the Anglican and Roman Catholic faiths, Wesleyans, Seventh Day Adventists, and I daresay others. None of these expend their time and energy reviling or holding up to ridicule the beliefs of any other community and I would urge the Indian community to exercise a like toleration.

In a Colony such as Fiji, where both Europeans and Indians have settled down in a strange land, surely both can work together loyally for the advancement of a common ideal, which should be the betterment of all classes in the land which has become their home—regardless of the religious faith of any particular section or individual.

I trust that it may not be too optimistic to hope that the ultimate result of this case will be a cessation of interference with the creeds of others.

Thus the Arya Samaj, and the Indians in general, were instructed to refrain from religious controversy. And further, the Arya Samaj was to regard the Sanatan Dharm as a "creed of others" and not interfere with it. Even before the debate book was composed and published, the Arya

Samaj had been losing ground in the Hindu community. While its leaders were still, after the obscenity case, regarded as Hindu and even supported by voters as the Hindu candidate in some races, the larger Samaj political project of a Hindu communal reorganization and political mobilization had already failed. The *sangathan* ("consolidation") project was moribund. By 1932 the Arya Samaj leaders were obviously frustrated and had been driven to an extreme measure. The debate book, an attempt to humiliate the Sanatanis, rebounded to their own humiliation. The final major campaign of the Arya Samaj battle for control and, by their lights, uplift of the Fiji Hindu community was over. It ended with a decisive defeat.

The Aftermath

In the years that followed, through World War II, Vishnu Deo was still a leader of influence in the Indian community. After five years he was again made eligible for Legislative Council and served several terms starting in 1937. But never again was his position unambiguous, and gradually overall priority shifted to the younger of the two barristers sent to Fiji by Gandhi, A. D. Patel, the man who eventually led the Fiji Indian representatives in the negotiations for Fiji's independence. Crucial for Vishnu Deo and the political project he had led in 1929 were the five years he was not eligible to run for office. He tried to get a pardon from the Governor to enable him to run again. Pearson was for it. One of his last memoranda, left for McGusty to have typed, concerned a possible application for pardon and argued in favor both on pragmatic grounds ("better in the Council than out of it with a semblance of a grievance") and on grounds of character ("As to the gravity of the offense and its moral delinquency . . . it is impossible to judge this matter by European standards. . . . Mr. Vishnu Deo has his defects, but he is certainly an able man."). McGusty wrote a note arguing against Pearson's view; addressing another of Pearson's points, he wrote, " I regard Mr. Deo's assumption of responsibility for the publication as an act of expediency, and not of virtue." Seymour, the Colonial Secretary, sided with Pearson, but only because the obscenity case did not truly reflect "moral turpitude"; otherwise he also had a dim view of Vishnu Deo's "personal character." Finally, Governor Murchison Fletcher flatly refused the pardon, noting that the offense was "most obnoxious" and the man "not a suitable representative of Indian opinion. There is the further objection that Mr. Vishnu Deo has thought it fit to flout the present Council, on which ground alone I would be unable to take any action which would in any way assist him to a seat in the new Council." Indian petitions for and against the pardon were ignored.

In 1932, when the government called for new elections, the 9 July *Fiji Samachar* called upon all Indians to remember Gandhi's instructions "to continue ceaseless agitation": "For the sake of your country, your nationhood, and most of all for the preservation of your dignity, let no candidates be nominated." However, the Indian Christian editor of Dr. Beattie's new journal *Vriddhi-Vani* had himself nominated, so Vishnu Deo engineered the nomination of one of the *sangathan* project schoolmasters, K. B. Singh. Singh won the election. But Vishnu Deo soon found that he could not control him. Singh eventually became a favorite of the Governor and even worked deliberately to frustrate continuing efforts to agitate for common roll. From this point onward, the Indians on the Legislative Council entered into what the Gramscians would call colonial Fiji's "normal politics," no longer contesting the basic framework.

After the banning of the Arya Samaj debate book and the convictions of Vishnu Deo and Babu Ram Singh in 1932, there was never again another intense public confrontation between the Arya Samaj and the Sanatan Dharm, nor another major public discussion of sexual morality among Fiji Indians.[13] Partly, perhaps, in awareness of the colonial scorn

13. In the 1980s slightly more than 10 percent of the Fiji Indian Hindus reported themselves as Arya Samaji. Some of these, I learned in the course of research, know little of Samaj history or theology and maintain *bhagwan sthan*, places for prayer to images of gods, including images and even deities rejected by the Samaj theologians. On Vanua Levu, Fiji's second-largest island, the Arya Samaj has come to be significantly more popular than it is on the main island, Viti Levu, leading whole settlements in some cases and defining a way of life and prayer there consistent with Samaj beliefs (see, e.g., Brenneis [1984] on "Batgaon"). On the main island of Viti Levu, the most faithful continuants of Samaj practice seem to be Samaj groups in the urban areas, often of elite and educated standing, who meet on Sunday mornings for worship services, including *havan* fire sacrifices. There are still many Arya Samaj schools in Fiji, but since the 1920s they have been more than rivaled by Sanatan Dharm schools, supported by local *mandali* groups and government grants-in-aid, and by Muslim schools and schools established by the government directly. The Fiji Arya Samaj no longer attempts a project of social transformation. Some of its leaders told me that the Arya Samaj had effectively accomplished what they intended to accomplish, since the Indian community was educationally, morally, and financially uplifted during the middle decades of this century. But since 1932 the Samaj has, by and large, followed the judge's instruction. Once the proponent of a vast social project, a Hindu nationalist revival and modernization, it has become a minority religious creed.

As to the debates over morality, in the 1980s the virtue of a woman was still a matter of extraordinary importance. Brenneis (personal communication) reports that for Fiji Indians on Vanua Levu, verbal or physical assaults on the virtue of a woman are one of the few matters that can motivate social out-casting. In both the city and the country in Viti Levu, young women and their parents are remarkably anxious about their marriages, parents domineering and strict in controlling their daughters' efforts to "date." And marriages are still major social events, no longer absorbing the proportion of income they did for prior generations, but still excruciatingly clear and important statements of family social and cultural affiliations and style. But public debate about these things is indirect and refor the Indian debates on sexuality of the early 1930s, and no doubt also concerned about further representations of their content, Fiji Indians with knowledge of them were reluctant to discuss these debates when I was in Fiji from 1984 to 1985. More generally I found a systematic forgetting, not only of the debates of the early 1930s but even of the discourse against indenture, especially in its depictions of abuses of women. At least until the more recent tribulations, the Fiji Indian community had willfully and collectively become a community of work ethic, piety, egalitarianism, sensitivity to insult, and repressed sexuality.

Fiji Indian political discourse moved from 1932 into new issues, options, challenges, and responses. By the late 1930s it had returned to the terrain of Bashishth Muni, to labor and sugar-growing issues. Labor unions and cane growers' unions were organized, and their leaders vied to be the "Gandhi of Fiji." New crises followed, especially over noncooperation in World War II. Eventually the unions, save one, coalesced into the National Federation Party, and it became the primary vehicle for Fiji Indian politics in the new nation. In 1987 the Fiji Indians briefly had a taste of victory in normal politics, when the NFP and a new Labour party in coalition won the election and formed a government—only to see the indigenous Fijians negate the terms of "normal politics" in a pair of military coups. These matters require their own treatment.[14] In independent Fiji, and even by the days of World War II, the political issues debated by Indians were different from those of 1929–1932, especially because the Fiji Indians were by then in dialogue with indigenous Fijians as well as, and finally instead of, with the British.

---

strained. Sexual and social morality are primary themes of very popular Hindi-language films imported from India, where the conflicts are usually between the girl's father and the boy, rather than between the young lovers. In these and other ways statements about sexual virtue are made and remade in public discourse and practice. But options in customary form are no longer debated and are less intertwined with other social, religious, and political issues.

14. On Fiji Indian egalitarianism and sensitivity to insult, see especially Brenneis 1983, 1984, 1987; on repressed sexuality, see also Brown 1984. For the best accounts of the coups, see Lal 1988 and Kaplan 1988; for a study of Fiji Indian political discourse from Fiji's "independence" to the coups, see Kelly 1988b. For other, broader accounts of Fiji Indian political history, see Mayer 1963, Ali 1980, and especially Gillion 1962 and 1977.

Hinduism, Sexuality, and
Countercolonial Discourse: A Politics
of Virtue and the Failure of the
Arya Samaj

We now ask *why*. The years 1929–1932 were a time of other changing
conditions, from world capitalist crisis to local debates official and unofficial about a wide range of administrative institutions, a time when it
might have seemed wiser for the Fiji Indians to have kept their public
discourse focused on the local conflict in electoral politics and the ongoing countercolonial action in India. Why did the Fiji Indians instead
become so engrossed in such a fatal debate about sexual morality?

Simple explanations are possible. Perhaps the colonial officials
provoked them, implicitly (or even explicitly) following Dr. McGusty's
principle, divide and conquer. But why then were the officials always out
to diffuse the pressures and suppress the debates? My sense is that the
European colonials were genuinely disgusted by the debates and their
topics and genuinely feared and disliked all forms of what they saw as
Indian "agitation." Perhaps this is not itself proof that the Fiji Europeans did not incite the Indians' discourse; imagining the colonial
strategies as unconscious and diabolical, one could argue that they did
not mind being disgusted, enjoyed provoking the Indians to live up to
their image of them as sinister and immoral, and perhaps even needed
the debates as continuing evidence of the Indians' alleged degradation
of character. However, we cannot find the links, outside of the Christian
literature of long standing, for direct European provocation of these
Indian debates *on sexuality*.

A second simple explanation would be that the debates in Fiji were a
reproduction of the debates in India, that the Fiji Indians followed irre-

sistibly the trends of social and political events of the "nation" of their nationalism. This approach does not explain the failure of their Congress; nor can it be formulated as a matter of Fiji Indian leaders following the lead of Indian leaders. The most important Indian nationalists advising the Fiji Indians, Gandhi, Andrews, and especially Benarsidas Chaturvedi, were critics of Hindu-Muslim provocations and the Hindu intramural disputes and called upon Fiji Indians to suppress sectional disagreements and act in unison. When such a call from Chaturvedi was published in *Vriddhi* in August 1930, it only provoked Vishnu Deo and *Fiji Samachar* to publicize heroes from the homeland who supported their efforts, especially Bhawani Dayal Sannyasi (Gillion 1977: 114). In short, if Fiji Indians followed India's political leads, the Fiji Indian leaders chose which leads from India to follow. Similarly, the leaders imported from India claimed to be fitting their plans to conditions in Fiji, from S. B. Patel, who so carefully worked for political coalitions, to Ram Chandra Sharma, who was convinced that the Tulsi Das Ramayan was the Veda for overseas communities. We might then look to conditions and relations in Fiji for a more complex answer.

Half of the issue for any causal explanation is the definition of the effect, and causal explanations in interpretive social sciences swing uneasily from Marxist and Weberian to Durkheimian definitions of cause and effect relationships. In the Marxist vocabulary effects can be imagined as "moments" in a terrain of "dialectically" related historical structures; in this approach everything is ultimately a cause of everything in history, but all manner of secondary vocabulary can be developed to privilege one lineage of historical relations or another. The Weberian critique insists on the infinitude of causes, emphasizes the privileging as an act of the scholarly observer, and redefines the effect as a compound but real "historical individual" rather than as a "moment" within a stage of ongoing world historical evolution. The Durkheimian method seeks a unitary cause for each effect and requires the scientist to redefine the effect into disaggregated effects when more than one cause is found; subsuming the disaggregated effects is the organic whole of society, whose cause is itself, the aggregation of all causes. In the Marxist analytic the effects are products of a history that is a structuring process; in the Weberian they are consequences of a history with intentional actions but also irreducible complexity and chaos; in the Durkheimian they are manifestations not merely of history but of the organic, interior time of society and its self-reproductive evolutionary growth. It would be possible at this point to read the Fiji debates on Hinduism and sexuality as moments in a structuring process, or as a manifestation of social reproduction and growth, or, as I do, as a conjuncture of intentional actions in a chaotically complex social universe, with motives understandable and outcomes neither fully intended nor inevitable.

We will continue to investigate the effect as we try to imagine its causes; first we will investigate the focus on sexual morality, and then we will reconsider the relationship between colonial authority and the Arya Samaj. The reader will find opportunity to remake the phenomena by his or her own lights. In my own view, it is a Weberian terrain that makes both the tragedy and its lessons conceivable.

The Focus on Sexual Morality

We discussed, at the end of chapter 2, the synthesis of nationalism and devotionalism Gandhi accomplished in his *satyagraha* ("insistence on the truth") campaigns. We also discussed how the Indian nationalists focused attention on the virtue or chastity, *satitva,* of Fiji Indian *girmitiya* women and made it an issue of devotional politics that led to the fall of indenture. Fiji Indian politics began with concern over sexual virtue, bound to a devotional image, the heroine struggling to be chaste, devoted to her lord-husband, while the agents of indenture sought to exploit her. The Fiji Indians of the late 1920s inherited this rhetoric, and also a continuing social contradiction. As in indenture days, there were more men than women, men growing older without wives and households of their own. And both in indenture days and after, there was no accepted way for women to exercise choice and control over marriage relationships.

With the demographic imbalance and the pollution of indenture, Fiji Indian parents demanded bridewealth and brideservice to consent to *kanyadan,* "gift" of daughter in marriage, but Fiji Indians were aware that dowry was more proper for high, refined people; once the gender demographics balanced, the bridewealth relations associated with low castes in India were replaced by dowry requirements, first for elite marriages and soon after for all marriages in the "tender egalitarian" community.[1] The superiority of dowry over bridewealth was not the topic debated; that was generally accepted. The point is rather that the marriage system was under pressure and in flux. Marriages became major social events, difficult to negotiate, occasions that put cane growers into long-term debt. Marriages not only required decisions about what

---

1. On "tender" egalitarianism see Brenneis 1983. On the structure and history of marriage practices see Jayawardena 1971, 1975, Mayer 1978, Brown 1981, and Kelly (n.d.b.). There may also be an untold story of female resistance within this marriage history.

kind of officiant and ritual to employ, but revealed local lines of boycott by presences and absences. One reason for the high expense was that the absence or noninvitation of anyone local implied that the person was boycotted. In this context the legal manipulations allowed by official Fiji's culturally distant marriage laws, and issues such as widow remarriage and the minimum age of marriage, all had practical consequences. Further, the indenture rhetoric emphasizing the virtue or chastity of women carried with it reprobation for a woman who did not follow the rules of *satitva*, dedication to the man who was her husband. Interviews with surviving *girmitiyas* conducted in the 1970s (Ali 1979; Naidu 1980) suggest that *girmitiya* women were measured against two extremes, pressured to be the good, chaste woman and not the wicked manipulator, while also pressured by circumstances and even by violence to leave one man for another. Only time would solve the demographic problem, and in the meantime even into the early 1930s the growing daughters of Fiji Indian households were the objects of significant competition.

To Europeans, continuing the vision of the unspeakable Indian morality of the plantation coolie lines, the "trafficking" engaged in by the unscrupulous was a matter of obscene sexuality. While there was certainly prostitution in some cases, in others witnesses insisted that the series of "husbands" married by custom and moving in to work for the parents of their bride were not in fact cohabiting with her—including, for example the pathetic bankrupt who was hanged after murdering his mother-in-law. What was desired was marriage and a household. Sex was much more readily available.

Finally, let us remember a third source for sexuality concerns and rhetoric. The Christian mission and its aspersions on the unclean, impure, nonwhite religions of the world both provided tropes and required replies. Thus we have three contexts informing the rhetoric on sexual morality: the virtue rhetoric in the anti-indenture campaign, the contradictions in marriage law and practice, and the sexual obsessions of the colonial Europeans, especially the Christian mission. With all this said, however, I would like to suggest that another problem also informed the debates. Along with these obligations and contests, rhetorical spaces and issues, another important element had entered the Fiji Indians' situation. The Arya Samaj, siding with the Indian Reform League to advocate women's education, delay of marriage, widow remarriage, and a chastity of sexual abstinence, were arguing something like a Christian morality—but a "modern" Christian morality, a *bourgeois* morality. They also sought to master, and integrate into their own social and political projects, a capitalist grammar. They tried to make their own version of a bourgeois respectability, to organize a life that would enable not only Vedic *dharm* and anticolonial struggle but also profit.

Studies of bourgeois culture in various places and times tend to find in it, across other differences, an extraordinary mixture of asceticism and hedonism. This combination of asceticism and hedonism lies in the grammar of capitalism and organizes aspects of otherwise varying bourgeois groups across capitalist history, from merchants in Asia, to the European colonial capitalists, to the bourgeoisie exploiting wage-labor in emerging political-economic Europe, to the bourgeoisies that emerge among the colonized.[2] On the one hand, bourgeois practice is ascetic: not only organized by a utilitarian, calculating skill, the sort of skill in maximizing or profiting that Adam Smith (1776), Bourdieu (1977), and others mistake as human nature, but as Weber (1958) perceptively shows in his discussion of Benjamin Franklin, dominated by a haunting, unrelenting sense of a duty to profit. On the other hand, bourgeois practice is hedonistic: not only a love of things and a desire to consume, but a sense of self defined by possessions, a self that is what it has, reducible to a quantity of things and experiences successfully connected-to, wherein this quantity, this accomplished hedonism, is also a moral synthesis because by its nature it reflects also the accumulation of the maximizing ascetic (see Simmel 1978: 389; Baudrillard 1981, 1987; Mukerji 1983).

Considering Foucault's analysis in *The History of Sexuality*, vol. 1 (1980) we can understand how sexuality can become another object for simultaneously ascetic and hedonistic evaluation, another capital resource for development. The focal figures of Victorian sexual discourse, the hysterical woman, the pervert, the masturbating child, and Malthusian couple, were all cases of sexual investments improperly managed, undisciplined and misdirected. The proper combination of hedonism and asceticism (before the "sexual revolution" and its discovery of a duty to develop techniques and accumulate experiences) was love in marriage. Marriage in this grammar was like a luxury investment, a big house or a great work of art, a form that enabled simultaneously the impulses to consume and to have and save. In European capitalist history, and increasingly in contemporary South Asian and Fiji Indian communities, the romantic ideal of the "love marriage" is held up as the perfect synthesis of interests. But in South Asia and among Fiji Indians it competes with a different form of calculating interest, the calculations of the bourgeois patriarch over the marriages of his sons and daughters for the benefit of his extended household. In India such bourgeois Hinduism

---

2. For a more detailed discussion of the grammar of capitalism see Kelly 1988a. I will also be discussing it in future works, including Kelly 1991 and n.d.b.

has led to dowry murders, murder of the new wife when her family refuses to, or cannot, pay the dowry promised with the marriage. In Fiji it has led to suicides of young wives. Neither love marriages nor dowry conflicts were issues for Fiji Indians until later, more demographically balanced and more thoroughly bourgeois, times. But the problems raise a new terrain for consideration. Can it be said that these are the problems of a "modernizing" or "westernizing" community, or a community learning to regard sexuality, family, and marriage as a calculable type of value?

So Foucault (1980: 57–58) would have it. To Foucault sex was constituted as a matter of calculable knowledge only in the West in recent history:

> Historically there have been two great procedures for producing the truth of sex.
>
> On the one hand, the societies—and they are numerous: China, Japan, India, Rome, the Arabo-Moslem societies—which endowed themselves with an *ars erotica*. In the erotic art, truth is drawn from pleasure itself, understood as a practice and accumulated as an experience; pleasure is not considered in relation to an absolute law of the permitted and the forbidden, nor by reference to a criterion of utility, but first and foremost in relation to itself; it is experienced as pleasure, evaluated in terms of its intensity, its specific quality, its duration, its reverberations in the body and soul. . . .
>
> . . . Our civilization possesses no *ars erotica*. In return, it is undoubtedly the only civilization to practice a *scientia sexualis;* or rather, the only civilization to have developed over the centuries procedures for telling the truth about sex which are geared to a form of knowledge-power.

To follow Foucault, then, we need not bother with the discourses on sexual substances and exchanges in the various elaborated medical systems of India. We need not wonder what the celibate ascetic is reserving, the householder producing. To Foucault there are no non-Western sciences of sexuality to be learned; his image of non-Western knowledge of pleasure is reminiscent of the overseer's story of the siren out to consume her lovers and herself in a total experience of pleasure for its own sake. If we follow Foucault, for the Indians themselves the movement to a bourgeois existence would be a break from such an Eastern way of pleasure, and into their first-ever calculated reckoning of the body. But if we reject Foucault's Orientalism, together with that of the colonial order, it opens new questions. The terrain for consideration is not simply a space discovered in modern Western ontology. The matter of sexual practices and social conceptions and arrangements related to them becomes more complex, and we might be as suspicious of depictions of pure "breaks" from "traditional" discourse and practice as we would of claims for pure cultural continuity.

If there is a characteristic capitalist grammar for sexuality, then, the question in a given instance is till articulation, not simply presence or absence. How is one to maximize one's sexual, one's social, one's familial profit? What are the projects and priorities? In coordination with other goals and other operations, different bourgeois sexualities, marriages, and families become possible. The bourgeois complex of combined asceticism and hedonism can be and has been articulated into many different historically and socially configuring paradigms for "virtue": the imperial British controlled the sexual passions of their savage natures with the prudence, restraint, and insight taught by civilization; political-economic man maximizes his sexual consumption along with the rest of his consumption, naturally balancing short-term passions with long-run self-interest; the Indian nationalist *swaraji* sought his path to purity, freedom, and divinity-within-self by means of experiments in self-restraint, without neglecting his duties as householder. If the imperialist virtue was teleological and the political-economic virtue naturalist, the *swaraji's* virtue was more akin to Gnosticism than either of these, insofar as it has a Western parallel. Nevertheless its emphasis, like the others, was on improvement and a superior satisfaction through a practice of superior discipline. And it was more open-ended than the others. The *swaraji* was far less certain than either the imperialist or the political economist about what his or her more virtuous future would be like. For the Fiji Indians, both ends and means were at issue as they debated how to uplift their society.

In the debates, and before and after them, the Arya Samaj attacked marriage institutions connected with "traditional" and "caste" Hinduism, especially child marriage and arranged marriage between strangers. The Samajis desired a more "modern" and individualist reckoning, and in the long run their point of view won out in the Fiji Indian community. In time the minimum legal marriage age was raised, and the age of marriage rose well above the legal minimum as the demographics righted and as girls were sent to school, part of the more general Fiji Indian pursuit of education (though parents of girls in their teens still begin to worry about finding suitable candidates, especially in rural areas). In this generation, especially with secondary education growing more frequent and romantic Hindi *filmi* movies a part of general social life, "love marriages" have become a serious challenge to arranged marriages, and an emergent norm is the "arranged love marriage," in which the parents meet to arrange the marriage after the girl and boy have chosen each other.

The Arya Samaj thus would seem to have represented a position destined for general acceptance. Was it then simply ahead of its time, more bourgeois than the community of the 1920s? It was, clearly, more bourgeois than the average Fiji Indian farmer of the 1920s. But the Arya Samaj was not, in a critical way, simply ahead of its time, as was demonstrated by the sharp and successful counterattack on the Samaj concept of *niyog*.

The *niyog* controversy, knowledgeable Arya Samajis told me, was a major misunderstanding. The doctrine was not, as it was accused of being, a general license for fornication and an excuse for sexual flings. It was in fact a principle rarely practiced, and then only for the sake of having children, especially for producing heirs. It was also quite strictly permitted by Veda. *Niyog* was lawful temporary sexual liaison between two people not married to each other, occasioned by circumstances such as sterility, injury, long absence, widowhood, or sexual impairment of a spouse. It was not only Veda-sanctioned, but it was justified by the principles of interpretation adhered to by the Arya Samaj. Generally, chastity in the form of sexual abstinence was enjoined, but for householders, reproduction was part of *dharma*. It was therefore righteous for them to pursue the aim of producing offspring and, when doing so by sanctioned means such as *niyog*, to enjoy the results.

The Samaj explanation of marriage, and by extension of *niyog*, ended therefore with enjoyment, with *kama*. It made sex, as part of life as a whole, part of a *dharma*-sanctioned utility calculus, working though life's aims to the enjoyment of life's pleasures. There are some forms of *bhakti* also that view the world as pleasureful, especially Krishna-centered *bhakti* depictions of the world as a pleasure-garden provided by Krishna for our enjoyment. However, the *bhakti* of the Fiji Sanatan Dharm *pandits,* teaching the Tulsi Das Ramayan as an exemplar of worldly duty, was very different. Here, as we have noted, when Sita and Ram become the paradigms of marital duty, the marriage relationship itself becomes a primary devotional relationship. For the wife, the husband is to be worshipped. The vows and attachments of marriage are not, then, part of a process wherein the individual comes to realize available and sanctioned pleasures. They are transformative of the self, the two people becoming permanently connected. The hierarchical relation between them enjoins duties upon both, but especially upon the wife, whose chastity and social nature are completely and newly defined. For the husband, protecting the wife becomes one of the duties of his ongoing life; for the wife, the husband is an instantiation of divine form.

It was, and is, possible for a devotional conception of the marriage relationship to articulate with a capitalist household. When one calculates, then, one is always (theoretically at least) calculating how to best serve God; what one receives and enjoys is not the end or purpose of action, but simply his blessing bestowed as one continues to work his will. As we saw, in 1930 McElwaine noted with "interest" and a tinge of scorn the doctrine of Sanatani *pandits:* that marriage at an early age was essential to establish the young woman's *satitva* or chastity, and management of marriage a life's duty for women. One need not view this, as McElwaine seemed to, as some type of indictment of the sexual threat posed by Indian men. It is still, in contemporary Fiji Indian society, a view Sanatanis articulate—though now deferred in practice and contested in principle by educated and career-oriented women.

In the disparaging rhetoric of the debates, the Samajis attacked the corruption and backwardness of child marriage, no doubt connecting the practice to local "trafficking" on the one hand, and the restrictive and unjust world of "caste" on the other. The Sanatanis attacked the utilitarian pleasure principle inherent in *niyog,* no doubt as a lack of submission to divine will in the outcome of the marriage, and more so as an inevitable violation of the chastity (*satitva*) of the woman involved, the violation of a divine relation.

More was debated in these encounters, however, than the sexual morality of women and men. The other point of contention, perhaps the main point of contention as far as the Arya Samaj was concerned, was the sexual morality of gods. If this too harkened back to the Christian attacks on Shiva and others, it probably had a much more specific target within the world of *bhakti* devotionalism: devotion oriented by *lila,* or concepts of "play."

As we have discussed, Samaj theology was founded on a *nirguna,* "formless," conception of god. While there was a commitment in a subordinate sense to a devotional attitude toward god, the principal duty and method in religious practice was to be knowledge, knowledge of this god without form and also knowledge of the world and its matter and souls. In debates in India as well as Fiji, Samajis sought to show that all theories of a god with a form (*saguna* conceptions of god) were inherently irrational. Recall their question for Muslims: is god in his true form naked?

The Sanatanis embraced a pantheon of divine figures, a pantheon of gods with form. Further, they focused their religious practice on devotion, attaching and orienting selves to divine form. The Samajis and the Sanatanis disagreed over fundamentals of Hindu theology, *nirguna* versus *saguna* conceptions of god, and *jnana* (knowledge) oriented versus *bhakti* (devotion) oriented paths to god. In the Fiji debates, much Samaji ridicule of the filth and corruption they saw in the stories of the sex play of gods was probably motivated simply by their desire to show the irrationality of the Sanatani *saguna* conceptions.

However, the Samajis seem to have had particular loathing for the mythos surrounding Krishna and his *lila*, his play. Stories about Krishna are often oriented by a particularly aggressive type of devotional longing, a longing to find Krishna and relate to him, even as an illicit lover beyond and apart from worldly relations. Krishna-oriented devotion can thus be radically dis-integrating of worldly relationships, regarding the world's *dharma* or law no more than divine *lila* or play, devaluing the world and its relationships in the search for divine form. To the Arya Samaj, this form of *bhakti* devotionalism in particular was an anathema, because of the Samaj's fundamental commitment to a *satya* and *dharma*, truth and duty, of political rebellion and struggle in this world as it is. To the Arya Samaj, Krishna *bhakti* was the height of the corruption of the true message of the Vedas.

A marvelous example of the attack on Krishna is the transformed parable called "Who Knocks on the Door?" printed in English in the *Fiji Samachar* on 14 February 1931. The story demonstrates not only how the Arya Samaj sought to preach its *satya* and *dharma* of political struggle, but also an extreme to which Christian forms could be worked into a version of Hinduism. A village girl named Daya "hears Voices in her heart . . . saying 'Krishna! Krishna!'" She is told that she can find Krishna in the forest, and "in the dark of night, she ventures out alone," evoking Radha and many others seeking Krishna as a lover. But instead of finding her Lord, she hears another voice, saying "Return to thy home! Not in the forest mayest thou find me!" Days pass, an old widow comes to the door begging, and the girl gives her food and clothes:

She presses the cup to the widow's lips. When lo! the widow is not there! Nor is her little cottage! A beautiful house has suddenly risen into view. Lights are shining. Music floods the place. And in the house is seated Krishna playing upon the flute! Daya falls at His feet. Krishna blesses her and says, "That poor old widow was my rupam (form). I was thirsty, and thou didst give me water to drink. I was hungry and thou didst feed me. I was naked, and thou didst clothe me. My vision is thy reward." Is this story a parable? Who knocks at India's door with pale face and hungry eyes? Behold! thirsty and hungry and naked stands Krishna, the Comrade of the poor!

Not only is the Christian parable borrowed to reject the image of Krishna as a lover in the forest, but also a radical political image is superimposed on the Christian parable of charity. The proper Krishna, and his proper devotee, are "Comrades of the poor."

The Sanatanis may have been the victors in the Fiji debates of 1931: the Samajis were humiliated by the obscenity trial, and the Tulsi Das Ramayan emerged as the defining text of Fiji Indian Hinduism. But it is my sense that the Sanatani side also suffered a major casualty, *lila*-oriented Krishna *bhakti*. As we have discussed in connection with the writings of Sanadhya and Chaturvedi, in the Gandhian nationalist reading the Tulsi Das Ramayan was also a text teaching a *satya* and *dharma,* "truth and duty," of political struggle, a social commitment to reverse the pollutions of colonial relations and struggle with evil colonial agents. In the Fiji of 1929–1932, a change was marked in Fiji Indian ritual practices, occasioned in part by the rise of the new commitment.

In November 1931 Beattie's *Vriddhi* noted with approval that Holi was declining in popularity and extravagance of celebration, while Diwali, a holiday devoted to Lakshmi, was gaining importance, and that the Tazia was being replaced by Ram Lilas as the principal Indian festival. From the Christian and moderate Reform League point of view, this was a sign of "social progress" in the Indian community. The festivals of riot and excess were fading from prominence. But the shift in fact was not so much one to a "modern" form of Hinduism as one within forms of devotional practice, the rise of the duty-oriented devotionalism of Ram.[3] Holi is often, and is in Fiji at present, associated with Krishna and his color-play (*rang lila*) with his *gopis* on the occasion of the holiday. Diwali is often, as in Fiji at present, celebrated as the day of Ram's triumphant return from exile and conquest of evil to his home and capital of Ayodhya.

In 1930 Muslim League protests to the government led to restrictions on performance of the Tazia (CSO 1113/30). Thenceforth only bona fide Muslims could get the license necessary to hold a full-blown public Tazia festival. The Tazia as performed by Hindus was a victim of the rise of Fiji Muslim separatism and the rise within the Fiji Muslim community of missionary-prompted consciousness of Sunni (not Husain-loving Shi'a) identity. The Tazia could still be performed if led by Muslims, and it did not simply disappear. As late as 1951 Mayer found a simple *tazia* tomb-replica being built by a rural Fiji Hindu household carrying out a vow to do so. But it was, as he said, "a far cry from the *taziya* rites of former times" (1973: 96). In any case, according to Pearson, the decline of Tazia performances had begun in fact before the Muslim moves to outlaw the Hindu-led versions of the festival. The Tazia prohibition did not enter into the contests between the Samajis and Muslims in 1930, because the Samajis had no love for the festival either. The Tazia and Holi, the festivals removing practitioners from the relations of the world, seem to have been losing their salience in postindenture Fiji. The rituals of reversal and self-abandon seem to have declined in the same years that the sexual morality of the gods was held up to scrutiny and the duty-oriented devotionalism of Ram and the Ramayan was propounded by the new leaders of the Sanatan Dharm.

3. For a fuller discussion of this ritual history see Kelly 1988b.

If such social change was encouraging to the reformers, the Arya Samajis wanted more. The fact that the struggle with colonial authority was already underway must only have intensified their concern for social uplift and social discipline. If their people were deluded by a corrupted tradition, they needed education to be strong. If they were asleep to their duties and prospects, they needed waking up. Suffering, then, not only in the stalemate of their political boycott, but in the face of resistance to their enlightenment Vedic asceticism, the Arya Samaj lashed out at the doctrines of what they, together with the Europeans and Christians, characterized as "traditional" or "orthodox" Hinduism. The Arya Samaj offered an explicitly "modern" retooled alternative, which encoded through the sanctions of *dharma* a utilitarian individualist calculus and made god morally impeccable, but less relevant than the problems of worldly politics.

The Arya Samaj discourse on virtue was influenced by both of the European versions of "virtue" discussed in chapter 1. Along with the political economists and their naturalistic sense of passions and interests, the Samajis often argued about biology as destiny and *dharma* as natural law. But their discourse on virtue was also, and more importantly, an effort to answer the colonial European privileging of a civilized self. The Samaj vision was of a new Indian civilization, to be made strong through social discipline and education. The effort to realize Indian potential and create the new Aryan self faced three obstacles: the impurities of the degenerated traditional Hinduism, the interference of Islam, and the competition from self-interested colonial civilization. With real problems in marriage custom and law at hand, the Arya Samaj in Fiji fought, and lost, on all three fronts at once.

The Sanatanis also struggled to locate themselves, their social roles, and their *dharma*, "religion" or "duty," in the postindenture colonial world of Fiji. But led by their missionaries, they found in the *bhakti* devotionalism of Tulsi Das a model for resolving their predicaments. In their exile from caste and community in India, within the colonial capitalist markets (including those of their own devising and control), they were not abandoned by, and did not have to abandon, a *saguna* ("embodied") god. Devotion to him could be expressed by carrying out the duties of householders in the new alien contexts, just as the problems of women could best be solved by securing and protecting their chastity (*satitva*). In the socially withdrawn Indian community of Fiji, Western sexual morality was still alien and chilling in its scorn, and the austere religion of knowledge and politics of Aryan civilization-building proposed by the Arya Samaj held no advantages over the promises of divine shelter and rescue offered by the commitment to divine form. In the mainly rural Indian settlements, bound financially between their land leases and the company cane prices, a fixed-income capitalism coordinated well with a duty-oriented devotionalism, centering virtue on god rather than on a historically achieved civilization or a fixed human nature. The synthesis of *bhakti* and capitalist principles at the core of later Fiji Indian culture was forged, despite the aggressive Arya Samaj challenge.

The Arya Samaj and Colonial Authority

Virtue is important especially if we are thinking within the colonial, "civilization"-oriented self-image, or if we are examining in a "politics of virtue" the challenges to that self and world understanding. Following Bakhtin rather than Foucault, we have placed discourses within dialogues and consequently have not restricted "virtue" to reality within only one discourse, or imagined (to mix two of Foucault's metaphors) that anyone who "deployed" the term would necessarily be "seduced" by the colonial vision of civilization that organized so much so effectively in the colonial world. But it is time to connect the failure of the Arya Samaj in Fiji, and the focus on virtue problems, with *their* effort to redeploy the term: why was their use of "virtue" ineffective? We move from a reading of the meanings in the debate about sexual morality to a reading of the sense in engaging in it, and from a reading of the tactical sense in engaging in it—the level at which Gillion deplored the quality of Vishnu Deo's leadership, the level at which one can wonder what would have happened if Ram Chandra and Murarilal had come later, or if Vishnu Deo had shared S. B. Patel's political style—to a reading of the strategy within the epistemology of an Arya Samaj. In this we also seek to see what we have learned about the conditions of political possibility, about the practice of discourse: about the connections between Arya Samaj epistemology, strategy, tactics, genres, utterances, and context, about what led Vishnu Deo and the other Arya Samajis to do what they did, when they did.

We find these Arya Samajis, in the abstract, as an instance of colonized people trying to articulate in the "new" and the "old" simultaneously. In concrete, in Fiji in 1929, they were the most articulate and popular anticolonial Indian force, riding a wave of success from school-building to newspaper publishing to Hindu Maha Sabha ("Great Society") organizing to National Congress organizing. To finish their story, we also need to complete our picture of their true nemesis, official Fiji: in the abstract, the monopoly holders of imperial authority; in concrete, the often confused and sometimes inept staff of a colonial backwater, bullied by colonial India, by local economic powers, and of course by the Colonial Office. We will start, then, with a final reckoning of official Fiji, then return to the Fiji Arya Samaj and the consequences of its efforts to transform its social terrain.

The Gramscians tell us that the hegemonic class in a social formation insulates itself from challenges to its authority by controlling the very forms available for challenges. In this light the debates between Pearson and the Fiji establishment over the institutions for Fiji Indian administration become very interesting. Both Pearson and his opponents in official Fiji expressed, and sought to implement, plans for ensuring the authority of the ruling colonial class, but the plans were different.

Pearson reflected what was perhaps the orthodoxy of colonial India. British colonial rule was necessary, and could be made necessary, to the degree that its own authorities certified and controlled the social hierarchies of the ruled. The ruled society would elaborate its own social hierarchy, with or without the involvement of the colonial rulers—but if allowed to "evolve" outside of colonial tutelage, the ruled would have no dependence upon the rulers. The goal, then, was to find a way to accommodate and reward "moderate" and "responsible" leadership, as Pearson put it, "in all sections" of the community. This plan was the vogue of official India in the 1920s, the decade in which Pearson finished his service there, a time when temporarily successful efforts were made to draw Congress *swaraj* advocates into positions of responsibility and authority in national and provincial governments in India (see, e.g., Wolpert 1982: 307–8). It would also seem to have affinity with the notion of indirect rule, the expediency of relying upon and manipulating local leadership, the wisdom of leading the ruled to rule themselves.

Most interesting then is the resistance of official Fiji to applying such an approach to the Indian community. Fiji's attitude, favoring the simple denial of Indian leadership and authority, can be traced clearly from the labor control techniques of indenture, through the strikes of 1920 and 1921, to the notion that the Indians were, in the first place, a class of natural workers with dangerous pretensions, and in the second place, mainly the business of their employers to control. Until the new "Indian problem" was realized, it was simply ignored that the Indians were in increasing numbers leaving the control of European employers, a trend already clear though really just beginning in the 1920s. Then, the new version of the "Indian problem" itself precluded concessions; fear and the need to fight a political threat "tooth and nail" governed policy. The Indians were left in the hands of the company overseers and the police, and under observation by the clerks and the censors. The colony thought itself safer if the Indians were granted no political authority at all, precisely because of an acute awareness of the contingency, the non-necessity, even the arbitrariness of the organization of its power. Even Pearson had seen the matter as one of *making* the colonial authority necessary for the growing Indian community. Even he had not seen European leadership as racially obligatory or historically inevitable.[4]

In 1929–1932, then, despite Pearson's advocacy of reform, official Fiji renewed its denial of authority to Indians and its denial of a place in law to Indian customary practices and relations. *Panchayats* were not given authority to consider disputes, even disputes concerned with Indian custom; attempts were made to remove Indian personal law, and stages such as betrothal from Fiji's marriage law, to reduce Indian marriage to status as a civil contract registered with the District Commissioner. The key agents in establishing the reaffirmed necessity to "keep the Indians down" were the European elected representatives, articulating the new version of the Indian problem, and official Fiji's own emerging Indian experts, led by Dr. McGusty. They were successful, and Pearson unsuccessful, for many reasons, notably Fiji's disgust with what was seen as a deteriorating situation in India. Also, they were successful in part because of the presence in Fiji of a group who could be identified as the Indian problem in concrete: the Arya Samaj. In such crucial moments as the Watchtower scare, McGusty and others identified the Arya Samaj itself as the enemy to be watched and denied, and this view carried over into a continuing denial of authority to the Indians generally. It was said that the Indian leaders lacked "character," that the Indian community did not have "the material" for responsible leadership. What was seen was the direction Indian leadership would take.

Repression of resistance made the colonial ruling class more self-conscious and vulnerable. Recall, for example, their panic at the prospect of Indian public events commemorating their fiftieth year in Fiji, or their fear that India would appoint a civil servant of Indian race to replace Pearson. All Indian voices worried them, and almost any occasion

---

4. The new Republic of Fiji, following the coups in 1987, also feels safer granting Fiji Indians no political authority at all. Contemporary indigenous Fijian leaders see a unique and superior value to themselves as the embodiment of Fijian custom, but they also see their authority as contingent in a world where they may not get the "respect" they require. They argue simultaneously for their own superiority and for their inability to compete in a "modern" historical terrain without complete control over law and order. Adopting and adapting the language of the civilizing project, they justify domination on the grounds of a reverse racism, the weakness and vulnerability of indigenous Fijians confronted by an Indian threat. On this see also Kelly 1988c.

for Indian authority threatened them. Pearson's challenge to the methods of official Fiji, and the social project of the Arya Samaj, failed simultaneously in the face of official fear of the Arya Samaj voice. In a wider perspective, relations with India generated both Pearson's and the Arya Samaj's efforts—and given Fiji's developed antipathy to India, guaranteed the opposition to both. However, the more abstract questions remain, the questions generated by understanding these results as an exercise of the power of a ruling class in colonial Fiji. To what extent did the self-insulating strategies of colonial Fiji determine the failure of the Arya Samaj project among the Fiji Indians? To what extent was the Indian community's turn away from the Samaj, in favor of the Sanatan Dharm, a product of colonial strategies and tactics?

There are several problems, in fact, with the hypothesis that colonial Fiji caused its Hindu Indians, by whatever mechanism, to become Sanatani. In the first instance, what constituted being Sanatani, especially in relation to the Tulsi Das Ramayan, was quite beyond the grasp of the colonial officers. At best, then, one might imagine that colonial intentions and colonial systems directed the Indians toward a Hinduism that was nonpolitical, only a "religion," toward a Hinduism that did not contest the colonial definitions of "civilization" and "virtue." Perhaps, in a pattern of rewards and punishments, the Arya Samaj project became untenable.

The evidence is overwhelming that, when given a chance, the colonial authorities did act to thwart the assumption of authority by Arya Samajis. Further, when given a final momentary license to do so, the Supreme Court did virtually outlaw the Samaj's final vehicle, public controversy. However, the Arya Samaj faced opposition in more quarters than from the government. The Indian opposition to the *sangathan* ("consolidation") movement, Hindu as well as Muslim, demanded attention from the government, as well as vice versa, and often got considerably less aid than was requested. The *sangathan* movement was clearly brought down by its own internal contradictions, as it went about factionalizing the community, calling for boycotts and out-castings, in order to unite it. Similarly, as we have seen, the Samaj was bound up in tensions and contradictions at other levels: importing Christian methods and metaphysics to find the true Hinduism; rejecting much of Hindu literature and imagery, but accepting Western science and the notion of the pursuit of happiness, to define the pure Vedic truth and law.

More light might be shed on the events of these tumultuous years if we reverse the proposition. Colonial strategies and tactics withheld further immediate gains from the Arya Samaj but could not by themselves have denied it the support of an Indian community willing to withdraw from the limited privileges of ongoing relations with Fiji Europeans. The Arya Samaj project failed among the Fiji Indians because of its own contradictions, as well as because of colonial antagonism. What, then, had led to the attempt of the Arya Samaj project, with all of its internal tensions and contradictions, in the first place?

The situation, I would argue, is the colonial variation on the paradox of revolutionary projects identified by Marx on the first page of *The Eighteenth Brumaire of Louis Bonaparte* (1963 [1852]):

> Men make their own history, but they do not make it just as they please; they do not make it under circumstances chosen by themselves, but under circumstances directly encountered, given and transmitted from the past. The tradition of all the dead generations weighs like a nightmare on the brain of the living. And just when they seem engaged in revolutionizing themselves and things, in creating something that has never yet existed, precisely in such periods of revolutionary crisis they anxiously conjure up the spirits of the past to their service and borrow from them names, battle cries and costumes in order to present the new scene of world history in this time-honoured disguise and this borrowed language. Thus Luther donned the mask of the Apostle Paul, the Revolution of 1789 to 1814 draped itself alternately as the Roman Republic and the Roman Empire, and the Revolution of 1848 knew nothing better to do than to parody, now 1789, now the revolutionary tradition of 1793 to 1795.

If the bourgeois classes in Europe fought feudal remnants with "names, battle cries, and costumes" of a heroic past, the revolutions of the colonies against colonial hegemonies borrow their "names, battle cries, and costumes," their "language" of revolt, not only from their own social past but from the past of their colonizers as well. Like French revolutionaries draped in Roman garb, the Arya Samajis were the advocates of a Vedic truth and a past Aryan greatness. But they were not only that. They were also, by their own lights, the Hindu enlightenment, the Hindu great awakening, Protestant Hinduism, and modern and scientific Hinduism. They were all of these, and also true Hinduism, reckoned by a particularly Christian search for the pristine essence of revelation. Rationalists and revivalists, they were also Hindu "nationalists" above all, proponents of an Aryan "civilization." In criticism of Ram Chandra's lessons on Tulsi Das, K. B. Singh preached about Bismarck. As Benedict Anderson (1983) has argued, the idea of nationalism is itself one of the most powerful "pirated" battle cries for anticolonial revolution, one of the most potent ways for a postcolonial community to be imagined and for European forms to be mobilized to challenge European rule. "Civilization" is surely another. But in what world is the revolutionary postcolonial nation possible? In what world are there non-Western "civilizations"? A world still using categories provided by Europe and its colonial project.

In my view, the least well understood problems in colonial history have to do with domination, but not with race, class, or gender in particular. They have to do with domination based on presumed temporal privilege (cf. Fabian 1983, which restricts the question to anthropological discourse). They have to do with "civilization." Colonial culture is an "intimate enemy" (Ashis Nandy's term) not only for the descendants of the colonized, but all the more, with less acknowledgment, for the descendants of the colonizers, many of whom still fight to affirm and teach their "civilization," now specified as "Western civilization" not to relativize it but to insulate it from the rest of the world. Thus current curricular battles are far from empty, but they are also far from our focus here. We are ready for a final reckoning of Fiji's Arya Samaj and the events of 1929–1932.

Shri Krishna Sharma (1966) represented the Arya Samaj not only as a dispeller of darkness but as a planter of seeds. The founding of the Fiji Samaj itself was a planting that grew into a tree that grants wishes. Other Samaj accounts of its history have used the metaphor of seeds, planting, and fruits differently, as they depict the relation of the Arya Samaj to Indian nationalism. The pamphlet *Arya Samaj—Its Ideals and Achievements* (Nardev 1975: 24) put it as follows:

Many persons, societies, and organisations have undoubtedly played a prominent role in the resurgence of India yet it could be said without hesitation that these bodies received their inspiration from the writings of Swami Dayanand and their activities have their origin in the work of the Arya Samaj. It is for this reason that Swami Dayanand has been called the "Maker of Modern India." Most of the fields in which Mahatma Gandhi toiled throughout his life had their beginnings in the works of Dayanand. Dayanand prepared the field; cleared the dense growth; removed the huge rocks and other hindrances; and he made the undulating lands level and fertile for others to cultivate the soil. The ground was well prepared for those who followed him to reap a rich harvest. He opened roadways and footpaths through rugged forests. It made the travels of those who came after him an easy one.

This rhetoric resonates with Rabindranath Tagore's tribute to Dayananda, which is quoted in the pamphlet; Tagore wrote that Dayananda was "the great pathmaker in modern India, who through bewildering tangles of creeds and practices—the dense undergrowth of the degenerate days of our country—cleared a straight path that was meant to lead the Hindus to a simple and rational life of devotion to God and service for man." The same imagery, in turn, has been used by a current Fiji Arya Samaj leader to explain the place of the Samaj in Fiji Indian history.

In 1984 a hagiographic *Fiji Times* article commemorated Gandhi's birthday and also remembered the life, triumphs, and death, on the same date, of A. D. Patel, the barrister sent by Gandhi to Fiji. A. D. Patel succeeded Vishnu Deo as the closest thing to the consensus leader of the Fiji Indians through several turbulent decades, the vicissitudes of which cannot detain us.[5] The article was written by the Deputy Leader of the NFP, the political party A. D. Patel had founded. An Arya Samaj leader—a man who had given me one of my copies of the Nardev pamphlet—wrote a letter to protest the representation of A. D. Patel as the founding spirit of Fiji Indian politics, citing Badri Maharaj, Manilal, Vishnu Deo, and others as key predecessors:

> For half a century, these organizations and leaders prepared the field, cleared the dense growth, removed the huge rocks and other hindrances and made the undulating land fertile for others to cultivate the soil. The ground was well prepared for them who followed them to reap the rich harvest.

Whatever the rhetorical excesses, these claims are interesting: not so much for Tagore's allegation that the original problem was degeneracy,[6] or for the happenstance that terrain is a favorite metaphor also for Foucault and others, but for the depiction of a different kind of revolutionary founder. In this depiction Dayananda and Vishnu Deo are not even the sowers of the seeds of change. Their work comes even earlier in a movement from bewilderment to capacity. Together the texts assert an analogy, and a claim about countercolonial discourse: as Dayananda was

---

5. Patel led a Gandhian-principled Fiji Indian cane growers' union to victories in the reorganization of relations of production, a process that eventually drove the Colonial Sugar Refining Company out of Fiji; at his death he was in the midst of negotiating the first constitution of independent Fiji. Gandhianism in Fiji faced several paradoxes. Not only did its implicit Hinduism alienate Muslims in Fiji as well as in India, but emphasis on specifically "Indian" nationalism contributed to the isolation of the Indians in Fiji, who could not hope to make Fiji, like India, a nation of their own. However, Gandhianism provided a synthesis of devotionalism and capitalism that enabled effective labor organizing and coordinated the anticolonial interests of Fiji Indian farmers, workers, and businessmen. For more on this history see Kelly 1988a, 1988b, and n.d.b.

6. On the definition of the problem, I find more appealing another of Tagore's formulations, quoted by C. F. Andrews: "'Do we not need,' he [Tagore] cries, 'an overwhelming influx of higher social ideals? Must we not have that greater vision of humanity which will impel us to shake off the fetters that shackle our individual life? We have begun to realise the failure of England to rise to the great occasion, and so we are troubled with a trouble which we know not yet how to name'" (quoted in Chaturvedi and Sykes 1949: 63). To Andrews, or at least the Andrews of 1910, the answer for India was Christianity.

to Gandhi, so was Vishnu Deo to A. D. Patel, the Arya Samajis a failure necessary for Gandhian successes.

There was nothing inevitable in the way the Fiji authorities handled the Fiji Arya Samaj, despite the antagonism the Samaj generated among the Europeans. Though it is not surprising that it was opposed, and in the process provoked the colonials to become more insecure, self-conscious, and hostile in general, other outcomes were possible. Pearson, appointed at India's behest, was able to convince Seymour, the Colonial Secretary, of the need for key measures for Indian education and often gained his support on other matters. If Seymour had been Governor from 1930 to 1936, instead of Murchison Fletcher, Fiji Indian history might have been different. If multiple measures to induce Indian leaders into positions of authority and power had been begun in 1930, the Arya Samaj might have been in a position to institute itself from the top down. It is not inconceivable that the Arya Samaj could have established for itself a position as broker between European civil society and an Indian community emerging from its social withdrawal, the position briefly held by the clerks of the Reform League. Instead it was frozen out, radicalized, and then frustrated by its inability to lead the Fiji Indians too far down an increasingly militant road. By the mid-1930s the Fiji Indian community was fragmented and confused as a political entity in the colonial sense, still fighting a doomed common roll battle, without a clear agenda for ordinary politics. The Arya Samaj project failed quite swiftly when opposed by colonial authorities. But the deeper influences of colonial power lay in the Arya Samaj project itself, in the intellectual tools the Samaj put to the job of clearing, preparing, and trying to plant seeds of change, in the self-contradictions of the Arya Samaj ontology and epistemology. The Samaj wanted an Aryan "virtue" and "civilization," but the ideas of virtue and civilization are clearest in the singular and unmodified. The Samaj wanted sameness with and difference from the colonizers, a place at the pinnacle of history, but their own pinnacle.

What was inevitable, not only for Fiji but for India as well, was that groups like the Arya Samaj would appear to offer leadership in the first efforts to mount a challenge to colonial power, that the preparers of the ground of social revolution would be groups that were internally hegemonized in the attempt to be revolutionary. The history of India's anticolonial and postcolonial political movements begins in the search for a synthesis, a search for ways to be modern and Hindu, nationalist and devout, effective and authentic. The first efforts, such as those of the Arya Samaj, were weighed down heavily by the colonial curriculum. They questioned much of the content of colonial relations, located and criticized the barriers between themselves and their colonial rulers while still insisting on difference. But their inquiry into colonial knowledge discovered more about its contents than its forms.

The Arya Samajis were among the first to realize that rule by European whites was not obligatory but contingent upon existing relations, that the European monopoly on "virtue" and "civilization" could itself be contested. In India they were among the first to call for *swaraj*. In Fiji Vishnu Deo, as much as anyone, established that the Indians in Fiji expected an end to British rule in India. Further, the Samajis could be critical of westernizing definitions of "virtue" and the process of civilizing, rejecting the Indian Reform League's "drinking and dancing," its adoption of Western social styles. But they accepted the time line asserted by colonial self-definitions, accepted that the British and therefore the world were "modern" and that being "modern" was something necessary to being "good." They sought, like the colonial British, to find ancient roots also for their modern virtues. But the old could not keep up with the new when, as the Fiji courtroom rhetoric put it, like Socrates they questioned their traditional Gods. The European colonials could take and leave from their ancients as they pleased, but they had no one ahead of them in "modernity" against whom they had to maintain a difference. The Samajis were faced, while trying to become "modern," with an equal but opposite obligation to find something old and powerful with which they could establish their alterity as well as their civilization. As with Marx's revolutionary (see quote in chapter 1), they learned the spirit of their new language and gradually lost the old, but unlike Marx's revolutionary they could not abandon the toga or the mask, could not avoid becoming a parody of their original intention.

The problem was not only epistemological or symbolic—it extended into their very tactics for challenging colonial power. Again, on the one hand, the Arya Samaj marshaled considerable skills in the practice of discourse. Completely beyond the likes of Jaisari Singh, and beyond even Manilal and Bashishth Muni, they were eloquent in the language and style and comfortable with the genres of colonial society. They managed not only schools but a successful multilingual newspaper, vital to their project. At the same time, unlike the westernized clerks and spies of the colonial world, their Hinduism and difference from colonial society were as authentic as any other "Hinduism" and recognized as such; they were eloquent also in the language and discourse beyond colonial control. However, they put these skills to the service of their epistemologically hegemonized project. Both in India and in Fiji, the Samajis saw themselves not simply as cultural brokers or mediators but as a historical vanguard. They saw in themselves the future of others, and they diagnosed their obligation to be the making of that future. The weakness of their position lay in fact in the incompleteness of their critique of colonial discourse; they thought it lay in the backwardness and corruption of the other Hindus. When they sought to "enlighten" the others, they isolated themselves.

But their efforts to connect the old and the new, to remake their colonized community, were indeed the beginnings of revolutionary action. As they preached their doctrines and tried to lead their version of social revolution, they opened new questions and provoked new kinds of answers from the colonizers. These answers revealed colonial power through its limits, revealed not the position of Empire at the cutting edge of History but the reliance of Empire on doctrines of History. The very idea that the British themselves were a historical vanguard could be called into question, and not only their "virtue" and "civilization" but even the idea of "modern civilization" could be examined as something less than an obligatory premise for knowledge of the world as it is.

Dayananda founded the Arya Samaj to make a modern civilization out of Hinduism. By 1921 Gandhi (1966: v. 20, p. 413) could describe his movement as part of a "world-revolt," "freeing mankind from the yoke of a system falsely called civilization." In 1925 Gandhi wrote, "The glamour of European civilization does not dazzle us. . . . The predominant character of modern civilization is the exploitation of the weaker races of the earth" (1986: 345). Colonial insistence on white Europe's moral and historical superiority was transformed by Gandhi from a truth to a symptom of profound delusion, the evidence of a lack of self-understanding. As Nandy (1983: 48–49) observes, Gandhi "implicitly defined his ultimate goal as the liberation of the British from the history and psychology of British colonialism." *Swaraj,* then, was not a desire to be like the Europeans, but a project designed to transform and free the Europeans, also, from colonial premises. "The peoples of Europe have no doubt political power but no *swaraj*" (1986: 349). Gandhi's *sat-yagraha* campaigns could articulate and insist upon such truths, and they shattered defensive opponents made increasingly aware of their own self-contradictions.

We can understand the relation between Arya Samaj failures and Gandhi's success and how, in histories of dialogue, an unsuccessful challenge to hegemony can be a condition of possibility for a more successful one. Some want more immediate lessons from this history of dialogue, lessons about what to do and how to live now. A few still seek such truths from the Arya Samaj (e.g., Forbes 1984), many more from Gandhi. Nandy (1983: 62–63) concludes that "Gandhi broke out of the determinism of history" and showed that "history can sometimes be made to follow from myths." Uberoi (1978: 86) hopes to find in Gandhi the basis of alternative science and calls upon scholars to "benefit us all by revaluing the field itself from a swarajist point of view." But the larger present trend is to measure Gandhi by the standards of that advanced and accomplished modern revolutionary theorist, his contemporary Gramsci (as we have implicitly done in this essay; see also Chatterjee 1984, Chandra 1988, Fox 1989, and many scholars in the "subaltern studies" movement, especially Guha 1989). Whether or not this is a good idea—and given the relative accomplishments of their politics, we might expect a Gandhian analysis of Gramsci to generate deeper insights —it also seems necessary, as discussed in chapter 2, for assessments of Gandhian discourse to come to grips with the irreducibility of his devotional ontology. Gramsci's history always works through vanguard groups, emergent classes, and the license of materialist teleology. Not only is the state, in his view, the "educator" that "aims to create a new type and level of civilization" (1957: 187), but the progressive parties that oppose hegemonies are also "aiming to raise the people to a new level of civilization" (1957: 152). But Gandhi's is not a story about the progress of civilization from level to level. Gandhi's *swaraj* and *satyagraha* undercut the conceits of "modern civilization" and evolutionary history by residing in a divinely grounded universe. As Gandhi (1986: 298) put it, "I have ventured utterly to condemn modern civilization because I hold that the spirit of it is evil." Can we find, from Gandhi or elsewhere, a way to condemn the colonialism still residing in "modern civilization" that neither reproduces elitist premises about history nor grounds our ontology in divinity or any other stasis? My sense is that this is worth working on.

Bibliography

Abu-Lughod, Lila. 1986. *Veiled Sentiments*. Berkeley: University of California Press.

Ali, Ahmed. 1980. *Plantation to Politics: Studies on Fiji Indians*. Suva: University of the South Pacific and the *Fiji Times and Herald*.

————, ed. 1979. *Girmit: The Indenture Experience in Fiji*. Suva: Fiji Museum.

Anderson, A. G. 1974. *Indo-Fijian Smallfarming*. Auckland: Auckland University Press.

Anderson, Benedict. 1983. *Imagined Communities: Reflections on the Origin and Spread of Nationalism*. London: Verso.

Andrews, C. F. 1915. Report of Mr. C. F. Andrews' Speech to the Planters' Association Executive Committee, Fiji, 7 Dec. 1915. Copy in Tippett Reference Collection, St. Mark's Library, Canberra, Australia.

————. 1937. *India and the Pacific*. London: George Allen and Unwin.

Andrews, C. F., and W. W. Pearson. 1916. Report on Indentured Labour in Fiji: An Independent Enquiry. Publisher not named (may be Benarsidas Chaturvedi). Copy in Fiji National Archives.

Asad, Talal. 1973. *Anthropology and the Colonial Encounter*. London: Ithaca Press.

————. 1983. Notes on Body, Pain, and Truth in Medieval Christian Ritual. *Economy and Society* 12:287–327.

Bakhtin, Mikhail M. 1986. The Problem of Speech Genres. In *Speech Genres and Other Late Essays*. Austin: University of Texas Press.

Ballhatchet, Kenneth. 1980. *Race, Sex and Class under the Raj: Imperial Attitudes and Policies and Their Critics*. New York: St. Martin's Press.

Barrow, G. L. 1921. *Fiji for the Fijians: A Protest and a Plea*. Pamphlet in the Turnbull Library, Dunedin, New Zealand.

Bateson, Gregory. 1958. *Naven*. Stanford: Stanford University Press.

Baudrillard, Jean. 1981. *For a Critique of the Political Economy of the Sign.* St. Louis: Telos Press.

———. 1987. *Forget Foucault.* New York: Semiotext(e).

Bauer, Janet. 1985. Sexuality and the Moral "Construction" of Women in an Islamic Society. *Anthropological Quarterly* 58 (3): 120–29.

Bavin, Cyril. 1914. The Indian in Fiji. In *A Century in the Pacific.* James Colwell, ed. Sydney: Methodist Book Room.

Bayly, C. A. 1988. *Indian Society and the Making of the British Empire (New Cambridge History of India).* Cambridge: Cambridge University Press.

Benedict, Ruth. 1974 [1946]. *The Chrysanthemum and the Sword: Patterns of Japanese Culture.* New York: New American Library.

Bernal, Martin. 1987. *Black Athena: The Afroasiatic Roots of Classical Civilization.* Vol. 1 of *The Fabrication of Ancient Greece 1785–1985.* New Brunswick, NJ: Rutgers University Press.

Bourdieu, Pierre. 1977. *Outline of a Theory of Practice.* Cambridge: Cambridge University Press.

Brantlinger, Patrick. 1988. *Rule of Darkness: British Literature and Imperialism, 1830–1914.* Ithaca: Cornell University Press.

Breman, Jan. 1989. *Taming the Coolie Beast: Plantation Society and the Colonial Order in Southeast Asia.* Delhi: Oxford University Press.

———. 1990. Introduction. In *Imperial Monkey Business: Racial Supremacy in Social Darwinist Theory and Colonial Practice.* CASA Monographs 4. Amsterdam: VU University Press.

Brenneis, Donald. 1983. The Emerging Soloist: Kavvali in Bhatgaon. *Asian Folklore Studies* 42: 63–76.

———. 1984. Straight Talk and Sweet Talk: Political Discourse in an Occasionally Egalitarian Community. In *Dangerous Words: Language and Politics in the Pacific.* D. Brenneis and F. Myers, eds. New York: New York University Press.

———. 1987. Performing Passions: Aesthetics and Politics in an Occasionally Egalitarian Society. *American Ethnologist* 14: 236–50.

Brown, Carolyn Henning. 1978. Coolie and Freeman: From Hierarchy to Equality in Fiji. Ph.D. dissertation, University of Washington.

———. 1981. Demographic Constraints on Caste: A Fiji Indian Example. *American Ethnologist* 8: 314–28.

———. 1984. Tourism and Ethnic Competition in a Ritual Form: The Firewalkers of Fiji. *Oceania* 54: 229–44.

Burton, J. W. 1910. *The Fiji of To-Day.* London: Charles H. Kelly.

———. 1912. *The Call of the Pacific.* London: Charles H. Kelly.

Chandra, Bipan. 1988. *Indian National Movement: The Long Term Dynamics.* Delhi: Vikas Publishing House.

Chatterjee, Partha. 1984. Gandhi and the Critique of Civil Society. In *Subaltern Studies* 3. Ranajit Guha, ed. Delhi: Oxford University Press.

Chaturvedi, Benarsidas, and Marjorie Sykes. 1949. *Charles Freer Andrews: A Narrative.* London: George Allen and Unwin.

Chaudhuri, K. N. 1985. *Trade and Civilization in the Indian Ocean.* Cambridge: Cambridge University Press.

Chauhan, I. S. 1969. Leadership and Social Cleavages: Political Processes among the Indians in Labasa, Fiji Islands. Ph.D. dissertation, Australian National University.

Clammer, John. 1973. Colonialism and the Perception of Tradition in Fiji. In *Anthropology and the Colonial Encounter.* Talal Asad, ed. London: Ithaca Press.

Cohn, Bernard S. 1983. Representing Authority in Victorian India. In *The Invention of Tradition.* Eric Hobsbawm and Terence Ranger, eds. Cambridge: Cambridge University Press.

———. 1985. The Command of Language and the Language of Command. In *Subaltern Studies* 4. Ranajit Guha, ed. Delhi: Oxford University Press.

———. 1988. *An Anthropologist among the Historians and Other Essays.* Delhi: Oxford University Press.

———. 1989. Visualizing the Peoples of India. Lecture for Department of South Asia Regional Studies, University of Pennsylvania, 22 March 1989.

Comaroff, Jean. 1985. *Body of Power, Spirit of Resistance.* Chicago: University of Chicago Press.

Conrad, Joseph. 1963 [1899]. *Heart of Darkness.* New York: W. W. Norton.

Corrigan, Philip, and Derek Sayer. 1985. *The Great Arch: English State Formation as Cultural Revolution.* Oxford: Basil Blackwell.

Das, Gyani. n.d. Fiji: An Indian Colony. Abstract in English of Bharatiye Upnivesh Fiji [India's Colony Fiji], ms. in Mitchell Library, Sydney.

Das Gupta, Ashin, and M. N. Pearson. 1987. *India and the Indian Ocean 1500–1800.* Calcutta: Oxford University Press.

Dayananda Saraswati. 1976. *Autobiography of Dayananda Saraswati.* K. C. Yadav, ed. New Delhi: Manohar.

Dumont, Louis. 1970a. *Homo Hierarchicus.* Chicago: University of Chicago Press.

———. 1970b. *Religion, Politics, and History in India.* The Hague: Mouton.

———. 1977. *From Mandeville to Marx: The Genesis and Triumph of Economic Ideology.* Chicago: University of Chicago Press.

Durkheim, Emile. 1915. *The Elementary Forms of the Religious Life.* New York: Free Press.

Fabian, Johannes. 1983. *Time and the Other: How Anthropology Makes Its Object.* New York: Columbia University Press.

———. 1986. *Language and Colonial Power: The Appropriation of Swahili in the Former Belgian Congo 1880–1938.* Cambridge: Cambridge University Press.

Fanon, Frantz. 1963. *The Wretched of the Earth.* New York: Grove Press.

Forbes, Richard Huntingdon. 1984. Arya Samaj in Trinidad: An Historical Study of Hindu Organizational Process in Acculturative Conditions. Ph.D. thesis, University of Miami. Ann Arbor: University Microfilms International.

Foucault, Michel. 1973. *The Order of Things: An Archeology of the Human Sciences.* New York: Vintage Books.

———. 1980. *The History of Sexuality,* vol. 1. New York: Vintage Books.

Fox, Richard G. 1989. *Gandhian Utopia: Experiments with Culture.* Berkeley: University of California Press.

Fox-Genovese, Elizabeth. 1988. *Within the Plantation Household: Black and*

White Women of the Old South. Chapel Hill: University of North Carolina Press.

France, Peter. 1969. *The Charter of the Land.* Melbourne: Oxford University Press.

Franklin, Benjamin. 1962 [1791]. *The Autobiography of Benjamin Franklin.* New York: Collier Macmillan.

Frazer, R. M. 1968. *A Fiji-Indian Rural Community.* Wellington, New Zealand: Victoria University.

Freud, Sigmund. 1965 [1933]. *New Introductory Lectures on Psychoanalysis.* New York: W. W. Norton.

Gandhi, M. K. 1928. *Satyagraha in South Africa.* Ahmedabad: Navajivan Publishing House.

———. 1966. *The Collected Works of Mahatma Gandhi,* vol. 20 (April–August 1921) Delhi: Publications Division Ministry of Information and Broadcasting, Government of India.

———. 1986. *The Moral and Political Writings of Mahatma Gandhi.* Vol. 1, *Civilization, Politics, and Religion.* Raghavan Iyer, ed. Oxford: Clarendon Press.

Garnham, Florence. 1918. *A Report on the Social and Moral Condition of Indians in Fiji.* Sydney: Kingston Press.

Geertz, Clifford. 1968. *Islam Observed: Religious Development in Morocco and Indonesia.* Chicago: University of Chicago Press.

Gibbs, Philip. 1924. *The Romance of Empire.* London: Hutchinson and Co.

Gill, Walter. 1970. *Turn North-East at the Tombstone.* Adelaide: Rigby Ltd.

Gillion, K. L. 1962. *Fiji's Indian Migrants.* Melbourne: Oxford University Press.

———. 1977. *The Fiji Indians: Challenge to European Dominance 1920–1946.* Canberra: Australian National University Press.

Gilman, Sander L. 1985. *Difference and Pathology: Stereotypes of Sexuality, Race, and Madness.* Ithaca: Cornell University Press.

Gramsci, Antonio. 1957. *The Modern Prince and Other Writings.* New York: International Publishers.

———. 1971. *Selections from the Prison Notebooks.* New York: International Publishers.

———. 1975. *History, Philosophy, and Culture in the Young Gramsci.* St. Louis: Telos Press.

Guha, Ranajit. 1989. Dominance without Hegemony and Its Historiography. In *Subaltern Studies* 6. Ranajit Guha, ed. Delhi: Oxford University Press.

Hansen, Karen Tranberg. 1989. *Distant Companions: Servants and Employers in Zambia, 1900–1985.* Ithaca: Cornell University Press.

Hobsbawm, Eric J. 1969. *Industry and Empire.* Vol. 3 of *The Pelican Economic History of Britain.* Harmondsworth, Middlesex, England: Penguin Books.

Hocart, A. M. 1970. *Kings and Councillors.* Chicago: University of Chicago Press.

Hutchins, Francis G. 1967. *The Illusion of Permanence: British Imperialism in India.* Princeton, NJ: Princeton University Press.

Inden, Ronald. 1990. *Imagining India.* Oxford: Basil Blackwell.

Jayawardena, Chandra. 1971. The Disintegration of Caste in Fiji Indian Rural

Society. In *Anthropology in Oceania: Essays Presented to Ian Hogbin*. L. R. Hiatt and Chandra Jayawardena, eds. Sydney: Angus and Robertson.

_____. 1975. Farm, Household, and Family in Fiji Indian Rural Society, part 1. *Journal of Comparative Family Studies* 6 (1): 74–88.

_____. 1975. Farm, Household, and Family in Fiji Indian Rural Society, part II. *Journal of Comparative Family Studies* 6 (2): 209–21.

Jolly, Margaret. 1987. The Forgotten Woman: A History of Migrant Labour and Gender Relations in Vanuatu. *Oceania* 58 (2): 119–39.

Jones, Kenneth W. 1976. *Arya Dharm: Hindu Consciousness in Nineteenth-century Punjab*. Berkeley: University of California Press.

Jordens, J. T. F. 1978. *Dayananda Saraswati, His Life and Ideas*. Delhi: Oxford University Press.

Kanwal, J. S. 1980. *A Hundred Years of Hindi in Fiji 1879–1979*. Suva: Fiji Teachers' Union.

Kaplan, Martha. 1988. The Coups in Fiji: Colonial Contradictions and the Post-colonial Crisis. *Critique of Anthropology* 8 (3): 93–116.

_____. 1989. *Luve ni Wai* as the British Saw It: Constructions of Custom and Disorder in Colonial Fiji. *Ethnohistory* 36:349–71.

_____. 1990. Meaning, Agency, and Colonial History: Navosavakadua and the *Tuka* Movement in Fiji. *American Ethnologist* 17:1–20.

Kelly, John D. 1988a. *Bhakti* and the Spirit of Capitalism in Fiji: The Ontology of the Fiji Indians. Ph.D. dissertation, University of Chicago, Department of Anthropology.

_____. 1988b. From Holi to Diwali in Fiji: An Essay on Ritual and History. *Man* (n.s.) 23: 40–55.

_____. 1988c. Fiji Indians and Political Discourse in Fiji: From the Pacific Romance to the Coups. *Journal of Historical Sociology* 1:399–422.

_____. 1989. Fear of Culture: British Regulation of Indian Marriage in Post-indenture Fiji. *Ethnohistory* 36:372–391.

_____. 1990. Discourse About Sexuality and the End of Indenture in Fiji: The Making of Counter-Hegemonic Discourse. *History and Anthropology* 5:19–61.

_____. 1991. Fiji Indians and "Commoditization of Labor." *American Ethnologist*. Forthcoming.

_____. n.d.a. Introduction and essays. In *My Twenty-one Years in the Fiji Islands*. Totaram Sanadhya. John D. Kelly and Uttra Singh, trans. Suva: Fiji Museum.

_____. n.d.b. *Capitalism, Colonialism, and Hindu Devotionalism in Fiji*. Work in progress.

Knapman, Bruce. 1987. *Fiji's Economic History, 1874–1939: Studies of Capitalist Colonial Development*. Canberra: National Centre for Development Studies, Research School of Pacific Studies, Australian National University.

Knapman, Claudia. 1986. *White Women in Fiji 1835–1930: The Ruin of Empire?* Sydney: Allen and Unwin.

Krishnamurty, J. 1989. *Women in Colonial India: Essays on Survival, Work, and the State*. Delhi: Oxford University Press.

Lal, Brij V. 1983. *Girmitiyas: The Origins of the Fiji Indians*. Canberra: Journal of Pacific History.

———. 1985a. Kunti's Cry: Indentured Women on Fiji Plantations. *Indian Economic and Social History Review* 22:55–71.

———. 1985b. Veil of Dishonour: Sexual Jealousy and Suicide on Fiji Plantations. *Journal of Pacific History* 20:135–55.

———. 1988. *Power and Prejudice: The Making of the Fiji Crisis*. Wellington: New Zealand Institute of International Affairs.

Legge, J. D. 1958. *Britain in Fiji*. London: MacMillan.

Macaulay, Thomas B. 1978 [1829]. Mill's Essay on Government: Utilitarian Logic and Politics. In *Utilitarian Logic and Politics*. Jack Lively and John Rees, eds. Oxford: Clarendon Press.

MacIntyre, Alasdair. 1984. *After Virtue: A Study in Moral Theory*. Notre Dame, IN: University of Notre Dame Press.

Macnaught, Timothy J. 1982. *The Fijian Colonial Experience: A Study of the Neo-traditional Order under British Colonial Rule prior to World War II*. Canberra: Australian National University.

McMillan, A. W. 1944. *The Indians in Fiji*. Government of Fiji, "for official use only." Pamphlet in Fiji National Archives.

Malthus, Thomas. 1985 [1798]. *An Essay on the Principle of Population*. Harmondsworth, Middlesex, England: Penguin Books.

Mamak, Alexander. 1978. *Colour, Culture, and Conflict*. Sydney: Pergamon Press.

Mangan, J. A., and James Walvin. 1987. *Manliness and Morality: Middle-class Masculinity in Britain and America 1800–1940*. New York: St. Martin's Press.

Mani, Lata. 1989. Contentious Traditions: The Debate on *Sati* in Colonial India. In *Recasting Women: Essays in Colonial History*. Kumkum Sangari and Sudesh Vaid, eds. New Delhi: Kali for Women.

Marriott, McKim. 1976. Hindu Transactions: Diversity Without Dualism. In *Transaction and Meaning*. Bruce Kapferer, ed. Philadelphia: Institute for the Study of Human Issues.

Marx, Karl. 1963 [1850]. *The Eighteenth Brumaire of Louis Bonaparte*. New York: International Publishers.

———. 1976 [1867]. *Capital*. New York: Vintage Books.

———. 1978. The Marx-Engels Reader. Robert C. Tucker, ed. New York: W. W. Norton.

Mayer, Adrian. 1952. The Holi Festival Among The Indians of Fiji. *Eastern Anthropologist* 6:3–17.

———. 1954. Interpersonal Relations Between Fiji Indian Kin. *Man in India* 34:1–15.

———. 1955. Aspects of Credit and Debt among Fiji Indian Farmers. *Journal of the Polynesian Society* 64:442–49.

———. 1960. *Caste and Kinship in Central India*. Berkeley: University of California Press.

———. 1963. *Indians in Fiji*. London: Oxford University Press.

_____. 1973. *Peasants In The Pacific.* 2d ed. Berkeley: University of California Press.

Mill, James. 1978 [1820]. Essay on Government. In *Utilitarian Logic and Politics.* Jack Lively and John Rees, eds. Oxford: Clarendon Press.

Mintz, Sidney, W. 1985. *Sweetness and Power.* New York: Viking.

Mishra, Vijay, ed. 1979. *Rama's Banishment.* Auckland: Heinemann Educational Books.

Moynagh, Michael. 1981. *Brown or White? A History of the Fiji Sugar Industry, 1873–1973.* Canberra: Australian National University.

Mukerji, Chandra. 1983. *From Graven Images: Patterns of Modern Materialism.* New York: Columbia University Press.

Mukherjee, Prabhati. 1978. *Hindu Women: Normative Models.* Calcutta: Orient Longman.

Naidu, Vijay. 1980. *The Violence of Indenture in Fiji.* Suva: University of the South Pacific.

Naipaul, V. S. 1981. *An Area of Darkness.* New York: Vintage Books.

Nandy, Ashis. 1983. *The Intimate Enemy: Loss and Recovery of Self under Colonialism.* Delhi: Oxford University Press.

_____. 1980. Sati: A Nineteenth Century Tale of Women, Violence, and Protest. In *At the Edge of Psychology: Essays in Politics and Culture.* Delhi: Oxford University Press.

Nardev Vedalankar, Pandit. 1975. *Arya Samaj—Its Ideals and Achievements.* Durban, South Africa: Veda Niketan.

Nardev Vedalankar, Pandit, and Manohar Somera. 1975. *Arya Samaj and Indians Abroad.* New Delhi: Sarvadeshik Arya Pratinidhi Sabha.

O'Flaherty, Wendy Doniger. 1980. *Women, Androgynes, and Other Mythical Beasts.* Chicago: University of Chicago Press.

Oldenburg, Veena Talwar. 1984. *The Making of Colonial Lucknow 1856–1877.* Princeton, NJ: Princeton University Press.

Pandey, Gyanendra. 1978. *The Ascendancy of the Congress in Uttar Pradesh 1926– 34: A Study in Imperfect Mobilization.* Delhi: Oxford University Press.

Pearson, M. N. 1976. *Merchants and Rulers in Gujarat: The Response to the Portuguese in the Sixteenth Century.* Berkeley: University of California Press.

Pletsch, Carl E. 1981. The Three Worlds, or the Division of Social Scientific Labor, circa 1950–1975. *Comparative Studies in Society and History.* 23:565– 90.

Polanyi, Karl. 1957. *The Great Transformation.* Boston: Beacon Press.

Prasad, Shiu. 1974. *Indian Indentured Workers in Fiji.* Suva: South Pacific Social Sciences Association.

Polak, Henry S. L. 1909. *The Indians of South Africa: helots within the Empire, and how they are treated.* Pamphlet.

Roseberry, William. 1988. Political Economy. *Annual Review of Anthropology* 17:161–85.

Ryan, Michael T. 1981. Assimilating New Worlds in the Sixteenth and Seventeenth Centuries. *Comparative Studies in Society and History* 23 (4): 519–38.

Sahlins, Marshall. 1985. *Islands of History.* Chicago: University of Chicago Press.

Said, Edward W. 1978. *Orientalism.* New York: Vintage Books.

———. 1985. *Beginnings: Intention and Method.* New York: Columbia University Press.

Sanadhya, Totaram. n.d. [1914]. *Fijidwip Men Mere Ikkis Vars* [My Twenty-one Years in the Fiji Islands]. John D. Kelly and Uttra Singh, trans. Suva: Fiji Museum.

Sangari, Kumkum, and Sudesh Vaid. 1989. *Recasting Women: Essays in Colonial History.* New Delhi: Kali for Women.

Sannyasi, Bhawani Dayal, and Benarsidas Chaturvedi. 1931. *A Report on the Emigrants Repatriated to India under the Assisted Emigration Scheme from South Africa, and on the Problem of Returned Emigrants from All Colonies: An Independent Enquiry.* Calcutta: Benarsidas Chaturvedi.

Scarr, Deryck. 1980. *Viceroy of the Pacific.* Vol. 2 of *The Majesty of Colour, a Life of Sir John Bates Thurston.* Canberra: Australian National University.

———. 1984. *Fiji: A Short History.* Sydney: George Allen and Unwin.

Schwartz, Barton M., ed. 1967. *Caste in Overseas Indian Communities.* San Francisco: Chandler.

Sharma, Ayodhya Prasad. 1962. *Kisan Sangh Ka Itihas* [History of the Kisan Sangh]. Lautoka: Fiji Kisan Sangh.

Sharma, Ram Chandra. 1937. *Fiji Digdarshan* [Fiji Survey]. Mandawar, UP: Shree Ram Chandra Pustkalaya.

Sharma, Shri Krishna. 1966. *Arya Samaj Fiji Dvip Ka Sucitra Itihas* [An Illustrated History of the Arya Samaj in Fiji]. Rajkot: Arya Printing Press.

Siegel, Jeff. 1987. *Language Contact in a Plantation Environment.* Cambridge: Cambridge University Press.

Simmel, Georg. 1978. *The Philosophy of Money.* Boston: Routledge and Kegan Paul.

Smith, Adam. 1937 [1776]. *The Wealth of Nations.* New York: Modern Library.

———. 1967 [1755]. Articles in the *Edinburgh Review* of 1755. In *The Early Writings of Adam Smith.* New York: Augustus M. Kelley.

———. 1976 [1759]. *The Theory of Moral Sentiments.* Indianapolis: Liberty Classics.

Steensgaard, Niels. 1985. Asian Trade and World Economy from the Fifteenth to Eighteenth Centuries. In *Indo-Portuguese History: Old Issues, New Questions.* Teotonio R. de Souza, ed. New Delhi: Concept Publishing Co.

Stoler, Ann Laura. 1989. Rethinking Colonial Categories: European Communities in Sumatra and the Boundaries of Rule. *Comparative Studies in Society and History* 31 (1): 134–61.

Subramani. 1979. *The Indo-Fijian Experience.* St. Lucia: University of Queensland Press.

Taussig, Michael T. 1980. *The Devil and Commodity Fetishism in South America.* Chapel Hill: University of North Carolina Press.

Thompson, E. P. 1963. *The Making of the English Working Class.* New York: Vintage Books.

Thornley, A. W. 1973. The Methodist Mission and the Indians in Fiji 1900 to 1920. M. A. thesis, University of Auckland.

Thursby, G. R. 1975. *Hindu-Muslim Relations in British India: A Study of Controversy, Conflict, and Communal Movements in Northern India 1923–1928.* Leiden: Brill.

Tinker, Hugh. 1974. *A New System of Slavery.* London: Oxford University Press.

————. 1976. *Separate and Unequal: India and the Indians in the British Commonwealth 1920–1950.* Vancouver: University of British Columbia Press.

Todorov, Tzvetan. 1984. *The Conquest of America.* New York: Harper and Row.

Tribe, Keith. 1978. *Land, Labour, and Economic Discourse.* London: Routledge and Kegan Paul.

Uberoi, J. P. S. 1978. *Science and Culture.* Delhi: Oxford University Press.

Vincent, Joan. 1988. Sovereignty, Legitimacy, and Power: Prolegomena to the Study of the Colonial State. In *State Formation and Political Legitimacy (Political Anthropology,* vol. 6). Ronald Cohen and Judith D. Toland, eds. New Brunswick, NJ: Transaction Books.

Viswanathan, Gauri. 1989. *Masks of Conquest: Literary Study and British Rule in India.* New York: Columbia University Press.

Voloshinov, V. N. 1987. *Freudianism: A Critical Sketch.* Bloomington: Indiana University Press.

Wadley, Susan Snow. 1975. *Shakti: Power in the Conceptual Structure of Karimpur Religion.* Chicago: Department of Anthropology, University of Chicago.

Wallerstein, Immanuel. 1980. *The Modern World-System.* Vol. 2, *Mercantilism and the Consolidation of the European World-Economy, 1600–1750.* New York: Academic Press.

Weber, Max. 1958. *The Protestant Ethic and the Spirit of Capitalism.* New York: Charles Scribner's Sons.

Whorf, Benjamin Lee. 1956. *Language, Thought, and Reality.* Cambridge, MA: MIT Press.

Williams, Eric. 1944. *Capitalism and Slavery.* New York: G. P. Putnam's Sons.

Williams, Raymond. 1977. *Marxism and Literature.* Oxford: Oxford University Press.

Wolf, Eric. 1982. *Europe and the People without History.* Berkeley: University of California Press.

Wolpert, Stanley. 1982. *A New History of India.* 2d ed. New York: Oxford University Press.

Worrall, Henry. 1894. Mission Work among the Indian Coolies in Fiji. *Australasian Methodist Missionary Review* 4 Jan. 1894, 10–11.

————. 1912. A Racial Riddle: The Clash of Alien Cultures in the Pacific. *Life* (Australia), 1 August 1912, 137–42.

Young, John. 1984. *Adventurous Spirits.* St. Lucia: University of Queensland Press.

Index